STORIES OF COSMOPOLITAN BELONGING

What does it mean to belong in a place, or more than one place? This exciting new volume brings together work from cutting-edge interdisciplinary scholars researching home, migration and belonging, using their original research to argue for greater attention to how feeling and emotion are deeply embedded in social structures and power relations.

Stories of Cosmopolitan Belonging argues for a practical cosmopolitanism that recognises relations of power and struggle, and that struggles over place are often played out through emotional attachment. Taking the reader on a journey through research encounters spiralling out from the global city of London, UK, through English suburbs and European cities to homes and lives in Jamaica, Puerto Rico and Mexico, the contributors show ways in which international and intercontinental migrations and connections criss-cross and constitute local places in each of their case studies.

With a reflection on the practice of 'writing cities' from two leading urbanists and a focus throughout the volume on empirical work driving theoretical elaboration, this book will be essential reading for those interested in the politics of social science method, transnational urbanism, affective practices and new perspectives on power relations in neoliberal times. The international range of linked case studies presented here will be a valuable resource for students and scholars in sociology, anthropology, urban studies, cultural studies and contemporary history, and for urban policy makers interested in innovative perspectives on social relations and urban form.

Hannah Jones is an Assistant Professor of Sociology at the University of Warwick, UK. She works on multiculture, belonging and inequality; policy making and public sociology; and critical and participative social research methods. Her first book, *Negotiating Cohesion, Inequality and Change: Uncomfortable Positions in Local Government*, won the 2014 BSA Philip Abrams Memorial Prize for best first sole-authored monograph in British sociology.

Emma Jackson is an Urban Studies Journal Research Fellow at the University of Glasgow, UK. She works on class, multiculture, homelessness and the relationship between everyday practices, mobility and place. She is currently writing a book on young homeless people and the city.

STORIES OF COSMOPOLITAN BELONGING

Emotion and location

Edited by Hannah Jones and Emma Jackson

Routledge
Taylor & Francis Group
LONDON AND NEW YORK

from Routledge

First published 2014
by Routledge
2 Park Square, Milton Park, Abingdon, Oxon, OX14 4RN

and by Routledge
711 Third Avenue, New York, NY 10017

Routledge is an imprint of the Taylor & Francis Group, an informa business

British Library Cataloguing in Publication Data
A catalogue record for this book is available from the British Library

Library of Congress Cataloging-in-Publication Data
   Stories of cosmopolitan belonging : emotion and location /
   edited by Hannah Jones and Emma Jackson.
   pages cm
   Includes bibliographical references and index.
   1. Identity (Psychology)—Social aspects. 2. Belonging (Social psychology)
   3. Social integration. 4. Home. 5. Cosmopolitanism.
   I. Jones, Hannah, 1980– II. Jackson, Emma, 1979–
   HM753.S765 2014
   155.2—dc23
   2013045630

ISBN: 978–1–138–00064–3 (hbk)
ISBN: 978–1–138–00065–0 (pbk)
ISBN: 978–1–315–77460–2 (ebk)

Typeset in Bembo
by Swales & Willis Ltd, Exeter, Devon

Printed and bound in Great Britain by
TJ International Ltd, Padstow, Cornwall

CONTENTS

PLATES

(between pp. 98 and 99)

CONTRIBUTORS

Les Back is Professor of Sociology at Goldsmiths, University of London, UK.

Kieran Connell is a Research Fellow in the Department of History, University of Birmingham, UK.

Melissa Fernández Arrigoitia is a Research Officer at the London School of Economics and Political Science, UK, and a Lecturer in 'Culture, Diaspora, Ethnicity' at Birkbeck, University of London, UK.

Kristina Grünenberg holds a Master's degree in Anthropology and a PhD in Sociology from the University of Copenhagen, Denmark. She has primarily done research in the fields of migration, urbanity and medical anthropology.

Suzanne M. Hall researches and teaches at LSE Cities and the Department of Sociology at the London School of Economics and Political Science, UK.

Helena Holgersson is a Researcher/Lecturer at the Department of Cultural Sciences at the University of Gothenburg, Sweden.

Emma Jackson is an Urban Studies Journal Research Fellow at the University of Glasgow, UK, working on class, multiculture, homelessness and place.

Rivke Jaffe is an Associate Professor at the Centre for Urban Studies and the Department of Human Geography, Planning and International Development Studies, University of Amsterdam, the Netherlands.

Hannah Jones is an Assistant Professor in Sociology at the University of Warwick, UK, working on multiculture, belonging, inequality and policy practice.

Adam Kaasa is a Research Fellow in the School of Architecture at the Royal College of Art, UK, working on circulations of architecture, modernity, public space and the commons.

Michael Keith has a personal chair in the School of Anthropology at the University of Oxford, UK, and is the Director of the Centre on Migration, Policy and Society (COMPAS).

Alex Rhys-Taylor is a Lecturer in Sociology at Goldsmiths, University of London, UK.

Anamik Saha is a Lecturer in Media, Communications and Promotion at Goldsmiths, University of London, UK.

Zeynep Turan Hoffman is a Faculty member in Architecture at Istanbul Bilgi University, Turkey.

Sophie Watson is Professor of Sociology at the Open University, UK.

ACKNOWLEDGEMENTS

First of all, we would like to thank all the authors who have contributed chapters to this book. It has been a labour of love but at the same time we have had to make editorial demands about deadlines, word lengths, form . . . and we are very happy to still count you as good friends after all of that. And we feel very privileged to be able to collect your wonderful chapters and ideas together in this way.

The book is also a product of a wider community of peers and colleagues, and some very supportive, collegiate and inspiring working environments. The editors would like to thank the Sociology PhD community of Goldsmiths, the NYLON research network, and our current homes of Urban Studies, University of Glasgow and Department of Sociology, University of Warwick. We would also like to thank Nicki Dennis and Alice Aldous for such helpful, efficient and cheerful editorial support.

Emma Jackson would also like to thank Adrian Lobb for all of his support and love, Michaela Benson, Tim Butler and Gary Bridge for being excellent and generous colleagues and collaborators on the research discussed in her chapter, and the Urban Studies Foundation for funding her post-doctoral fellowship.

Hannah Jones would also like to thank Carla, Gwen, Hrishikesh and Rick Jones and Judith Kahn for support, celebration and inspiration, Christy Kulz and Maria do Mar Pereira for reading and commenting on earlier versions of her chapter, the participants who agreed to be interviewed in the research discussed in that chapter, and all those who have encouraged and supported this project since its beginnings.

Thanks also to The Frick Collection for permission to reproduce *The Temptation of Christ on the Mountain*, Duccio di Buoninsegna in Plate 1.

INTRODUCTION

Moving and being moved

Hannah Jones, Emma Jackson and Alex Rhys-Taylor

Moving and being moved

The twenty-first century has seen a move towards increasingly concentrated forms of habitation, with more and more people collecting in increasingly dense areas. However, in the main, people are not just fixed into those spaces. From the early Chicago School studies of migration into the city's margins (Park 1928), through to more recent studies of 'mobility' (Urry 2010) and flows (Appadurai 1996; Hannerz 1996), social scientists have placed movement at the centre of our understanding of late modernity. Zygmunt Bauman (1998) argues that motion is so important to contemporary life that *the* two definitive social types of the contemporary age are the tourist and the vagabond. The tourist, for Bauman, is the voluntarily mobile business person or traveller, flitting across the planet irrespective of borders or local demands. Despite the apparent homogeneity of the 'non-places' (Augé 1995) through which they move, such individuals might be identified, or at least identify as, cosmopolitan. The vagabond, on the other hand, is involuntarily mobile, swept along on the winds of economic necessity, displaced by ethnic violence or relocated by urban planners.

It is clear that the 'citizenship' of these two types of 'citizens of the world' is quite different; and where 'cosmopolitan' is applied in its everyday sense, it would be to the elite 'tourist' (and passport holder) and his privileged consumption of the world, and not to the 'vagabond' – or indeed to the non-traveller who stays 'in place' but may nonetheless, in our thinking, be considered cosmopolitan in her connections in and across the world.

While we problematise these two figures in this volume, the study of those who move – in a range of circumstances and with a range of choice over their movement – and the journeys they undertake, as well of those who remain 'in place' but nevertheless experience the cosmopolitan, is central to challenging the methodological nationalism that, as Beck and Sznaider (2006) warned, continues to blind us to the facts of cosmopolitan existence.

While the social sciences have come to understand the importance of movements of labour, capital, culture and commodities, existing methods and epistemological positions have limited understanding of the full spectrum of those movements' effects. Amongst the greatest omissions, grounded in a preference for tracing quantifiable and abstracted flows, has been a consideration of the experience of being moved. Literally, the experience of a passage from one place to another, but also the experience of passage from one emotional state to another that can accompany motion – being moved to tears, moved to laughter, moved to hate, love, pride or fear. In this volume we seek to address that oversight. Taking global circulations of people, commodities and capital as established, and somewhat banal, facts of contemporary life, the contributors draw on an array of empirical entanglements in seeking to understand the emotional dimensions of moving, or of its aftermath. In doing so, we highlight the importance of understanding the sometimes pleasurable – and often painful – realm of emotional experience that modulates the (re)constitution of the social world.

The connections between motion and emotion, however, are more than just wordplay. As the reader will discover, each empirical example of emotion and its social consequences emerges out of, quite literally, being moved or 'affected'.

In the emotional/affectual geography debate (see Pile 2010; Bondi and Davison 2011), emotion/affect are laid out by Pile as belonging to two separate and distinct perspectives. Pile portrays emotional geography as necessarily warm and fuzzy. His critique frames the field as naive and sentimental, as 'presenting superficial accounts because it is mesmerised by expressed accounts of emotional life' (Pile 2010: 8). Indeed, the dualisms presented by Pile have a distinctly gendered undertone: 'emotional geographers want to talk to people about their feelings, affectual geographers don't' (Pile 2010: 10). Much of the work in this book is based on emotional accounts of place; however, we refute the notion that this is cosy work underscored by a 'valorising of the personal' (Pile 2010: 11). Indeed, many of the accounts of participants in the studies presented here are infused with decidedly unpretty emotions: disgust, dislike, anger, unease – alongside happiness and pleasure – and are fraught with ambivalence. 'The personal' is neither cosy, nor ever separate from the social and political. Underpinning this book is the notion that exploring such uncomfortable emotions and their circulation is essential for understanding social and spatial processes.

Neither do we use emotion in isolation from affect; following Bondi and Davidson (2011), we find affect and emotion rather too messy for this demarcation to be useful. If affect is a 'prepersonal intensity corresponding to the passage from one experiential state of the body to another' (Massumi 1987: xvii), emotion or feeling is the biographically specific meaning ascribed to that change. Wetherell argues that what is crucial is to consider how these affective practices (and circulations) are repeated, how they form patterns, how they 'thread' between people, how they are spatialised and how power becomes manifested or reproduced ('How are practices clumped, who gets to do what when, and what relations does an affective practice make, enact, disrupt or reinforce?' (Wetherell 2012: 17)).

Ahmed's (2004) 'emotionality' gives us a conceptual framework for interpreting the relationship between repeated stories, emotion, power and value. She argues that emotions about objects, texts and places circulate and accumulate through repetition and 'stick' to objects. If we theorise emotions in this way, then we can approach emotions not as merely personal but as linking biography to power, the circulation of feeling and the production of spaces and places. Ahmed's key question is 'What do emotions do?'

Let us take an example. In July 2013, a billboard commissioned by the UK Home Office and ostensibly targeted at 'illegal immigrants', reading: 'In the UK illegally? Go home or face arrest', was mounted on the back of a van in order that this message might literally be circulated as the van drove around a selection of London boroughs with large migrant heritage populations. This is a government intervention in place, a promise/threat of a cleansing of London and an intervention that is steeped in and productive of distinct emotions (unease, worry, hate, reassurance) as well as affective responses (shudders, twitches). Thrift has pointed out that: 'systematic knowledges of the creation and mobilisation of affect have become an integral part of the everyday urban landscape' and that this is deployed politically (2004: 58). Circling super-diverse areas of London, the advertising campaign sought to stir specific emotions: of fear of the state among irregular migrants, and capitalising on a presumed fear within the wider population of 'uncontrolled' migration, assuaged by a sense of security that 'something is being done' about an invisible bogeyman (while reinforcing a feeling that the bogeyman lurks among them/us).

However, this is not an abstract and unnameable affect. Using the racist taunt of 'go home' which previous generations of migrants had faced in streets, workplaces and playgrounds and now thought largely confined to past decades, it adds to a circulation of fear, striking a chord within individuals' memories, while seeking to promote an attachment of this fear to bodies out of place. Others, who do not recognise the resonances of that taunt of 'go home', fail to see why a campaign clearly aimed at 'illegal' activity (or persons) has been deemed 'racist' (Goodhart 2013). Here, personal biographies and physical bodies are what create different responses – both affective and emotional – when confronted with the same sign. And these different responses create and reinforce political cleavages, social divisions and mobilisations of action (both anti- and pro-migrant, anti- and pro-government). Indeed, the intention of the campaign was to affect social and political relations by working on emotional reactions.

Emotion is, then, more than the personal or internal consequences of movement. In a social context, emotion produces its own effects as it feeds back into the social world. It colours the pain that can emerge from having been moved from elsewhere (see chapters by Grünenberg, Turan Hoffman), it gives meaning to the experience of being ushered into another time (as in the chapters by Holgersson, Kaasa) and it drives the establishment of new forms of attachment amidst the experience of the here and now (see chapters by Connell, Jones). In these terms, this volume looks beyond 'being moved' or affected, to the specific feelings that emerge from that movement. As the collected chapters make plain, if various types of motion are at the heart of the contemporary condition, then understanding ways in which bodies are moved – affected – and the meaning that they give to the experience of being moved – emotion – is integral to understand the human and social consequences of this mobility.

And yet, there are a variety of nuances in which each contributor to this volume uses the analytical categories of emotion, affect or even feeling. We make no apologies for this; this is theory-in-use and in development, and the connection to empirical research demonstrates Bondi and Davidson's (2011) argument that these categorical definitions need to be kept open and used relationally, if they are to be any use at all. Broadly, each contributor to the volume engages with emotions not simply as experience within the self, but in terms of involvement in and production of the power relations of cosmopolitan urban life. In doing so, we consider the emotional and affective power of place, but also of the stories that make spaces into places.

Place/space and the connections between them

> Stories thus carry out a labour that constantly transforms places into spaces or spaces into places. They also organize the changing play between places and spaces.
>
> *(De Certeau 1988: 188)*

While the writers in this book use place/space in various ways, the constitutive role that emotions play in processes of *making* cities, towns and suburbs cuts across all of the following chapters. Collectively, we argue that emotions are intrinsic to, first, the social, political and economic production of urban space; and second, to the processes by which places become linked through transnational connections.

Whereas 'place' is often construed as more fixed and permanent – for example, de Certeau describes place as 'proper', the world of the planner rather than the walker (1988) – 'space' is often used to describe a more dynamic set of relations. Lefebvre's theory of 'the production of space' is useful in breaking down the distinction between the city of the imagination and the material city (Tonkiss 2005; Harvey 1993). Rather than split the street of the planner and the walker into place/space, he distinguishes between three categories of spatial production: spatial practice, representations of space and representational space. While we do not strictly adhere to these categories, the notion of space as produced by a combination of practices, official representations and imaginings underpin this book.

However, a focus on space (as in progress and dynamic) does not make place (as something imagined as more stable and particular) a redundant concept. Places, on a variety of scales, retain their potency in people's narratives, imaginings and spatial practices. In turn, what happens in specific places affects spatial relations. This links places together: Downtown Kingston with New York, Toronto and London (Jaffe), 'Africa' with Handsworth (Connell), Nykøbing with Višegrad (Grünenberg), Peckham with Lagos (Jackson). However, whereas Tuan argues: 'From the security and stability of place we are aware of the openness, freedom, and threat of space, and vice versa' (1977: 6), following Massey (1994) we point to the coexistence and practice of multiple places in the same space. For example, in Holgersson's chapter, residents live different versions of their neighbourhood as a place. In addition, the intervention of official representations in this neighbourhood can be seen as an attempt to transform a story of a particular place, to privilege one version of place over the others and to make it manifest in space.

The focus in this volume on the connections across places and spaces, and their co-constitution through felt relations, brings out repeated themes of disjuncture and familiarity. Jackson's description of the 'creeping familiarity' with notes of Lagos, Nigeria felt by new residents in Peckham, London captures this banal cosmopolitanism, as the 'exotic' becomes 'everyday' – whether this is by seeing reassuring resemblances between a bridge in Nykøbing, Denmark and one in Višegrad, Bosnia (Grünenberg); or coming to feel a solidarity with Turkish people once seen as colonial vanquishers by the Armenian diaspora (Turan Hoffman). The relationship between shock and boredom, exotic and banal, or *unheimlich* and *heimlich*, is above all an emotional one. It is also a connection across time and space which invites the tools of the ethnographer, with her mission to 'make the familiar strange, and the strange familiar'.

Cosmopolitan belonging

The chapters of this book draw on experiences of cosmopolitan belonging in the sense of 'belonging' – or not – to different places at different times, or to several places at once, and to how this belonging – or not – remakes places as well as people. Cosmopolitanism is important for both the subjects and the approaches in this book. The strict etymological sense of 'cosmopolitan', as 'citizen of the world' is not quite right, however. We are pointedly approaching our writing here as an empirically driven project, and doing so means grappling with the realities of differential experiences of mobility, belonging and power, and of citizenship, for different people as they reside or travel through the world. And yet we want to stay open to the connections, both material and felt, that are made between people and places, and the relationship between these constant remakings and the social relations – global and local – in which people live.

Others have attempted to develop and use the concept of cosmopolitanism in ways closer to what we mean here, moving beyond 'methodological nationalism' (Beck and Sznaider 2006) in order to recognise that the nation state is rarely the most useful unit of analysis for understanding interconnected social processes. But while Beck and Grande call for a 'methodological cosmopolitanism' which 'takes the varieties of modernity and their global interdependencies as a starting point' for thinking and research (2010: 412), this has been critiqued for a residual

Eurocentrism of focus which must be defeated in order to 'enrich European socio-logical understanding by folding the way it has been understood by its Others back into its operations' (Gilroy 2010: 622) and thereby produce the 'planetary human-ism' of a 'cosmopolitanism from below' (Gilroy 2004). Such 'planetary humanism' has in turn being critiqued (Jazeel 2011), with the argument that some form of closed universalism is inherent in cosmopolitanism, if this is equated with 'planetary consciousness' where the planet has a closed-off edge and is seen with a 'view from nowhere' (after Haraway 1988). Jazeel's problem with cosmopolitanism is that he sees this as synonymous with a call for 'living together' and 'toleration', which assumes a privileged agent doing the 'tolerating' (2011: 86). This contrasts with the way we are using 'cosmopolitan', which is not about a normative descriptor of settled or desired multicultural relations, but about a way of understanding the ongoing relations between people and social formations which make one another up, across distance and time. This is closer to Delanty's call for a 'critical cosmopoli-tanism' of the 'cosmopolitan imagination' which 'occurs when and wherever new relations between self, other and world develop in moments of openness' (Delanty 2006: 27), though this still remains abstract and indeed so open as to be vague.

These arguments between social and political theorists over what could and should be the way we think about a concept are just one example of the limita-tions of theory divorced from empirical engagement. A more promising model for the way we are trying to engage with theory, materiality and political intervention may be found in the work of Rosi Braidotti on 'nomadism'. For Braidotti also rejects the 'methodological nationalism' of academic disciplinarity, which limits understandings of the social world by trapping habits of thought within one set of traditions rather than gathering resources from wherever available, this latter move being what she calls 'nomadic theory' (Braidotti 2011). She also argues that the social world we study is inherently 'nomadic' (or what we are calling cosmopoli-tan) in the sense that it is in movement and without fixity, that each element is not separate but connected, relational and constantly being remade – that, following Deleuze and Guattari, we should conceive of the social world not as 'things' but as 'processes' (Braidotti 2011: 15). And finally, she applies this nomadic perspective of rejecting fixity to the mission of the scholar – to produce knowledge, but not to imagine this is an intellectual process separate from existence and intervention in material relations (Braidotti 2011: 19; see also Keith 2005).

Where we use the term 'cosmopolitan' in this book, it is largely in parallel with Braidotti's 'nomadism'. However, where 'nomadism' is a useful term for Braidotti because of her emphasis on movement and on rejecting fixity, its suggestion of a lack of 'home' is not quite right for the stories we explore in this book. In their different ways, each of the empirical chapters here explores 'belonging' to a place, or the idea of a place, which might be close to an idea of home – even where that home is changing, is far away, has never been visited or never existed. We want to take that sense of openness rather than fixity, of becoming rather than being, of pragmatism and eclecticism, of critical thinking as well as material and political engagement, of seeing the connections with the global or distant in the local and specific, as what we mean by cosmopolitan stories, cosmopolitan belonging and cosmopolitan sociology.

Connecting place, power, feeling

All of the chapters in this book engage with the ways that emotion and place constitute one another by considering everyday interactions where people live, work, choose and feel. As a group of authors, we think it is important to pay attention to this empirical world, to hear and see with and through the experiences of others, as well as through our own. This is one way of pursuing the sociological mission espoused by C. Wright Mills (2000 [1959]), to link 'private troubles' to 'public issues'. Just as Back and Keith argue in their opening chapter, both sides of this equation are important to the authors in this book: to understand the minutiae, the daily moments of feeling, what engenders feeling and what action feelings inspire; and to consider where these feelings come from, what power relations they reflect, reinforce or undermine. The personal is the political; equally, the political is personal.

Empirical, ethnographic research with real people is messy, it's hard. Though it may sound banal to spend time watching TV outside a cafe (Jaffe), or to sit on a bus with a group of tourists (Turan Hoffman), these humdrum occasions are where theory ought to matter, if it matters. The project of this book is to build on existing empirical work examining how emotions are lived in space/across place (e.g. Davidson et al. 2005; Smith et al. 2009) and to infuse this with sociological, political attention to how feeling functions within (and as) regimes of power. In this type of work, we test what people tell us, what we see, what we feel, against the theories that develop in the process.

The ethnographer's most important tool is herself (Coffey 1999). In different ways, each author in this book uses an ethnographic sensibility to explore social reality mediated through our own interpretations. Interpretation, elaboration, connection is a poetic business, using instinct and inspiration, and weighing ethical responsibilities (Gunaratnam 2009: 59). We do not shy away from that element of ethnographic work, but we make a case for this openly interpretive work also being rigorous, using skills of listening and connection that are honed over time, expertise of spending time, paying attention to the people we meet and the wider social context in which they exist (Back 2007). As Yasmin Gunaratnam puts it, we aim to 'practise our . . . crafts in ways that aspire to the honing of technique and skill and that give recognition to our being touched' (2009: 59). That is, the life of the researcher is no less situated that the lives we set out to study, and one aspect of bringing in attention to feeling is to recognise our writing of research and theory is always already mediated through our feelings as researchers, writers and theorists.

This situatedness is similarly recognised in the form of the volume, which makes transparent our own starting point and attachments, beginning as a cluster of researchers working in and on London who are in dialogue with a wider group of researchers working across the world. There is no claim or attempt to cover 'case studies' from the whole globe in an exhaustive and representative way. Rather, we pick out just some of these stories of cosmopolitan belonging, following emotional transnational connections that criss-cross the globe and shape urban spaces through the experiences of the people who inhabit them. We have written this location into the structure of the book, rather than glossing over it, in order to acknowledge this rather than attempting to speak from nowhere.

The chapters

This volume is an attempt to figure an understanding of the lived, felt and political experience of global and intimate connections. Authors come from backgrounds in sociology, geography, anthropology, cultural studies and contemporary history and each draws on theoretical and empirical influences from across and beyond these disciplines. As such, the reader will find our usages of terms like 'emotion', 'affect', 'belonging', 'place', even 'cosmopolitan' shift between chapters. This reflects our version of a cosmopolitan work: an eclecticism which is reactive, responsive and contingent, and is no less rigorous for being so. Rather than seeking out grand theory that will incorporate and tame the complexity of urban formations or flows of feelings, we seek to expand and examine the complexity of the everyday. In doing so, we do not aim for, or expect to achieve, an overarching theory or form.

Nonetheless, there is coherence and continuity between the chapters, the connecting threads drawn out in this introduction and the conclusion to the book. What we share is a common interest in paying critical attention to the role of emotion in cities. This offers a way to understand the relationship between the experience of cities and the power structures from which those experiences are constituted, and which, in turn, they constitute. Beyond contributing to our understanding of individual cities, emotion and affect reveal the ways in which urban space is produced through connections, and disconnection with elsewheres. As Back and Keith argue in their introductory reflections, urbanism has too often been framed as a choice between theoretical abstraction and ethnographic forms of empiricism, between 'macro' and 'micro'. In this volume, each author in her or his different way draws on original research into the everyday lives of people who live in and across urban spaces. They consider how those everyday lives are felt, and how feelings work on and within structures of power and inequality.

One key intention of this book is political; to draw attention to the political aspects of emotions and emotional reactions. This is part of a feminist tradition of engaging with the importance of the domestic, in the sense of the mundane and unacknowledged emotional labour in which we all engage, all the time. We are not, for the most part, writing about the 'micro-biopolitics' which Thrift (2004) tries to reach through non-representational theory getting at twitches, facial expression and pre-cognitive affect; nor about the overt play on feeling in political advertising, rhetoric or branding. Rather, a shared focus of the book is what people do, say and feel when affected by cosmopolitan reality.

The volume is structured around narrative and geographical journeys which spiral outwards whilst linking across the globe, and across the volume. We start with a cluster of studies which explore affective connections between inner London neighbourhoods (Southwark, Hackney and Peckham) and their global 'external geographies'. The second section shows how emotion shapes the production of other 'urban regions' through narrative journeys that start – or rather, are intercepted by the researchers – elsewhere in England (Peterborough and Barking, Birmingham, and Redbridge). This is followed by a section which follows affective journeys from and to other European countries (Bosnia and Denmark, Sweden, Armenia). The final section engages with cities of North America (in Jamaica, Mexico, and Puerto Rico) and their connections across the globe. Each section builds the book's consideration of the role of emotion at local and global scales in the production of urban forms.

Part I: Local worlds/cosmopolitan formations: London and/in the world

The book begins with three chapters based on research in inner London, which is where this book project began. In each of these chapters we see how, in different ways and different parts of the city, super-diverse London is made up of historic and present transnational trajectories. Hall's perspective on the south London borough of Southwark presents a consideration of how 'home' in the public housing estates of this borough has become stigmatised by national discourses which are intertwined with international neoliberal pushes (see also chapters by Fernández Arrigoitia and Kaasa). Hall considers how 'the street' appears to provide more possibility for living interaction, and seems to offer, in this context, more chances for place-based hope and affection. While the cosmopolitan tourist vision of the polished Southbank Centre for arts is within walking distance of the estates Hall studies, it is a contrasting experience of migrant heritage and global connections, as mundane and 'thrown-together', which she uncovers on the Walworth Road.

This everyday sharing of space with memories and attachments of far-away places and times is evoked poetically and materially in Rhys-Taylor's focus on the mango as a simultaneously shared and differentially experienced artefact of cosmopolitan urban becoming in an east London street market. While food and its consumption are very often invoked as central to exchanges of cosmopolitanism, foodstuffs are more usually treated as symbols of an existing culture to be shared, learned of and consumed by 'others' (hooks 1992; Hage 1998), or the fusion of foods as a symbol of new hybrid cultures (Cook 2001). For the people Rhys-Taylor meets in the market, however, the mango is a shared everyday object of desire, yet evokes specific and different memories, feelings and attachments through its smell, taste and touch, relating to migratory histories from across the world. The mangoes themselves are cosmopolitan objects, and Rhys-Taylor shows their cosmopolitan provenance and their importance as national symbols to nations across continents. In this market, they are part of a quintessentially London environment, in part because of how they invoke and overlay these transnational connections and memories.

In Jackson's chapter, we are back again in south London, this time in Peckham, but a Peckham which evokes resonances with Lagos in its sights, sounds and smells. Again, symbols of home are sometimes non-human, this time not the dissonant familiarity of a mango, but the mundanity of the pigeons and the 'weave hair in the road' which conjure an affection for home – for some – and a fear of encroaching change – for others. While there is sensationalist disgust and repulsion at the physical signifiers of 'elsewhere' in some of the stories Jackson uncovers here, for others the belonging and affection felt by locals is expressly related to the cosmopolitan nature of the place they are in.

Part II: Places that don't exist: England(s) and elsewheres

Moving from the super-diverse spaces of inner London, this next section of the book intersects with trajectories of belonging in parts of England less obviously conceived as 'centres' of cosmopolitan transit. First, Jones considers how local policy practitioners working on national agendas of 'community cohesion' (relating to fostering shared local belonging in a context of ethnic diversity) consider their own place in networks of local and multiple belongings. The two interviewees on whom she focuses share contrasting stories of how they understand their local connections and their relationships to the transnationally embedded changes taking place where they live and work. These two emotional and emotive retellings of belonging and connection are both strikingly different, in their own ways, from the more sanitised narratives of policy within which the two interviewees work. For one, there is a feeling of profound loss and fear connected to a sense that a childhood home 'no longer exists' because of the changing populations moving there through intranational, as well as international migration; while the second story is from someone whose childhood home no longer exists on a modern map, but for whom the narrative is of building new solidarities in new places which are always becoming.

Connell's chapter continues to explore this vein of transnational connections to places which don't 'exist' in a physical sense, but whose affective consequences are important in making sense of local worlds. Piecing together oral histories of Handsworth in Birmingham, he considers the importance that the notion of 'Africa' had for a generation of young black Britons, many of whose parents had migrated from the former British colonies of the Caribbean. The experience of racist exclusion in the country of their birth was met by many of this generation by an engagement in music and poetry movements which drew explicitly on images of belonging to Africa. Connell shows how the emotional connections built through the affective experience of reggae, sound systems and poetry linked anger and pride in inner-city Birmingham to an imagined Africa, but suggests through the experience of one group's attempted migration to Africa that it was the affective connections to an idea, rather than a physical space represented by the continent, that made Handsworth liveable.

For the interviewees in Saha and Watson's chapter, the place that no longer exists is a remembered version of the outer London borough of Redbridge. This is not a clichéd story of a dispossessed melancholic whiteness but part of how 30-something British Asians make sense of the neighbourhoods in which they live. They uncover a feeling of loss for what went before, 'life and soul' and 'pride in tradition', and they uncover how this appears in the narratives of second- and third-generation migrants, and how they relate this to an expanding local population of residents from the same ethnic group as themselves. This reopens those questions of who 'belongs', and the complexities of power relations both within and between ethnic and migrant groups within wider circuits of power.

Part III: Displacement, its aftermaths and futures: Tracing connection to, from and through Europe

Part III engages with dispersals of populations within and from Europe. First, Holgersson considers a space in Gothenburg, Sweden which had long been used by marginalised groups and activities, more recently coming to the attention of developers and city authorities as a place that might suit a different vision of the future. While working-class Swedish-born locals and immigrants from Finland, Iran and the Gambia have made this space into a local place of belonging through use for community, business and religious activities, this present/past is being erased by a vision of the future which imagines these lived and felt connections as never having existed. The future housing developments may be designed to attract the cosmopolitan, in the sense of Bauman's tourist, but to do so it will erase the transnational belongings which already exist as well as removing the bodies which constitute these links. Tenaciously, one Iranian butcher has been able to insert herself into this future, disrupting the futures imagined by the planners while staking a physical and financial as well as felt claim to the place.

Grünenberg's chapter engages with subjects of more violent and extreme displacements, as she reflects on her ethnographic work with Bosnian refugees in Denmark. By considering fieldwork both in the new place of settlement in Nykøbing, Denmark, and with returnees to the places from which they have been exiled, Grünenberg uncovers complex relationships between belonging, place and power. Like many diasporic groups, many of the stories in this chapter are of a feeling of not being at home either in the former or current place of dwelling. But she also shows how some elements of new and old belongings reconfigure through specific moments, interactions and resonances between the two places – as the resemblance between a bridge in the new home creates a connection with the old place which enables new paths to be taken.

Turan Hoffman also considers a diasporic community, but in this case the displacement was of previous generations from Armenia, dispersed across the globe. Using frameworks borrowed from social psychology, she examines how an attachment to a place one has never visited is meaningful both emotionally and politically. Following tourists returning to the land from which their forebears were exiled, she explores the feelings this engenders and what it means to be moved, not just by seeing the sites one has heard of and studied, but encountering the descendants of those who remained, and reconsidering the relationships between individual encounters (between Armenian-heritage tourists and local Turkish people) and the geopolitical histories of nations.

Part IV: Cosmopolitanism in the home: North American belongings

Part IV brings us back to 'home', a circular movement from Hall's opening chapter as we return to the street (Jaffe) and estate (Fernández Arrigoitia, Kaasa), but with cases thousands of miles from where the book started. These chapters engage not with Bauman's simplified cosmopolitan figures of 'vagabond' and 'tourist', but with people 'at home' and not (necessarily) migrants, but nonetheless entwined in cosmopolitan circuits of power and meaning which impact on the shape and feel of everyday life. It is probably worth noting that while each chapter in this section is based on empirical work in the continent of North America, the work is not in the mainland US or Canadian contexts which this might immediately conjure, but in territories with a different relationship to the geopolitics of cosmopolitan belonging and histories of migration, colonisation and nationhood.

Jaffe's chapter focuses on social moments in cookshops and cafes of West Kingston, Jamaica. In particular, she analyses the emotional and affective responses of locals with whom she watched locally circulating crime documentaries made in the UK, US and Canada, focusing on Jamaican gangs in those locations and making sensational links to images of drugs, guns and squalor in Kingston. Jaffe notes how, rather than responding with offence at a negative portrayal of their area, the people with whom she watched these videos expressed pleasure at other aspects of the films – recognising familiar faces from the neighbourhood, or spots in other cities where they had lived or visited. While the documentary-makers linked Kingston to international networks of fear and exclusion, this audience demonstrated a more intimate connection across distance, of shared history and familiarity. This is not to belittle the impact of stigmatisation through cosmopolitan cultural production focused on Kingston. Jaffe also highlights more hostile reactions to the outcomes of previous popular ethnographic writing, its harmful effects on local lives, and the negotiations of this which she made in her own relationship to research.

Fernández Arrigoitia's work on a housing estate in San Juan, Puerto Rico takes us into another stigmatised public housing scheme, again echoing themes from Hall's earlier chapter. Fernández Arrigoitia's research with residents of Las Gladiolas reveals the connection between physical, affective and emotional impacts of the post-colonial context of this place. She shows how, from the creation of public housing schemes in Puerto Rico as a technology of the colonial relationship between the island and the US, intended to regulate and manage 'uncivilised' populations, persistent structural inequality remained and trapped residents in what then became treated as 'flawed dependency'. This technology of civilisation was deemed to have failed, and it, and its inhabitants, have been increasingly treated as objects of disgust. The consequent attempts by government authorities, inextricably linked with the quasi-colonial relationship with the mainland US, were played out locally in physical and legal actions documented by Fernández Arrigoitia, in turn provoking reactions of resistance from residents mobilised through complex mixtures of feeling including fear, defiance and love.

This relates closely to our final chapter, Kaasa's study of a public housing scheme in Mexico City. Like Las Gladiolas, the CUPA was initially built as part of an explicit ideological project to link the intimate practices of domestic life with the ambitions of national government, in this case an ambition to celebrate and create a vision of revolutionary, modernist nationhood. While part of an international architectural movement the design, presentation and experience of the CUPA were all intended to create a specifically Mexican experience, and Kaasa demonstrates how the interrelations between specific parts of the housing, and the lives of inhabitants – doing laundry, walking up stairs – created intimate moments of connection, and affect (specifically 'love'), which lasted well beyond the inaugural attempts to connect this affection with a visceral attachment to the revolutionary state.

★ ★ ★

It should be clear that a central concern of the book as a whole is to demonstrate the importance of narrative in producing place through feeling. Our editorial decision to organise the volume in this geographical 'outward' movement from an imagined point of origin provides a narrative logic for the book. Importantly though, this simple trope will also highlight the absurdity of imagining a one-way flow of ideas, emotion or belonging; of supposing the isolation of any 'place'; or of suggesting that there is a single 'origin' of any of the narratives, connections and flows we trace.

References

Ahmed, S. (2004) *The Cultural Politics of Emotion*, Edinburgh: Edinburgh University Press.

Appadurai, A. (1996) *Modernity at Large: Cultural Dimensions of Globalization*, Minneapolis, MN: University of Minnesota Press.

Augé, M. (1995) *Non-Places: Introduction to an Anthropology of Supermodernity*, London: Verso.

Back, L. (2007) *The Art of Listening*, London: Berg.

Bauman, Z. (1998) *Globalization: The Human Consequences*, New York: Columbia University Press.

Beck, U. and Sznaider, N. (2006) 'Unpacking cosmopolitanism for the social sciences: A research agenda', *British Journal of Sociology*, 57 (1): 1–23.

Beck, U. and Grande, E. (2010) 'Varieties of second modernity: The cosmopolitan turn in social and political theory and research', *British Journal of Sociology*, 61 (3): 409–43.

Bondi, L. and Davidson, J. (2011) 'Lost in translation', *Transactions of the Institute of British Geographers*, 36: 595–8.

Braidotti, R. (2011) *Nomadic Theory: The Portable Rosi Braidotti*, New York: Columbia University Press.

Coffey, A. (1999) *The Ethnographic Self*, London: Sage.

Cook, R. (2001) 'Robin Cook's chicken tikka masala speech', *The Guardian*, 19 April. Available at www.guardian.co.uk/world/2001/apr/19/race.britishidentity (accessed 1 October 2013).

Davidson, J., Bondi, L. and Smith, M. (eds) (2005) *Emotional Geographies*, Aldershot: Ashgate.

De Certeau, M. (1988) *The Practice of Everyday Life*, Berkeley, CA: University of California Press.

Delanty, G. (2006) 'The cosmopolitan imagination: Critical cosmopolitanism and social theory', *British Journal of Sociology*, 57 (1): 25–47.

Gilroy, P. (2004) *After Empire: Melancholia or Convivial Culture?*, London: Routledge.

—— (2010) 'Planetarity and cosmopolitics', *British Journal of Sociology*, 61 (3): 620–6.

Goodhart, D. (2013) 'At last we are talking about, and dealing with, illegals', *London Evening Standard*, 30 July. Available at www.standard.co.uk/comment/comment/david-goodhart-at-last-we-are-talking-about-and-dealing-with-illegals-8738189.html (accessed 1 October 2013).

Gunaratnam, Y. (2009) 'Narrative Interviews and Research', in Y. Gunaratnam and D. Oliviere (eds) *Narrative and Stories in Healthcare: Illness, Dying and Bereavement*, Oxford: Oxford University Press, 47–62.

Hage, G. (2000) *White Nation: Fantasies of White Supremacy in a Multicultural Society*, New York: Routledge.

Hannerz, U. (1996) *Transnational Connections: Culture, People, Places*, London: Routledge.

Haraway, D. (1988) 'Situated knowledges: The science question in feminism and the privilege of partial perspective', *Feminist Studies*, 14 (3): 575–99.

Harvey, D. (1993) 'From Space to Place and Back Again', in J. Bird, B. Curtis, T. Putnam and L. Tickner (eds) *Mapping the Futures: Local Cultures, Global Change*, New York: Routledge, 3–29.

hooks, b. (1992) 'Eating the Other', in hooks, b., *Black Looks: Race and Representation*, New York: South End Press, 21–40.

Jazeel, T. (2011) 'Spatializing difference beyond cosmopolitanism: Rethinking planetary futures', *Theory, Culture and Society*, 28 (5): 75–97.

Keith, M. (2005) *After the Cosmopolitan? Multicultural Cities and the Future of Racism*, London: Routledge.

Massey, D. (1994) *Space, Place and Gender*, Cambridge: Polity Press.

Massumi, B. (1987) 'Notes on the Translation and Acknowledgments', in G. Deleuze and F. Guattari (eds) *A Thousand Plateaus*, London: Continuum, xvii–xx.

Mills, C.W. (2000 [1959]) *The Sociological Imagination*, Oxford: Oxford University Press.

Park, R.E. (1928) 'Human migration and the marginal man', *American Journal of Sociology*, 33: 881–93.

Pile, S. (2010) 'Emotions and affect in recent human geography', *Transactions of the Institute of British Geographers*, 35 (1): 5–20.

Smith, M., Davidson, J., Cameron, L. and Bondi, L. (eds) (2009) *Emotion, Place and Culture*, Aldershot: Ashgate.

Thrift, N. (2004) 'Intensities of feeling: Towards a spatial politics of affect', *Geografisker Annaler*, 86 B(1): 57–78.

Tonkiss, F. (2005) *Space, the City and Social Theory*, Cambridge: Polity Press.

Tuan, Y. (1977) *Space and Place: The Perspective of Experience*, Minneapolis, MN: University of Minnesota Press.

Urry, J. (2010) 'Mobile sociology', *The British Journal of Sociology*, 61 (s1): 347–66.

Wetherell, M. (2012) *Affect and Emotion: A New Social Science Understanding*, London: Sage.

REFLECTIONS

Writing cities

Les Back and Michael Keith

In Duccio's *The Temptation of Christ on the Mountain* – painted some time between 1308 and 1311 – the painter depicts Christ looking down from on high at the venal city below (see Plate 1). In the painting the white son of God turns away the blandishments of the black devil. The Sienese painter was well known for his innovative takes on perspective and representation. In this famous image this God-like perspective speaks to a way of thinking about the act of social observation, the pleasure of the gaze that captures the object in its field of vision like a specimen on a petri dish. In the Bible Matthew references Christ seeing all the kingdoms of the world from his mountain-top position. In Duccio's representation a black devil gestures to the urban delights but the angels at Christ's shoulder help to hold the high ground.

If the racialised dimensions of the imagery can be over-read, abusing the temporality of the Renaissance iconography, the geometry speaks profoundly to a Judaeo-Christian juxtaposition of nature over culture, to a sense that the city symbolises the worldly and the man-made, a disposition or a way of thinking about the world as much as an object of analysis. This distinction between an urban disposition and the attempt to make sense of urban form has long roots in both the scholarship of urban studies and more deeply cultural urbanisms that structure our ways of thinking about the metropolitan.

So how should we approach the city? From what vantage point should we write? From a high perch of abstraction – physical or conceptual – or do we get our shoes dirty scurrying around knowing the city 'from below' on streets, in communities, in neighbourhoods and urban interiors? Or should we think about how these vantage points might intersect with the research imagination? There is nothing inherently oppressive about the view from above or necessarily positive about intense proximity. It is not simply a matter of the closer we get to the city, the better our account.

The city is beguiling but its multiplicities commonly confound easy rationalisation, its scale jumping and time travelling, rendering it the locus of here and elsewhere, yesterday, today and tomorrow simultaneously. As Salman Rushdie in his
love letter to London that became the famous novel *The Satanic Verses* plaintively
describes:

> Everything happens by magic. Us fairies haven't a fucking notion what's
> going on. So how do we know if it's right or wrong? We don't even know
> what it is. So what I thought was, you can either break your heart trying to
> work it all out, or you can go sit on a mountain, because that's where all
> the truth went, believe it or not, it just upped and ran away from these cit-
> ies where even the stuff under our feet is made up, a lie, and it hid up there
> in the thin air where the liars don't dare come after it in case their brains
> explode. It's up there all right. I've been there.
>
> *(Rushdie 1988: 313)*

But we cannot escape the city's embrace; its creativities and deceptions define the
increasingly urban human species:

> 'The modern city' Otto Cone on his hobbyhorse had lectured his bored
> family at the table, 'is the *locus classicus* of impossible realities. Lives that have
> no business mingling with one another sit side by side upon the omnibus.
> One universe, on a zebra crossing, is caught for an instant, blinking like a
> rabbit, in the headlamps of a motor-vehicle in which an entirely alien and
> contradictory continuum is to be found. And as long as that's all, they pass in
> the night, jostling on Tube stations, raising their hats in some hotel corridor,
> it's not so bad. But if they meet! It's uranium and plutonium, each makes the
> other decompose, boom.'
>
> *(Rushdie 1988: 314)*

We will explore the idea of perspective and the challenges of writing city life
through a series explorations of mode, concept, form and end.

Mode: How do views shape words?

We will illustrate how views shape accounts through Sukhdev Sandhu's extraordinary little book called *Night Haunts* (2007). Sandhu's account of London at night
is not only a book; it was first conceived as an interactive website produced by
Artangel which contained writing, as well as soundscapes and sound pieces. You read
it and listened to it simultaneously.[1] Silent reading is a modern phenomenon – in the
early days of the book religious texts had to be read aloud in order make sure there
was no seditious silent contemplation going on (Morrison 2000). There is something wonderful in this idea: of writing the city simultaneously through words and
sound (see also Back 2011a; Lyon and Back 2012). Social science writers can learn a

great deal about how to better represent urban life from the many good examples of contemporary writers and artists whose work is about the life of cities.

Night Haunts is an attempt to take the genre of Victorian nocturnal exposé and reinvent it. One of the chapters involves an encounter with the Avian police – The Metropolitan Police Air Unit – who begin their excursions from the former military base hinterlands of London in Lippetts Hill, Essex. During WWII the base was a prisoner of war camp for German and Italian prisoners of war. Sandhu explains:

> These avian police see, not just a side, but the entire face of London. The rest of us, victims of gravity, stranded down on the ground, have to make do with squinting from the windows of EasyJet planes or going for an evening ride on the London Eye. They do a job many of us can only dream of doing.
>
> *(Sandhu 2007: 21)*

They become what de Certeau referred to as 'voyeur gods' and clearly their presence in the skies is about surveillance, control and perspectival governmentality. Sandhu talks about the way this has taken on a new intensity in the atmosphere of incessant terror alert where thermal-imaging cameras irradiate the city. London from above looks 'skeletal, postmortemed'; even the most innocent thing seems menacing once bleached and decoloured. There is something else though that is striking in this beautiful account. Here's another passage about what the view from the sky offers:

> Things invisible at ground level suddenly rear into view: industrial parks – there seem to be hundreds of them. And while, even from the Primrose Hill or Greenwich Park, the city melds into one largely unindividuated flat-scape, at night time it becomes more composite in character, a loose and disconnected set of Lego pieces. One pilot describes Croydon as 'an oasis of high-rise buildings, sitting there like downtown Dallas'.
>
> *(Sandhu 2007: 23)*

The shift in scale can help him see things that are imperceptible from ground-level. Unlike de Certeau, Sandhu understands the duplicity of perspective. The romance of the street's horizon might be as partial and mirage-like as the seductive certainties of critical distance from on high. Sandhu ends the passage with a discussion of the sense of wonder and mastery that the pilots express as they break suddenly from 'operation speak' into a kind of urban love poetry:

> When I was working on the ground I certainly didn't like the city. Quite the opposite. But everywhere's lovely from the air. Even the worst bits look good. Like King's Cross: I never noticed the architecture of St Pancras before – all the stations and the buildings are fantastic. To be honest, I'd rather spend more time in the air than on the ground. Whatever you see on the horizon you can go to. You feel like a giant because the world is smaller.
>
> *(Sandhu 2007: 26–7)*

This invokes Roland Barthes' famous essay on *The Eiffel Tower* which paradoxically allows those who ascend it to feel 'cut off from the world and yet the owner of it' (Barthes 1979: 17). But as Barthes himself cautioned, the very presence of the new structure shaped the way the city thought of itself; he reminds us that Montesquieu dined regularly in the Tower because he thought it the only place in Paris where you could avoid its presence towering over you. In a London framed by starchitects' creations with branded monikers – the cheese grater, the gherkin, the walkie-talkie, the Shard – we are reminded of Noel Coward's wry complaint that he was not too sure what London was coming to: the higher the buildings, the lower the morals.

In contrast to the iconic landscapes of architectural conceit, a reflexive engagement with the prosaic and the sublime everyday sites of the city cautions us to consider the stories that make the city visible, and what sort of narrative forms make the city comprehensible.

Such an inflection suggests a historical sensibility that is cautious about how time serves as narrative driver; a geographical disposition that understands how space serves as narrative driver; an attitude that is sensitive to the logics of history and geography but is suspicious of the easy spatial determinism of some urban theory and the dubious inevitability of some forms of chronology.

It implies a project of scholarly urbanism that takes forward but never finishes Walter Benjamin's great unfinished *Arcades Project*, accumulating incommensurable collections of material cultures, representations and prose and playing with their curation. It also implies the occasionally speculative connection of different forms of evidence that has the power to surprise and to challenge our ways of thinking as much as proving an argument; as when Benjamin himself suggested that:

> Empire is the style of revolutionary terrorism for which the state is an end in itself. Just as Napoleon failed to understand the functional nature of the state as an instrument of domination by the bourgeois class, so the architects of his time failed to understand the functional nature of iron, with which the constructive principle begins its domination of architecture. These architects design supports resembling Pompeian columns, and factories that imitate residential houses, just as later the first railroad stations will be modelled on chalets. '*Construction plays the role of the subconscious.*'
>
> *(Benjamin 1999 [1935]: 4; original emphasis)*

This in turn implies an urbanism that peels away at the surface of the material fabric of the city, asks how regimes of power and law are translated into bricks and mortar, which stories the built form is meant to tell the spectator and how we might read against the grain, to see the ruins that are yet to come in the hubris of architectural conceit. It approaches the project Christine Boyer outlined when trying to describe what a city of collective memory might consider:

Architectural writing relies on imagery and artifacts, visual tropes that form the basic elements of its selective and combinatory system. An 'analogous city' text, not quite a real city nor entirely a fictitious one, is a composition of images produced by two kinds of generators: concrete images drawn from a memory archive or architectural types, or imaginary figures and archaic symbols retrieved from the deep structure of memory. City texts consequently are visual constructions overlapping and superimposing architectural images that contaminate and bleed into each other. This visual montage of real and imaginary objects relies on the viewer to *round out the whole.*

(Boyer 1996: 175; emphasis added)

But if we are not careful we move from the moment of reading the city to a logic of privileging the visual form, a fallacy of the visual ordering of things when we know that the visible deceives, the invisible may be more open to other forms of sensory archaeology – the tell-tale marks of routinised bodily hexis, the smells of the city, the chat and chatter of the gossip, the rumour-monger and the democracy of the senses that make us at once at home and a stranger in the places we have known for years. There is value but also a limit to the power of considering the metropolitan landscape as text that displays a hidden meaning: 'The trope of the palimpsest is inherently literary and tied to writing, but it can also be fruitfully used to discuss configurations of urban spaces and their unfolding in time without making architecture and the city simply into text' (Huyssen 2003: 7).

Our point is that views shape the city and the city is shaped by the view; the question is to what purpose. Sandhu's purpose is clear – he wants us to sit alongside him and feel the twitches of the war on terror's nervous system and yet at the same time he wants us to imagine that which is hard to appreciate from sea level. In another wonderful experiment in urban observation Artangel with Living Architecture ran an international architectural competition called *A Room for London*. They offered an open brief for a site on the roof of the Queen Elizabeth Hall at London's Southbank Centre with panoramic views of the iconic tourist sites along the Thames. The tender was won by David Kohn Architects with artist Fiona Banner for a boat-shaped replica of the *Roi des Belges* – the paddle steamer Joseph Conrad captained up the Congo River, an experience he used for his novella *The Heart of Darkness*. The boat on top of the Queen Elizabeth Hall looked like it had been marooned by a freak high tide. In the course of London's Olympic year (2012) a range of established writers were invited to ascend the high perch and contemplate the life of the city (Artangel 2013).

Of course the ground-level view retains an essential value for students of city life. China Miéville's *London's Overthrow* is a description of London in the midst of a faltering neoliberal revolution. Miéville offers an attentiveness to all that Londoners see and ignore routinely – the visible traces of social polarisation and ruined lives to the intrusive soundtrack of young people playing grime music on their phones on the bus. *London's Overthrow* is an ethnography written in the form of a prose poem.

Miéville's observations are acute and give banal and unspectacular aspects of urban culture an enchanted significance. 'You can do a class analysis of London with Christmas lights' he writes astutely (Miéville 2012: 29). In December, class distinction can be discerned through peering through the windows of most London homes. In cheaper and poorer plebeian homes 'the season is celebrated with chromatic surplus', while the rich and middle class 'strive to distinguish themselves with White-lit Christmas trees' (Miéville 2012: 30). His point might be extended; in the suburban council estates of Bexley and Croydon the entire brick and mortar is illuminated with multi-coloured electric excess, while middle-class passersby mutter 'tasteless Chavs'.

The suburban spectacle contains a deep connection to emerging class segregation in London. As Miéville explains, class diversity in London neighbourhoods – 'All those streets with many-coloured Christmas lights and white' (Miéville 2012: 66) – is due to the availability of affordable council housing for low income families. It was a Londoner's right to have a home and it meant families were not priced out of life in the heart of the city. This is changing now, and like Parisian *banlieues*, cheap housing is pushed out to the fringes of the city. By comparison, the middle classes, as Benson and Jackson point out, invest in inner city neigbourhoods and deploy their cultural capital in making such places as Peckham, south London fit for people like them to live in (Benson and Jackson 2013; see also chapters by Jackson and by Hall in this volume). 'The *banlieue*fication of London is underway' Miéville concludes. Class division and territorial stigmatisation are intensifying as the poor are concentrated in places like New Addington, Croydon where residents light up their homes at Christmas in lurid technicolour.

China Miéville's wonderful book is a reminder of the importance of wandering attentively into the interstices of city life. Proximity and getting close to the local can also be intellectual entrapment. Answers are not confined to postcodes. Zygmunt Bauman makes this plain: 'There are . . . no local solutions to globally generated problems' (Bauman 2003: 115). Solution and perspective have to be scaled to the proportions of the problem. Our perspective and vantage points have to be able to move through and across the scale of what we want to call a global sociological imagination. We need to guard against the provincialism of the particular, while paying local circumstances careful attention.

The limits of localism are a reminder of the importance of an attentiveness to the relationship between the elsewhere and the near at hand. Suzanne Hall's wonderful mapping of these global threads on London's Walworth Road is a useful example of what this can look like (Hall 2012: 34 and in her chapter in this volume). One of the issues of our time is the inability within public and political debate to take seriously the task of describing these relationships, to develop an inventory of the elsewhere on every street – or what Doreen Massey called *a global sense of place* (Massey 1994). These sonorous traces are everywhere and yet at the same time they are ignored or at best acknowledged superficially.

To sum up, we are suggesting that there are lessons that social scientists can draw from the examples we have discussed in order to make our writing and research craft more imaginative. For as Hannah Arendt once commented: 'imagination alone enables us to see things in their proper perspective' (Arendt 1993: 323). This means thinking differently about the relationship between the vantage point of observation and scale, so that nearness is not automatically coded positively and distance negatively. The scale of that imagination needs to shift, so that we can oscillate from the view from the sky to the view from the bridge, or the window.

Concept: Encounter, difference, paradox

How do we conceive of the city? There will be as many answers to this question as there are people. As a whole? As fragments? A political unit? A kaleidoscope? What keeps us interested in cities is the paradoxical stage they provide for both the encounter with difference and brutal and enduring forms of division, exclusion and violence: debarred and bridged, convivial life and the melancholic obsession with a world lost (see Back 1996, 2007; Keith 1993, 2005).

There has been so much talk in recent time about the 'death of multiculturalism' and the wounded nationalism that needs to be repaired and reinvented (Back 2009; Keith 2007). Isn't there something deeply telling in the notion of 'managing diversity': the language of the UK Home Office and their Immigration Enforcement wing betrays something important: 'control, manage, cohere'. This is not to argue the merits of social attrition or rootlessness or an empty cosmopolitanism. As Jean Amery commented: 'one must have a home in order not to need it' (Amery 1980: 46).

We are mindful of those who are precisely struggling to make a home in the damaged landscapes of our cities. It is assumed in so much of the discourse about community that disorder, or lack of cohesiveness is an inherent problem or a lack for society. Rob Sampson argues that the issue of disorder becomes a societal obsession, be it in the famous 'Broken Window Theory' or the Victorian reformer's disgust with the poor keeping pigs in the street (Sampson 2009). Controlling disorder is a vehicle for purifying or perfecting community. But isn't the modern experience precisely a matter of a release of forces through disorder: 'All that is solid melts into the air, all that is sacred is profaned' as the modernist Marx proclaimed? We certainly saw this in the responses of the UK Labour government to public concern after the 7 July 2005 London bombings. But is a socially cohesive society always a good one?

Out of the interstices of the city emerge creativities forged out of disorder, informality and extemporisation. What are sometimes understood as cramped spaces of the metropolis might equally be considered as the paradoxical consequences of attempts to control and rationalise the city that pluralise the territories of opposition to regulation.

Aren't there also huge hypocrisies to be found in the way the rich scramble for gated worlds and riverside views to be enjoyed from the window of a sound-proofed luxury flat? Michaela Benson has documented British lifestyle migration of middle-class people to France and their claims to distinctiveness and aspiration to an authentic rural life (Benson 2013). While Benson doesn't develop issues of post-coloniality and whiteness in her insightful discussion, it is also the case that some lifestyle migrants are running from what urban Britain has become. There is a clue in the cheerful description of Nick Griffin – the British National Party's Chairman – summer holidaying in the French countryside with the soundtrack of Bonnie Tyler's 1977 hit 'Lost in France' playing in his villa.[2] Hiding out on renovated pig farms, some complain about being exiled from their own 'green and pleasant land'. The irony being that their postcolonial melancholia (Gilroy 2004) about foreigners at home is voiced at the same moment when they are staking a claim as migrants in rural France.

Is the encounter with difference always doom, stillborn, fated and fatal? Paul Gilroy (2004) has articulated another vision of convivial multiculture – it has to be said to very mixed reviews – that tries to give us a name for the unspectacular, loose, unruly rhythms of encounter (see also Back 2009; Lyon and Back 2012). He and others like him stand accused of romanticism, sometimes peculiarly for not paying enough attention to racism, or for being naïve. A deficit remains in the public discussion of multicultural life with regard to a capacity to represent the unspectacular ways in which multiculture works as a daily routine of life in cities like London (see also Hall 2013).

Viewing multiculture as normal invites a different kind of imaginative enquiry: it is not an end-point but a starting point for thinking and attention. The challenge of writing the city is how to develop an inventory of encounters, albeit insisting that these encounters are paradoxical ones. Remember that the difference between a contradiction and a paradox is that a contradiction holds out the possibility of some resolution. On the other hand, paradoxes – and the incommensurable cultural and political contained within them – do not; rather they have to be lived with, like the co-existence of racist hatred and convivial sociability on the same streets, and sometimes in a single citizen. This returns us to the issue of form and how adequately we represent the complex paradoxical nature of city life.

Form: Aside from words and figures what other forms of writing?

On 19 August 2013, the *Daily Mail* headline screamed – 'Britain's crime hotspots: Astonishing new figures identify the most lawless postcodes in the country . . .'. The story reported that East London's E15 1AZ postcode was the worst place for crime in the country with 3,440 offences committed between January 2012 and June 2013. The newspaper claimed it was little more than 'a magnet for muggers, pickpockets and thieves' – despite the multi-million investment in East London prior to the London Olympics.[3]

Behind the tabloid headline is a series of interesting issues about representing the social life of the city. Drawing on statistics available on the Home Office website, the newspaper exports details of crimes and correlates them with postcodes. Nick

Herbert, the former Policing Minister who championed crime maps, was reported as saying: 'The power of crime mapping is putting information in the hands of people.' Big data speaks to new modalities of representation. Where the photograph changed the way the world understood itself and the moving image made a certain sense of presence visible – not least the maelstrom of the crowd and the crowd's power in populist demonstration – the multiplicities of GPS create their own seductive buzz, a mass of material that can be organised, taxonomised, topologised and correlated against behavioural forms and social norms, more often by those mapping market formations than urban scholars.

Part of the empirical crisis facing social researchers is that telling society is no longer the sole privilege of urban sociologists (see Savage and Burrows 2007). What place then for the urban researcher in the midst of the proliferation of freelance fact-makers and folk analysts? In this sense, part of the challenge of the current moment is to make a case for what is distinctive about the attentiveness we train on the city.

The other issue that the *Daily Mail* story helps bring into focus is the enduring dominance of statistics and quotations in providing the measures of urban culture. The current crisis in sociology is certainly about its jurisdiction (see Savage 2010) at a moment in human history when society is producing more information than ever before – this is only part of the story though. We can no longer write about social life by relying exclusively on statistical surveys or narrative interviews (see Back 2012).

Part of the unprecedented opportunity we have to write and represent the city is to augment our presentational modes and research devices. The current crisis has also stimulated an important debate about the politics of method (see Ruppert et al. 2013; Law and Ruppert 2013). Margaret Mead commented some time ago that we work within and are limited by disciplines of words and we might also add that accounts of city life have been dominated by numbers.

John Law and John Urry argue that the attention paid to social life in social science is limited to a narrow range of cultural and emotional textures:

> [Social research methods] deal, for instance, poorly with the fleeting – that which is here today and gone tomorrow, only to reappear the day after tomorrow. They deal poorly with the distributed – that is to be found here and there but not between – or that which slips and slides between one place and another. They deal poorly with the non-causal, the chaotic, the complex. And such methods have difficulty dealing with the sensory – that which is subject to vision, sound, taste, smell; with the emotional – time-space compressed outburst of anger, pain, rage, pleasure, desire, or the spiritual; and the kinaesthetic – the pleasures and pains that follow movement and displacement of people, objects, information, and ideas.
>
> *(Law and Urry 2004: 403–4)*

Earlier we stressed the importance of developing ways to attend to the fleeting and the distributed, and the value of careful description and the capacity to evoke the sensuous urban experience in all its complexity. Paul Stoller calls this 'sensuous scholarship' (Stoller 1997) and many of these themes resonate within the contributions in this volume. There is much talk about trying to get beyond text but we are a little sceptical about this because a photograph cannot argue in quite the way a sentence can. There is a possibility for re-imagining the ways we write the city, forms of argument and representation.

The cultures of audit that are preoccupied with paper, citation indexes and ranking are going to take some time to catch up with the possibility of creating sensuous and lively accounts of city life. This should not inhibit our imagination. We want to propose that we start thinking seriously about what it would mean to write within a 'democracy of the senses' following Berendt (1985). Would we represent the city differently if we stopped relying primarily on an epistemology of the look and a methodological fixation with the interview?

Twentieth-century urban sociology dulled its senses – it is time, as Stoller suggests, to 'awaken the urban scholar's body' (Stoller 1997: xi). We would extend this to expand the senses we use to make sense of the city. Alex Rhys-Taylor's extraordinary olfactory surveys of multiculture in a London market produce a different kind of inventory of the relationship between the here and the elsewhere (Rhys Taylor 2013a; see also Rhys-Taylor, this volume). Also, Rhys-Taylor (2013b) points to the complex ways in which disgust and racism operate outside of an explicit narrative form. Urban hatred does not need to be spoken and announced in order to be socially alive (Back 2011b).

This brings us to the final issue: the purpose or the end of urban writing. If our writing aspires to change the quality of attentiveness to urban cultures, we also shape cities differently as a result.

End: For whom do we write?

In September 2013, Marshall Berman passed away. The poetic urbanist of modernity, he strived to displace the certainties and pieties of hubrisitic politics with a profound humanism that saw contradiction and ambivalence in the soul of the city. In his late reflections on his great work *All That Is Solid Melts into Air*, Berman (1999: 99) suggested that Karl Marx's melting metaphor of a seductively mutable capitalism had inspired William Butler Yeats' formulation of tumult:

> Things fall apart, the centre cannot hold . . .

Yeats goes on a few lines later to suggest:

> . . . The best lack all conviction, while the worst
> Are full of passionate intensity.

In the mutable metropolis maybe it is time for slightly less conviction and slightly more inspection, reflexively, up close and then at a distance, in moments of perspicuous contrast, methodological invention and ethical mediation.

What is the real impact of our writing on cities? There is a lot of talk about impact and relevance in the academy these days. It seems that those who audit us want to be provided with evidence that our words will be translated into societal impacts. It is a measure, we think, of the instrumentalisation of impact as value. The last thing we are against is engagement and public conversation. We are not arguing for a return to the ivory tower; it is the academy that is promoting a kind of knowledge as policy or worse still research as governmentality. The Human Terrain teams containing sociologists and anthropologists operating in Afghanistan and Iraq are a warning in this regard. Should we be legislators or interpreters? We think the latter.

The call for a more public sociology is something that urban sociologists need to heed. But hyper-political posturing is not politics. Books and writing are actually quite weak instruments for social change. Perhaps their value is in another register. The importance of developing an attentiveness to the world and the urgency of developing a different kind of urban story and an inventory of vital encounters in and across difference.

We stress the paradoxical nature of these encounters: the everyday conviviality between white shopkeepers and their diverse clientele alongside racist melancholia. Shut-outs and racial exclusions are part of the world in which London minority businesses practise their 'multicultural edge' (see Lyon and Back 2012). There is also the marketing of difference that sometimes verges on caricature and also the tensions surrounding the London cosmetics trade that sells to a solely black market and trades in hair relaxing agents and skin lightening creams. This is all paradoxical urban multiculture.

We have argued for expanding our modes of writing. There is an opportunity to contemplate the creation of new kinds of vital texts like Sandhu's extraordinary *Night Haunts* project. This is not just a matter of using technological devices to achieve sensuous correspondence: to see seeing, hear hearing or to smell the whiff of the world! We are not arguing for a technological fix. Rather we want to explore how we might achieve evocation, allusion and movements of imagination through using the repertoire of multi-modal resources that are now within our reach.

We are arguing for a more artful approach to writing cities that acknowledges that we produce or re-enact the city as we write about it. The description we write of a cityscape will not hold still. The jars of food stacked on the shopkeepers' shelves or crates of fish photographed on the weekend market day will not be there the next time it springs to life for midweek trade. These accounts are epitaphs to a life passed in living rather than eternal truths.

We also want to propose that writing the city needs to be artful. We should aspire to an aesthetic sensibility beyond the limits of what passes as academic style and be crafty like Dickens's gamine hero, the Artful Dodger. This passage quoted earlier from John Law and John Urry is suggestive of what is at task in bringing a bit of craftiness into the craft. They continue:

> If methods are not innocent then they are also political. They help *make* realities. But the question is: which realities? Which do we want to help make more real, and which less real?
>
> *(Law and Urry 2004: 404; original emphasis)*

Perhaps, in the end this is the politics of what we are doing – magnifying some things, blowing them up, projecting them onto a screen, turning up the volume of the background and making it larger than life. At the same time, the end of studying city life is to cut pompous certainties down to size and challenge the arrogance of politicians and urban ideologues. Maybe this is what writing the city is needed for. To question confident pronouncements – be they about the death of multiculture or anxieties about urban disorder – while at the same time pointing at the things that cannot be said and remarking on that which is deemed unremarkable.

Notes

1   See www.nighthaunts.org.uk
2   See British National Party website 'Lost in France', available at www.nickgriffinmep.eu/content/lost-france
3   'Britain's crime hotspots: Astonishing new figures identify the most lawless postcodes in the country . . . and zero in on east London's Westfield shopping centre', *Daily Mail*, 19 August 2013. Available at www.dailymail.co.uk/news/article-2389085/Britains-crime-hotspots-Astonishing-new-figures-identify-lawless-postcodes-country--zero-Londons-Westfield-Shopping-centres.html (accessed 30 September 2013).

References

Amery, J. (1980) *At the Mind's Limit: Contemplations of a Survivor on Auschwitz and Its Realities*, Bloomington and Indianapolis, IN: Indiana University Press.

Arendt, H. (1993) *Essays in Understanding 1930–1954*, New York and London: Harcourt Brace and Company.

Artangel (2013) *A London Address*, London: Granta.

Back, L. (1996) *New Ethnicities and Urban Culture: Racisms and Multiculture in Young Lives*, London: UCL Press.

—— (2007) *The Art of Listening*, Oxford and New York: Berg Publishers.

—— (2009) 'Researching community and its moral projects', *21st Century Society*, 4(2): 2001–14.

—— (2011a) The Academic Diary, London: Free thought. Available at www.academic-diary.co.uk (accessed 1 October 2013).

—— (2011b) 'Trust your senses? War, memory, and the racist nervous system', *Senses and Society*, 6(3): 304–22.

—— (2012) 'Tape Recorder' in C. Lury and N. Wakeford (eds) *Inventive Methods*, Abingdon: Routledge.

Barthes, R. (1979) *The Eiffel Tower and Other Mythologies*, Berkeley and Los Angeles, CA, and London: University of California Press.

Bauman, Z. (2003) *Liquid Love: On the Frailty of Human Bonds*, Cambridge: Polity.

Benjamin, W. (1999 [1935]) 'Paris, the Capital of the IXth Century: 1935 Exposé' in *The Arcades Project*, Cambridge, MA: The Belknap Press/Harvard University Press.

Benson, M. (2013) 'Living the "real" dream in la France profonde? Lifestyle migration, social distinction, and the authenticities of every life', *Anthropological Quarterly*, 86(2): 501–26.

Benson, M. and Jackson, E. (2013) 'Place making and place maintenance: Practices of belonging among the middle classes', *Sociology*, 47(4): 793–809.

Berendt, J.-E. (1985) *The Third Ear: On Listening to the World*, New York: Henry Holt.

Berman, M. (1999) 'All That Is Solid Melts into Air: Marx, Modernism and Modernization' in M. Berman, *Adventures in Marxism*, London and New York: Verso.

Boyer, C. (1996) *The City of Collective Memory: Its Historical Imagery and Architectural Entertainments*, Cambridge, MA: MIT Press.

Duccio di Buoninsegna (1311) *The Temptation of Christ on the Mountain*. Available at http://commons.wikimedia.org/wiki/File:Duccio_di_Buoninsegna_-_MaestÓ_ (back,_predella).The_Temptation_of_Christ_on_the_Mountain.JPG (accessed 1 October 2013).

Gilroy, P. (2004) *After Empire: Melancholia or Convivial Culture?*, Abingdon: Routledge.

Hall, S. (2012) *City, Street and Citizen: The Measure of the Ordinary*, London and New York: Routledge.

—— (2013) 'Multilingual citizenship', *Discover Society*, 1 (October). Available at www.discoversociety.org/multilingual-citizenship (accessed 1 October 2013).

Huyssen, A. (2003) *Present Pasts: Urban Palimpsests and the Politics of Memory*, Stanford, CA: Stanford University Press.

Keith, M. (1993) *Race, Riots and Policing: Lore and Disorder in a Multi-Racist Society*, London: UCL Press.

—— (2005) *After the Cosmopolitan? Multicultural Cities and the Future of Racism*, London and New York: Routledge.

—— (2007) 'Don't sleepwalk into simplification: What the Commission on Integration and Cohesion really said', Open Democracy, 12th August. Available at www.opendemocracy. net/ourkingdom/articles/commission_on_integration_and_cohesion (accessed 1 October 2013).

Law, J. and Ruppert, E. (2013) 'The social life of methods: Devices', *Journal of Cultural Economy*, 6(3): 229–40.

Law, J. and Urry, J. (2004) 'Enacting the social', *Economy and Society*, 33: 390–410.

Lyon, D. and Back, L. (2012) 'Fishmongers in a global economy: Craft and social relations in a London market', *Sociological Research Online*, 17(2): 23. Available at www.socresonline. org.uk/17/2/23.html (accessed 1 October 2013).

Massey, D. (1994) *Space, Place and Gender*, Cambridge: Polity Press.

Miéville, C. (2012) *London's Overthrow*, London: The Westbourne Press.

Morrison, B. (2000) *The Justification of Johann Gutenberg*, London: Chatto and Windus.

Rhys-Taylor, A. (2013a) 'The essences of multiculture: A sensory exploration of an inner-city street market', *Identities: Global Studies in Culture and Power*, 20(4): 393–406.

—— (2013b) 'Disgust and distinction: The case of the jellied eel', *The Sociological Review*, 61(2): 227–46.

Ruppert, E., Law, J. and Savage, M. (2013) 'Reassembling social science methods: The challenge of digital devices', *Theory, Culture and Society*, 30(4): 22–46.

Rushdie, S. (1988) *The Satanic Verses*, London: Random House.

Sampson, R.J. (2009) 'Disparity and diversity in the contemporary city: Social (dis)order revisited', *British Journal of Sociology*, 60: 1–31.

Sandhu, S. (2007) *Night Haunts*, London and New York: Artangel & Verso.

Savage, M. (2010) *Identities and Social Change in Britain since 1940: The Politics of Method*, Oxford: Oxford University Press.

Savage, M. and Burrows, R. (2007) 'The coming crisis of empirical sociology', *Sociology*, 41(5): 885–99.

Stoller, P. (1997) *Sensuous Scholarship*, Philadelphia, PA: University of Pennsylvania Press.

PART I

Local worlds/cosmopolitan formations

London and/in the world

1

EMOTION, LOCATION AND URBAN REGENERATION

The resonance of marginalised cosmopolitanisms

Suzanne M. Hall

Introduction: The emotional resonance of marginalised places

What are the interplays between emotion, location and urban regeneration? I focus on a 'marginal' inner city area and connect the cultural resonance of location, with how emotions advance certain trajectories of urban renewal. The place in question is Walworth, an inner city south London neighbourhood described across official, media and on-the-ground sources as deprived and ethnically diverse. By contrasting the emotional registers of 'estate' and 'street' within the same place, I explore side-by-side forms of marginalisation and cosmopolitanism, where relegation *and* prospect, and containment *and* mixing abide together. While this chapter acknowledges the intensely discriminatory processes of territorial stigmatisation through both ghettoisation and marginalisation, it engages with the different spaces of 'estate' and 'street' to deviate from the discourse of absolute relegation and segregation. Rather, this chapter engages emotion to explore the resonance between affect and effect: how feelings about places are proliferated between spheres of power and everyday life. I draw on Sara Ahmed's (2004) essential conceptualisation of 'emotionality', tracing how emotions are circulated, accumulated and how they endure or 'stick'. My aim is to connect how the emotionality of stigmatised places secures distinctive paths for urban regeneration. In failing to consider the urban poor in visions of a prosperous urban future, regeneration by dispossession ultimately advances limited prospects for cosmopolitan belonging.

Walworth is an inner city place that is physically proximate to yet culturally distanced from central London. It is a mark on the map of south London close enough to the centre to catch glimpses of the London Eye and to hear the chimes of Big Ben, while remaining distant from the cultural register of urban prestige and 'World Class' prospect to its immediate north. A ten-minute red double-decker bus journey from the north of Walworth takes you to the recently regenerated Southbank Centre, where festivals, skateboarding, Public Space and Public Art aggregate in the palpable presence of the successful, cosmopolitan city: 'The complex, one of the trendiest in London . . . is truly multicultural and cosmopolitan' (www.tripadvisor.co.uk 2013). By contrast, Walworth offers a somewhat different trope of cosmopolitanism, an altogether different mix of class and ethnicity, with an emotional register of a more down-at-heel place. Despite Walworth's vast cultural distance from the Southbank Centre's orbit, Walworth is an extremely well-located, inner city location with a number of sizeable, strategic pieces of publicly owned land. Large-scale regeneration is therefore on the cards for Walworth: two of its social housing estates, the Heygate and the Aylesbury, are being regenerated; and plans to transform the Elephant and Castle public transport interchange and its associated shopping centre are underway.

As regeneration efforts emerge in Walworth, it is instructive to explore the links between emotional affect and political effect: how the emotive impressions attributed to a place come to be shared, and how these feelings advance certain trajectories of urban regeneration. I use the two different spaces of the social housing estate and the high street to explore overlapping but different processes of urban renewal. Through the estate, I focus on the persistent relegation of Walworth through the emotionally charged trope of deprivation, and how this sponsors a morally charged trope of intervention and urban redevelopment. But the narrative of urban marginality that I explore is arguably less predictable than the inevitable decline abetted by the advanced marginalisation attributed to the ghetto (Wacquant 2007). For Walworth has layers of life that lie below the radar of official scrutiny; a host of possibilities and animations that are able to exist precisely because they are rendered invisible by the authorised mask of 'deprivation'. Territorial stigmatisation frequently reveals a highly mediated process of relegation that coincides with processes of regeneration, displacement and gentrification (Smith 2002). Less visible in the gentrification literature, however, is that the stigma effect potentially also produces a mask whereby other processes of diversification emerge below the surface. In Walworth, this is particularly evident during fallow regeneration cycles, when there is limited interference from the market or state.

As a local resident of Walworth from 2004 to 2010, during which time I undertook an ethnography of the Walworth Road (Hall 2012), I became aware of a *complex urban marginality*, where historic cycles of limited economic growth were iteratively followed by economic booms and targeted regeneration. These cyclical economic periods have led to an urban landscape of complex marginality, where relegation intersects with prospect, and where class intersects with pronounced ethnic diversity sustained by periods of urban migration. In the last half century Walworth has incurred two large-scale processes of regeneration with no significant state-led redevelopment between the two periods. Authorised regeneration in the 1960s and 1970s took the form of *en masse* social housing provision together with the rationalisation of the Elephant and Castle transport interchange. State-facilitated regeneration since 2008 involves a process of dismantling the same *en masse* housing estates and over-determined transport interchange, in the process releasing substantial redevelopment opportunities to the open market. However, state-led or state-facilitated regeneration endeavours coexist, even if uncomfortably, with much smaller, much more diverse and ongoing acts of urban renewal. The exploration of a complex urban marginality through the spaces of 'estate' and 'street' arguably leads to a more cluttered view of urban marginalisation. It is therefore possible to trace the registers of relegation imposed on the urban poor in Walworth, alongside practices of border crossings across containments of class, ethnicity and demotion, where alternative, albeit less visible, cultural registers emerge.

To explore how the spaces of 'estate' and 'street' are rendered culturally visible, I directly draw on Ahmed's (2004) three processes by which emotions are socially produced. Emotions *circulate* by moving 'outside in': meanings are impressed from the outside onto objects and texts, and buildings and places, gradually acquiring and resonating a social measure of value. Individuals read the social 'worth' of these symbols, interpreting and responding to their social value. Emotions *accumulate*, their increase in shared impact secured through the distribution, repetition and subsequent inflation of affect or cultural reach. Emotions *endure*, they 'stick', creating a shared, intractable response to objects, people and places. Through tracing the circulation, accumulation and endurance of collectively shared emotions, Ahmed shows that the power of emotion in making and securing collective meaning is that it is evoked before it is rationalised. To add to Ahmed's 'emotionality' I trace the role of emotions in the *transformation* of buildings and places, and how the power of emotion is used to gain cultural momentum for political traction. The collective feelings associated with the scale, shape, mass and texture of built form is used to project an attitude to objects, people and places, thereby procuring legitimation for intervention or regeneration.

This chapter focuses on the work that emotion does in defining place, by tracing the circulation, accumulation, endurance and transformative potential of affect in the making and remaking of Walworth. Two related questions guide the analysis: first, how do the attributes of a place socially circulate; 'what sticks' in the shared impressions of a place? And second, what modes of urban transformation do the place-oriented impressions of deprivation and diversity sponsor? Emotionality, I argue, allows us to see the 'social syntax' of place: the emotive political and cultural constructions of territories, people and objects that come to register a public or shared sense of place. The register opens up fertile ground for further emotive claims as to how and why certain places require 'fixing'. Regeneration claims often result in further withdrawals of state investment from a place, thereby compounding segregation by class and race. However, in the seemingly simplistic analogy of cheek-by-jowl 'estate' and 'street' the significant narrative of a complex urban marginality emerges. The histories of urban poverty formation intersect with those of urban migration and the cultural diversification of the city, arguably most pronounced in London's most deprived areas. In the two sections that follow I focus on the cultural resonance of estate and street, to trace varied forms of belonging alongside varied practices of urban renewal.

The registers of relegation: Estate

> We lived in Peckham, in a council house my family, big family. We had a garden, we had a dog, and then when I was five years old the council decided to regenerate Peckham and they tore all those houses down. I mean it was miles and miles of, of, council housing, and destroyed the communities that lived there and built the notorious North Peckham Estate, which was opened in the 70s. So what really happened was the tight-knit kind of community that I first lived in was just literally destroyed overnight. I mean it was a terrible, terrible thing that happened to the area. I don't think the area ever recovered, because since then, as you know, they have regenerated Peckham again, by tearing down the North Peckham Estate. So what I say is, 'What Hitler failed to do during the Blitz, Southwark Council have done twice in my life-time.' (laughs) . . . My grandparents ended up in Wood Dene in Peckham, which is now about to be, at last, demolished. We called it 'The Kremlin', and in fact the bus conductor used to say, 'anyone for the Kremlin?' and we used to jump off the bus. It was awful. A horror estate . . . Big double page spread in 'The South London Press' about horror estates.
>
> *(John, self-proclaimed 'social housing tenant', Interview 2007)*

There is surely no form of architectural invention in the UK so intensely the object of heart-felt grievance (Hanley 2007), literary degradation (Amis 1989), social analysis (Power 1987) and ongoing official intervention than the modernist social housing estate. The cultural notoriety of this singularly symbolic spatial and social form has, as John's words above show, subjected the diverse inhabitants of *en masse* housing estates to repetitive iterations of displacement, demolition and renewal. How are these disruptive repetitions justified as 'regeneration'? Ahmed refers to 'processes of intensification' (2004: 45) where the emotive currency of an object or issue is publicly heightened, even exaggerated, to induce pronounced, shared emotional reactions. Although these reactions may be individually felt, they are widely procured, circulated and maintained through highly emotive symbols. John refers to his grandparents' fortification in Wood Dene through the symbol of 'The Kremlin', whilst other council inhabitants in an east London housing estate refer to their place of residence as 'Alcatraz', evoking imprisonment rather than residence (Foster 1995). As Ahmed suggests, highly emotive symbols – in this case fortification and imprisonment – travel 'outside in' through permeating broader societal registers, acquiring widespread connotations, and resonating in the perceptions of housing estate residents. Finally, emotive symbols serve to justify targeted political interventions. It is instructive to trace the emergence of stigma or what Goffman aptly refers to as 'the management of spoiled identity' (1963) through spatial symbols, and to connect stigma to Ahmed's 'emotionality' through how emotions are socially produced in the mass and materiality of social housing estates.

Until recently, there were three large-scale social housing estates adjacent to Walworth Road that together provided some 5,000 social housing units. The diverse individuals and families of the Heygate, Aylesbury and Brandon estates were able to benefit from comparatively affordable housing within close proximity to good public transportation links, an array of public amenities and inner city work opportunities. To deflate the overextended association of 'sink' estates with 'low life' inhabitants (Haylett 2001), it is important to note that social housing estates in London typically aggregate a comparatively wide economic mix of inhabitants, and historically have provided state-subsidised and affordable housing opportunities in a city where property values continue to dramatically increase, despite the current impact of the global economic crisis. Substantial proportions of Great Britain's twentieth-century housing were provided through publicly rented housing stock, reaching a climax in 1979 where 32 per cent of housing was publicly rented (Stone 2003: 14). A significant number of highly diverse individuals lived, and continue to live, in social housing.

But well outside this sanguine perspective, two of the three social housing estates within Walworth – the Aylesbury and Heygate estates – are recipients of heightened stigmata. The Aylesbury, located halfway down the Walworth Road, was described in the press on the dawn of its recent regeneration, as 'hell's waiting room', a literal demonisation that in an evocative swipe denigrates the diverse residents of the Aylesbury (Muir 2005). How is it that the monolithic forms of the estate are all too readily translatable into reductive social monoliths? Built in 1963 and comprising 2,700 units, the Aylesbury was the largest housing estate in Europe within one contained area. The sheer scale of the development was matched with individual building mass, and the 120 metre block of housing along Thurlow Street has the dubious honour of being the longest prefabricated stretch of housing in the UK (Boast 2005). The Heygate estate, located to the north of the Walworth Road and adjacent to the strategic public transport interchange at the Elephant and Castle, was built between 1970 and 1974 and comprised of 1,194 units. Providing well-located inner city housing to diverse individuals, this estate too is relegated in the media as 'a concrete warren . . . with a grim reputation for crime, poverty and dilapidation . . . a monument to the failure of post-war mass housing' ('Daily Mail Reporter' 2013).

In 2007, clearance and regeneration programmes commenced on both estates. The stated objective from the London Borough of Southwark (LBS) – to regenerate poor quality housing stock – drew links between spatial and social degeneration to justify redevelopment. Who gained from the circulated notoriety of these estates? At the Aylesbury, the regeneration process has been led by a housing association, the Creation Trust, and has depended on an increase in housing density from 2,700 to 4,900 units. While 2,288 units are secured for social housing, the remainder will be sold on the open market to fund the regeneration project. The ongoing densification process has resulted in limited demolition, as the new housing blocks are inserted amongst existing fabric, but has also yielded a housing mix with a shift in emphasis from public rental to private ownership. Arguably, the mass of the Aylesbury has been disaggregated in social mix, spatial form and material textures, despite the increase in units (Lees 2013 provides an important, less sympathetic perspective of the process).

By contrast, the regeneration process at the Heygate estate has been facilitated by the LBS and led by the private developer, Lend Lease. Regeneration commenced in 2008 with the eviction of all of the Heygate's residents. By 2012 a deal was struck for the balance of profit and populace to be feasible for the developers, where 75 per cent of the new housing would be released to the market and 25 per cent would be 'affordable housing' (for details: http://londonist.com/2012/02/heygate-estate-residents-rebuff-lend-lease-masterplan.php). Five years on from the eviction of its residents, the vast estate remains boarded up, the *tabula rasa* development logic tampered by an economic recession in which it is increasingly difficult to rebuild housing, and particularly social housing, at scale without significant state intervention. In the context of substantial government cuts to public funds, and an increasing appetite to assist in the raising of urban land values, the state effectively withdrew from its holding at the Heygate. In April 2013 Southwark Council sold the estate and its land to Lend Lease for £50 million pounds. It has emerged that only 79 of the 2,535 new housing units will be available as rented public housing. While this process animates Smith's (2002) argument that economic globalisation has produced a revanchist urbanism where gentrification is a primary strategy, Ahmed's emotionality allows us to trace the historic and contemporary modes through which regeneration logics are publicly secured.

The process of rupture – captured in the Heygate example as *en masse* social displacement, is integral to the *circulation* of estate stigma. During the post-war period from 1950 to 1970, numerous large-scale territories of well-located inner city land became available for an accelerated, *en masse* social housing initiative, and some 2.9 million social housing units were built (Stone 2003). The production of large-scale social housing in London emerged from the intersections of post-war rupture, a strong political commitment to house the working classes accelerated by the Wilson government between 1964 and 1979, and limited appetite for property speculation. The political production of housing was matched with an ideological commitment to find new spatial forms of living that would exemplify a modern age afforded by the new possibilities of industrial mass fabrication (Le Corbusier 1923). The commitment of the international movement in architecture and its geographic spread perpetuated a widely shared vocabulary for social housing, thereby accelerating its insignia initially as modernity and subsequently of failure: 'Affect does not reside in an object or sign, but it is an effect of the circulation between objects and signs . . . the more signs circulate, the more affective they become' (Ahmed 2004: 45)

The stigma of failure was similarly internationalised through the symbolic forms of the demise of, for example, Cabrini Green in Chicago (1940), Pruitt Igoe in St Louis (1954) and Biljmermeer in Amsterdam (1966). Despite the noble intentions behind the large-scale provision of well-located urban housing, a powerful perceptual paradigm of *en masse* urbanism came to negatively signify many of these social housing estates, including the Heygate and Aylesbury estates in Walworth. While the standardisation of built form relied on the homogenisation, repetition and geographic spread in the *accumulation* of estate stigma, the materiality and scale of these visibly monolithic, concrete social housing estates evoked overt characterisations of people and place. A standardisation of built form came to correspond with a standardisation of language reiterated in the media through the short hand of the 'sink' estate:

- '10 steps to turning around a sink estate: Graffiti. Muggings. Fly tipping. Drug taking. Vandalism. What to do when a housing estate is this blighted?' (Lane 2008).
- 'The end of sink estates? Council to give more homes to those WITH jobs to help break the benefits culture: Council houses are to be set aside for people who work for a living . . . The aim is to stop the slide of social housing estates into benefit dependency and crime and restore their original status as decent places for respectable working families' (Doughty 2011).
- 'North's sink estates are "beyond saving": Crime, vandalism, chronic unemployment . . . Many rundown housing estates in northern England should be considered beyond redemption and demolished, according to a devastating report published yesterday. The report concluded that some neighbourhoods, particularly in the north-east and north-west, could not be saved because they suffered from insurmountable problems ranging from crime and heavy unemployment to a poor image' (Hetherington 2006).

The emotive portrayal of 'sink' estates is strongly evoked through registers of disgust – 'drug taking, vandalism, muggings, crime, benefit dependency' – which serve to secure the alterity of the estate as a flawed but isolated micro-world. But as Lawler shows (2005: 429), 'disgust' is not simply the 'violation of taste in relation to class'; it is also a means of preparing the grounds for the expulsion and exclusion of the working class, a regeneration rhetoric prompted in these media excerpts through reformation; 'turning around' and 'breaking the benefits culture' providing the antidote to the cause of disgust. The intentional physical detachment of the estates from their surrounds has assisted in the formation and *endurance* of estate stigma. The logic of containment insists that it is the 'sink' estate, and its 'low life' inhabitants that is the problem, where the 'cure' lies in estate regeneration (commensurate with profiteering), without the need for broader structural redress.

Who gains from the circulated notoriety of social housing estates, and why is social transformation so difficult to achieve once estate stigma has stuck? The regeneration of the Heygate and Aylesbury estates including the eviction and displacement of thousands of diverse council tenants who lived in the Heygate estate has been accompanied by the highly emotive, singular relegation of these estates and their inhabitants in both planning and media discourse. Pre-2008, these regeneration schemes were promoted as public–private partnerships, in which local people were to be central. The economic crisis has been used to tip the terms of the social compact in favour of profit. *En masse* building in the 1960s and 1970s has heralded the follow up of *en masse* displacement post-2008, and social housing tenants will be forced further away from the prospects and conveniences of the city. In exploring the 'emotionality' of the estate as both the material and social production of relegation, we come to see the affect and effect of what Williams (2001 [1958]) described as 'the masses formulae'. If 'cosmopolitan' urbanism offers a more disaggregated, diverse antithesis to the *en masse* urbanism of the 1960s and the revanchist urbanism of the global era, it cannot be imagined simply as cultural diversity. Our framing of 'cosmopolitan belonging' must incorporate class diversity and recognise inequality, and it is arguably in the landscapes of well-located inner city social housing that crucially diverse forms of cosmopolitan belonging are best secured (Hall 2013).

The registers of the everyday: Street

> In its way, Dragon Castle's presence in so dispiritingly hideous a centre of urban deprivation is just as incongruous as finding Jim's sitcom crumpet on the bridge of the USS Enterprise. Certainly, it's a shock to walk through a door on such a gruesome main road and be greeted by a gently splash-ing fountain, and to find an ocular feast of red paper dragons, tassel-strewn lanterns and golden chandeliers so luminescently vulgar, they'd be asked to leave a Las Vegas casino on the grounds of taste. Myself, I liked this retro gaudiness, and loved how it was framed, through smeary windows, by dirty red buses trundling down a filthy road on a dank, drizzly day.
>
> *(Norman 2008)*

Norman's brief sojourn to south London to dip in a bit of urban exotica-come-filth is lavish in its lack of restraint. Were he to brave it past the Dragon's Castle restau-rant and the first hundred yards of the Walworth Road, he may have encountered a somewhat different ocular feast, albeit one that might be invisible to a stereotypi-cal inclination. Here is a mile-stretch of street where 128 independent proprietors converge, their countries of origin spanning a global web of Afghanistan, China, Cyprus and Northern Cyprus, England, Ghana, India, Iran, Ireland, Italy, Jamaica, Malawi, Malaysia, Pakistan, Nigeria, Sudan, Sierra Leone, Trinidad, Turkey and Vietnam (Hall 2012). Unlike the explicit visibility of the 'estate' and its *en masse* insignia of physical and moral dereliction, the Walworth Road is a linear aggrega-tion of parts, activated by the everyday pragmatisms of making do and getting by. The apparently banal activities of buying a lotto ticket, visiting the Council's One Stop Shop, returning a library DVD, or stopping off for milk and a paper on the way home, render an everyday, apparently unremarkable, urban collage.

For those who penetrate beyond the surface exteriors of the shop fronts, there are a collection of small interiors where bespoke suits, bacon-egg-and-chips, ornate furniture, betting, legal claims, holidays to Nigeria, and hair and nails can all be acquired. It is not that the social housing estates adjacent to the street are with-out their intimacies and intricacies, but domestic etiquette on estates limits public access, while the street's everyday banality arguably reduces emotive hype and with it more totalising portrayals of relegation. (Although Jackson's portrayal in this book of a totalising and emotional reading of Rye Lane in Peckham as an 'African' street points to the contrary.) While the housing estate is socially read through its static, monolithic exterior, it is the street's collection of dynamic interiors that allows for its legibility and its more diverse cultural *circulation*. Angela, an ex-art student comments, 'I used to go down to the Walworth Road whenever I needed something for an art project' reflecting on the street's cheap and peculiar assortment of goods.

For others, it is the assortment of people that makes for its value. Mustafa, a pensioner who visits the Walworth Road a few times a week says, 'I like the Walworth Road very much. It's one of the best roads in Southwark. Got all nationalities, everyone's doing what they want to do.' Rags, a retired Bermondsey boxer and former welterweight champion who grew up in Walworth offers a more qualified affirmation: 'The Walworth Road has changed dramatically. It's a really multicultural society, a multinational society. Put it this way, I don't feel racism around here, I don't think colour matters so much around here . . . except with the police.' Rags' 'feel' for racism is an important navigator for his daily and life choices. While he chooses to regularly frequent the Walworth Road, as an emerging boxing talent he forfeited his welterweight title, rather than defend it in the then apartheid South Africa.

For others still, the street has altered in ways that 'feel' outside their habitus. Mike who is in his seventies and moved to Walworth from east London comments, 'Walworth Road was ordinary Cockney-type society. Most of 'em in the graveyard now . . . There was big changes when the migrants came here, 50s onwards . . . There was small shops, no supermarkets, run by English people'. Rhys-Taylor captures these ways of emotionally navigating places and how they change through 'culturally bequeathed gut feelings for the boundaries of one's own class' (2013: 237) as evoked by a 'sensoria' of sight, smell, touch. Jack, for example, feels change as more gradual, marked by the loss of shared cultural practices within a place:

> There's been subtle changes. Take the changing role of the pubs. Every street had a pub, and that was like a community centre. You could come home of an evening, take off your working-class clothes, get your newspaper and go down to the pub . . . It wasn't just a question of drinking, it was a social club. The way I got to know people was the pub . . .
>
> *(Fieldwork Interview, 2007)*

But the street adapts, unlike the more brittle form of the estate, its physical architecture acquiring new social morphologies. Kebab shops and barbers offer a different clientele the social venues that are not unlike Jack's reference to the pub as shop-cum-community centre. These street interiorities host opportunities for casual and habitual associations invisible to the passer-by. And while Jack has lost his regular pub, he still frequents Nick's Caff: 'I've been coming for years and years. Since my divorce, I come for supper on my way home. It's very much like a social club. What you'd call "caff society" – know what I mean?' The *accumulation* of the diverse cultural repertoires of the street that span Mustafa, Rags, Mike and Jack's associations are tied in part to its disaggregated physical form and its incremental

adaptability. But land values have also played a key role, and Walworth's comparatively deflated value from industrial to contemporary times has allowed for a host of
newcomers to set up shop over the span of a century. The *Post Office London Street
and Commercial Directory* (1881–1950) reflects waves of immigrants occupying the
retail spaces along the length of the Walworth Road, from eastern European and
Irish immigrants in the 1880s, to Greek, Italian and Cypriot immigrants in 1950,
to the array of proprietors who occupy the interior edges of the Walworth Road
today representing over 20 countries of origin.

The *endurance* of the street's actual and perceptual diversity is in part hardwired
by its particular urban infrastructure, which has generated high levels of footfall and
therefore good retail opportunity along the length of the street. There are some
15,000 people living and working in close walking distance of the Walworth Road
(CABE 2007), while some 180 buses shift up and down the street per hour. These
thresholds of support allow this street, located within a comparatively deprived
urban area, to sustain an economic vitality largely based on convenience, and
shaped by diverse small-scale entrepreneurial endeavours including those established by the waves of migrants from the late 1800s onwards. Indeed, the total
estimated weekly expenditure for residents living in proximity to and served by
the Walworth Road in 2007 was £4.3 million, as compared with £4.8 million
within the far more affluent, 'upmarket' High Street Hampstead catchment area
(CABE 2007). Although the Walworth Road is surrounded by a less affluent population, the population density in proximity to it sustains a diverse, small-scale retail
economy that has fared comparatively well – 32 per cent of proprietors have been
in place for 20 years or more, pointing to duration as an important measure of economic and social value (Hall 2011).

The *transformation* of the street has been incremental, driven largely by the
small scales of individual property ownership, the range of proprietors along
the street and the needs of ethnically diverse clientele. Design interventions by the
LBS through the 'Walworth Project' in 2010 (http://www.nsl.co.uk/case studies/
transformation-of-walworth-road) were low key, attending to safer crossings and
wider pavements together with fairly demure insertions of trees and benches. But
with the imminent changes to the Heygate and Aylesbury estates it is likely that the
pace of change on the Walworth Road will be increased. Will the LBS and its next
cohort of development partners be able to recognise the diverse cultural, economic
and social value of the street? Will their measures of 'successful' cosmopolitanism
extend past places like the Southbank Centre, where retail chains that are familiar
across the city prevail, and the public is largely constituted by a middle-to-upper-
class presence?

Complex urban marginality and cosmopolitan belonging

> I am delighted to publish my spatial development strategy for London – a
> keystone in realising my vision for London as the best big city in the world
> . . . My vision for London embraces two objectives. London must retain and

build upon its world city status as one of three business centres of global reach
. . . London must also be among the best cities in the world to live, whatever
your age or background. We need enough homes, meeting a diversity of
needs . . . We must close the unacceptable gaps in life chances, opportunities
and quality of life between Londoners; tackle disadvantage and discrimination and ensure opportunities accessible to all . . . These objectives are not
opposites. We can't achieve one without the other. But there can be tensions
between them . . .

(Boris Johnson's introduction to the London Plan, GLA 2011)

Tensions between 'world city status' and increasing disadvantage and displacement
abound in post-2008 London. As urban land values increase in London and as public resources decrease, 'the best big city in the world' appears to favour privilege. By
exploring the role that emotion plays in urban regeneration processes, it is apparent
that feelings are procured and heightened to rationalise the eviction of inhabitants
in favour of profit-oriented redevelopment. Buildings and places, materiality and
surface, are key to accumulating the symbols of decline. At the same time, the narrow narratives of 'cosmopolitan belonging' that circulate through the spaces and
textures of the city present particular narrow views of cultural diversity, where
architectural forms merge with social compositions. Social housing estates and everyday multi-ethnic streets don't fit with the aesthetics of cosmopolitanism promoted in places like the Southbank Centre, only a short bus ride from Walworth.

This chapter has contrasted the estate and street of Walworth's diverse and comparatively deprived urban landscape, directly challenging the singular narratives
and images of 'cosmopolitanism' that essentially promote middle-to-upper income
mixing. But the contrast of estate and street also serves to reveal a complex urban
marginality, as opposed to an advanced marginality, to show how Walworth exists
as an inner city location with both relegation and prospect, and containment and
mixing. The emotions that circulate, accumulate and endure across the microcosms
of the Heygate and Aylesbury estates, and along the Walworth Road, are as varied
as their material compositions. However, stigma tends to stick precisely where it is
easier to procure a singular image, a standardised notation, so explicitly embodied
in the form of the modernist housing estate.

Finally, there is a necessary response to the myopic and cynical act of decant-
ing the Heygate estate and relinquishing it to the open market with the most
cursory, minimal requirement for social housing. The prospects for 'cosmopolitan
belonging' are substantially limited in a city that is becoming increasing disparate, and where the dispossession of low-income individuals from well-located
urban housing is being actively pursued. Dispossession will be further advanced
with the Conservative–Liberal Democrat government's 2011 rearrangement of the
terms of social housing rental through the 'Affordable Rent' scheme (http://www.
homesandcommunities.co.uk/ourwork/affordable-rent), allowing for social housing rentals on new or re-let public property to be let at 80 per cent of market
value. Low-income exclusion from well-located urban housing will therefore be

particularly exaggerated in inner city areas such as London where market values are already inflated. Any prospect for a richly diverse and more equitable belonging cannot be left to the logics of revanchist urbanism. Securing and giving shape to a more diverse, more cosmopolitan future, that has more varied social and spatial form will require different social and architectural imaginaries. More explicitly, it will require state intervention of the sort that recognises that social housing, accessible education and a range of livelihoods are central to the diverse vitality of London's landscapes.

References

Ahmed, S. (2004) *The Cultural Politics of Emotion*, New York: Routledge.

Amis, M. (1989) *London Fields*, London: Jonathan Cape.

Boast, M. (2005) *The Story of Walworth*, London: London Borough of Southwark.

CABE (2007) *Paved with Gold: The Real Value of Good Street Design*. Available at www.cabe.org.uk/files/paved-with-gold.pdf (accessed 1 October 2013).

'Daily Mail Reporter' (2013) 'Secret twilight of the high-rise housing awaiting demolition', MailOnline, 28 April. Available at www.dailymail.co.uk/news/article-2316072 (accessed 1 October 2013).

Doughty, S. (2011) 'The end of sink estates?' MailOnline, 3 November. Available at www.dailymail.co.uk/news/article-2057183 (accessed 1 October 2013).

Foster, J. (1995) 'Informal social control and community crime prevention', *British Journal of Criminology*, 53: 563–83.

GLA (2011) *The London Plan: Spatial Development Strategy for Greater London*, July 2011.

Goffman, E. (1963) *Stigma: Notes on the Management of a Spoiled Identity*, New York: Simon & Schuster.

Hall, S.M. (2011) 'High street adaptations: Ethnicity, independent retail practices and localism in London's urban margins', *Environment and Planning A*, 43(11): 2571–88.

—— (2012) *City, Street and Citizen: The Measure of the Ordinary*, London: Routledge.

—— (2013) 'The politics of belonging', *Identities: Global Studies in Culture and Power*, 20(1): 46–53.

Hanley, L. (2007) *Estates: An Intimate History*, London: Granta.

Haylett, C. (2001) 'Illegitimate subjects? Abject whites, neoliberal modernisation, and middle-class multiculturalism', *Environment and Planning D*, 19: 351–70.

Hetherington, P. (2006) 'North's sink estates are "beyond saving"', *The Guardian*, 6 January. Available at www.guardian.co.uk/uk/2000/jan/06/britishidentity.peterhetherington (accessed 1 October 2013).

Lane, M. (2008) '10 steps to turning around a sink estate', BBC News magazine, 1 April. Available at http://news.bbc.co.uk/1/hi/magazine/7318556.stm (accessed 1 October 2013).

Lawler, S. (2005) 'Disgusted subjects: The making of middle-class identities', *Sociological Review*, 53(3): 429–46.

Le Corbusier (1923; 2007) *Towards a New Architecture*, trans. J. Goodman, Los Angeles, CA: Getty Research Institute.

Lees, L. (2013) 'The urban injustices of New Labour's "New Urban Renewal": The case of the Aylesbury Estate in London', *Antipode*. Available at doi: 10.1111/anti.12020

Muir, H. (2005) 'Deliberately demoralising', *Guardian Society Supplement*, 18 May. Available at www.guardian.co.uk/society/2005/may/18/guardiansocietysupplement.politics2 (accessed 1 October 2013).

Norman, M. (2008) 'Restaurant review: Dragon Castle', *Guardian Weekend*, 8 November. Available at www.guardian.co.uk/lifeandstyle/2008/nov/08/restaurant-review-dragon-castle (accessed 1 October 2013).

Post Office (1881–1950) *Post Office London Directory: Streets and Commercial Directory*, London: Post Office.

Power, A. (1987) *Property before People: The Management of Twentieth-Century Council Housing*, London: Unwin.

Rhys-Taylor, A. (2013) 'Disgust and distinction: The case of the jellied eel', *The Sociological Review*, 61(2): 227–46.

Smith, N. (2002) 'New globalisation, new urbanism: Gentrification as a global strategy', *Antipode*, 34(3): 427–50.

Stone, M.E. (2003) *Social Housing in the UK and US: Evolution, Issues and Prospects*, Working Paper, 1–83. Available at www.gold.ac.uk/media/Stonefinal.pdf (accessed 1 October 2013).

Wacquant, L. (2007) *Urban Outcasts: A Comparative Sociology of Advanced Marginality*, Cambridge: Polity.

Williams, R. (2001 [1958]) 'Culture is Ordinary', in J. Higgins (ed.), *The Raymond Williams Reader*, Oxford: Blackwell Publishers.

2

INTERSEMIOTIC FRUIT

Mangoes, multiculture and the city

Alex Rhys-Taylor

There is not, it seems, a single morsel that cannot be bought and consumed in contemporary London. From crocodile steaks through jellied eels and fried chicken to pink peppercorns, purple broccoli, halal hotdogs, kosher crumpets, truffles, tripe, salt-fish and zebra (yes, really), the city's food court is as multifarious as it is multitudinous. Every day an assortment of grocers, supermarkets and restaurants successfully satisfy the palates of most of the city's 8.3 million. The effect of this gustatory diversity is that, from one angle, the shelves of London's grocers and kitchens appear an ideal playground for omnivorous cosmopolites with little emotional investment in anything specific. However, if we shift perspective to consider the meanings that people ascribe to the myriad commonplace flavours, textures and smells, we get a sense of a different cosmopolitan reality. That is, we see the extent to which many of the city's residents hold deep affection for specific sensoria, affection that culminates in locally specific culture. Moreover, if we consider the trajectories of ingredients that predominate the most 'everyday' spaces of the city we see that this local culture has distinctly post-colonial facets. More precisely, the regimes of taste and distaste that characterise the city have their roots in the routes mapped out in previous centuries of European colonialism. This is not to say that the cultures of, and relations between, colonisers and the colonised are automatically remade in the city's food court. Rather that in many instances, the tastes bequeathed through colonial circuitry lend themselves to the production of novel senses of identity and articulations of culture that inevitably disrupt and destabilise the borders, binaries and hierarchies upon which colonial asymmetries were founded. In doing so, they ground new forms of cosmopolitan belonging in a sensuous and emotional relationship with the city. As this chapter aims to demonstrate, global food in London is at once central to forging affection for the city's locales and to maintaining connections to elsewhere. Drawing on an ongoing ethnographic exploration of taste and culture in the streets, kitchens and shopping baskets of inner-city London, it reveals the role of 'globalised' food stuffs within the production of distinctly local forms of post-colonial, multiculture.

Paul Gilroy describes the 'convivial multiculture' that characterises aspects of the contemporary British city as emerging around sites of cultural 'overlapping' (Gilroy 2006: 28), where difference exists alongside shared points of signification and emotional attachment. And indeed, some of the points of overlap cited by Gilroy, such as the Highland shortbread craved by Mancunian Guantanamo detainee, Jamal al Harith (Gilroy 2005: 439), are gustatory. However, moving beyond considerations of the role of recognisably 'British' points of overlap, and the binaries of 'native' and 'migrant' they play into, this chapter hones its attention on 'tastes of elsewhere' in the affective production of the post-colonial city's local culture. Focusing particularly on a specific collection of non-indigenous fruits, berries, spices and vegetables – each of which was propagated around the tropics by European colonisers – the aim is to foreground the roles of these objects within the city's multiculture.

To get a sense of what I am talking about it serves to move the focus of this discussion away from generalisations, to a precise location in London, halfway up Ridley Road Market, Dalston, east London. Since its formal establishment in the 1920s the market has been an enduring source of 'a variety of wares, and . . . a great deal of spontaneous entertainment' (Benedetta 1936: 138). Particularly notable for its ability to cater to the tastes and budgets of a wide range of the city's most marginalised migrant groups (Rhys-Taylor 2013), the unruly space is also the site of some of the most remarkable cultural activity undertaken by the city's inhabitants. It is a space through which transnational connections are made and out of which new local cultural formations emerge. As remarkable as it is, however, much of that activity appears at first to be banal. Consider, for instance, Marcia, who patters her way slowly through the lively throng of the street market on an early summer morning, an old wicker basket hanging from the crook of her elbow. Her movement is stiff but efficient as she shuffles between hollering vendors and absent-minded strollers towards a small huddle. She joins the disorderly queue congealing around the sweet, woody-floral scent of freshly cut mangoes. A grocer is offering them on a paper plate for the delectation of passers-by while his colleague handles the exchange of fruit for money. The man with the change in his belt greets the first in queue.

'Ni Hao, Ni Hao, four for a pound.'
'I'm Vietnamese,' she replies in a cockney chirrup, smiling and unbothered.

Over the next two minutes the grocer banters his way through the group of ostensibly Bengali, Ghanaian and British women, the crowd occasionally sharing a laugh at one of the grocer's armoury of jokes. Finally he reaches Marcia. Like the others before her, she swaps a pound coin for a box of four mangoes. Lifting the corrugated lid to check the fruits nestled in shredded blue paper, she sees – and smells – that they are ripe and need to be eaten quickly. She resolves to share them with her children and grandchildren. Moments later, explaining her choice of the mangoes to me, Marcia tells of how, as a young girl in Saint Lucia, she was occasionally given the mango stone to suck on as a treat, teasing residues of pulp from the fibres around the stone. These Pakistani mangoes, she complains, 'have *so* little fibre around the stone' and also have less flavour because, she says, although they're ripe, 'they pick them too young'. For Marcia, the fruit is a poor analogue of the fruits that she remembers from childhood. They are, nonetheless, evocative of childhood landscapes to which she remains attached. As such, the syrupy drupe is an important source of dietetic and emotional nutrition.

The memories that Marcia rekindles around the kernel of the fruit are, naturally, related to a very specific cultural and personal story. She is, however, far from alone in finding succour in the ochre flesh. As I discovered, following Marcia's tip-off about the passion that mangoes evoke, each individual in the queue likely finds their own meaning and comfort in the fleshy drupe. As demonstrated below, this meaning is always inflected by specific biographies and culture. Yet, as specific as the individual experience of a particular fruit might be, they emerge out of what Edward Said (1993: 1) referred to as the 'intertwined histories and overlapping territories' of colonialism. Moreover, having emerged out of intertwined histories of colonialism, these experiences unfurl into the post-colonial futures of the city. That is, while the consumption of exotic fruit can become a site for the reiteration of colonial power relations, it also offers points of mutual affection and overlap out of which a convivial metropolitan multiculture (Gilroy 2006) can be made.

The senses and cultural attachment

The colours and patterns in which people dress, the sounds to which they move, the flavours they imbibe and the scents with which they adorn their bodies are often saturated with explicit and implicit cultural meaning. As such, these sensoria are important components in the production, and reproduction, of cultural identity. They give texture to everyday life, shape how individuals think about themselves and also determine how they identify, and think about, 'others'. Beyond offering props in the performance of identity, specific sensoria and sensations are often key points for anchoring emotional attachments to culture. This is particularly so for both the smells and the flavours with which humans infuse their lives. As anthropologists have separately detailed (Howes 1987; Classen 1990, 1997; Caplan 1992; Sutton 2001; Korsmeyer 2002), both scents and taste have long been the most affective of sensoria and central to the embodied processes through which cultural attachments are made. This can be seen clearly if we turn our noses toward religious rites and cultural festivals, a great number of which often feature a specific set of scents and flavours. From the cinnamon and cloves that inflect the atmosphere of a northern European Christmas (Mason and Muir 2013), through the spiced vegetarian wedding platter of Chennai's middle classes (Caplan 1992: 10) to the quiet fragrance of Japanese tea ceremonies, flavours and aromas are the frequent centrepiece of culturally formative rituals.

There are a number of reasons why these two types of sensations might be so important to such an array of culturally significant events. Not least amongst them is the fact that we are, quite literally, what we eat. The same might be said of what we breathe. That which passes through our gullet or into our lungs becomes a physical part of us. As such the arbitrary cultural meaning ascribed to the differentiated flavours and aromas of particular foodstuffs can be particularly efficacious in determining embodied cultural identity. It would, for instance, be inconceivable that one of Madras's middle-class Brahmin would be able to sustain their embodied identity if they imbibed meat (Caplan 1992: 6). If we are to understand these sensations' cultural importance, it is also worth noting that when experienced communally, the sense of both smell and taste are also socially integrative (Classen et al. 1994: 123). For example, in a Greek Orthodox church full of incense or a Rastafarian drum circle infused with ganja, all of those participating are enveloped by the same sensations, affected by them communally and are taught to find meaning in those sensations, together. The most important factor, however, in the pronounced ritual importance of smell and taste, lies in their connection to memory (Caplan 1992: 4; Waskul et al. 2009). Entire biographical memories, complete with multi-sensory atmospheres and concomitant emotions, can be rekindled through an encounter with the most dilute substance from the past. In the case of religious rites and cultural festivals, the repetition of sensations alongside the sharing of stories, memories and lessons enables individuals to habitually relate emotion and meaning to sensation. Over time, it becomes possible to firm up embodied and affective relationships with culture by way of only the slightest sensory nudge.

The taste of home

Vannini et al. (2011: 145) describe the sights, sounds and smells of a given milieu or tradition as part of the 'sensory order' of that culture. The sensory order is then interpreted through the specific 'somatic rules' of that culture. Far from simply weaving the backcloth against which cultural activity takes place, 'sensory order' and the 'somatic rules' for decoding it, combine as one of the key modalities through which culture is produced and reproduced. The 'sensory order' of any individual evocation of culture does not, however, merely comprise of the scents, sounds and flavours of seasonal and religious rituals. Rather, for the main part, the 'sensory orders' (Vannini et al. 2011: 145) people are most dependent on and emotionally bound to, are often a far more banal assortment of the odours we wash in, the flavours we fill our shopping basket with and, as Tacchi (2003: 281) argues, the radio stations that we tune into. Such is the extent to which this 'sensory order' shapes who we are that most of the time we do not even notice it. That is, until the sensations that colour our lives disappear.

In this respect, the importance of taste and smell to cultural reproduction is only amplified in globalised cities characterised by extreme forms of mobility and dislocation (Bauman 1998). One of the consequences of this increased mobility is a preponderance of 'culture shock' (Kim 2001; Leong and Ward 2000) amongst arrivals to today's cities, a phenomenon that has clear sensory dimensions. This shock emerges largely from the fact that upon arrival into a new location, the embodied praxis out of which home and culture is made often 'dissembles' in the absence of 'sensory familiarities' (Edensor 2006). Because of their cultural potency, it is quite frequently the aromas and flavours of home that the 'stranger' both misses, and seeks out first.

A yearning for the sensorium of home is present in the experiences of tourists (Edensor 2006) and expats (O'Reilly 2002: 93). The imperative of locating familiar sensoria is, however, even greater for the involuntarily mobile residents of contemporary cities, the 'vagabonds' caught on the winds of global conflict and economic necessity (Bauman 1998: 77–102). As anthropologists have demonstrated (Seremetakis 1996; Law 2001; Sutton 2001) the unfamiliar sensory realm of a new home often engenders a distinct sadness and sense of loss. However, the encounter with even the faintest of flavours from elsewhere or another time – a peach (Serematekis 1996) or a sprig of basil left in a glass on the windowsill (Sutton 2001) – enable migrants to rekindle cultural memories, complete with a strong sense of emotional attachment, in the present. In this sense, the nose and taste buds help anchor dislocated bodies, by locating moorings amidst the most vaporous of materials.

While providing a sense of comfort by way of a connection to elsewhere, remaking the sensorium of home in a strange land can often breed its own hostility. Not least because 'new arrivals', who are often required to make considerable efforts in order to visibly 'pass' as 'locals' in the contemporary city (Valenta 2009), might be marked out, by olfaction in particular, as different. As Manalansan (2006) demonstrates, the food smells of particular metropolitan streets, transport links and neighbourhoods have come to play an important part in the social construction and racial codifying of urban space. This often results in undesirable consequences for new migrants to the city, for while aromas of difference might not be, objectively speaking, noxious, as Classen (1992: 134) writes, 'the odour of the other . . . often serves as a scapegoat for certain antipathies toward the other for whom . . . an animosity [is felt] for unrelated reasons'.

The mirage of the mosaic

Providing both a source of anxiety and fear, as well as foundations upon which identity and culture can be remade in a new home, the fruits, herbs, scents and spices of migrant lives also have special economic functions. For a start, they present an opportunity amongst a 'captive market' (Kloosterman and Rath 2001) of homesick co-ethnics. In many cases today, sensations derived from elsewhere are initially imported into cities like London to be sold to a network of similarly relocated families and individuals. Often sequestered from the primary commercial zones and central public spaces of the city, these sensoria are sold in specialist grocers, cooked in domestic kitchens and often eaten in familial settings. The flavour and scent of elsewhere is not, however, always kept so private. Nor is it necessarily met with anxiety when it osmoses into more public spaces of the

city. In some cases, carefully marketed and augmented versions of these sensoria 'cross over' (Cook and Harrison 2003) into, or at least are appropriated by,
the local culture and geography into which migrants move. A number of British
city authorities have actually honed in on the marketable novelty of particular
migrant sensoria and, often based on patterns of initial settlement, have assidu-
ously worked with 'ethnic entrepreneurs' to curate themed quarters within the
city. As a result a number of cross-cultural economic opportunities for migrant
groups have emerged. At the same time, however, these themed spaces have been
accused of peddling distinctly colonial ideas about other cultures (Anderson 1987:
581) and perpetuating false understandings of ethnicity (Beebeejaun 2004; Holmes and Beebeejaun 2007). While presenting economic opportunity, such spaces
also play their part in maintaining ethnically accented hierarchies of power. We
need only consider the way in which east London's 'Banglatown' was originally
named as such by the Far Right before being re-appropriated by local officials to
see the synergy between the master-planned cultural quarter and the racial codifying of space. Both acts of naming rely on the idea that discrete migrant groups
coagulate around specific 'essences', ultimately shoring-up ethnic enclaves and
ghettos. What I want to argue, however, is that in many respects both the master-
planned mosaic of consumable multiculture and the xenophobe's image of 'smelly
immigrants' are simply wrong in their understanding and representations of the
relationship between the senses, emotional attachment and cultural identity in
many of today's cities. In what follows I want to demonstrate how, through the
senses of smell and taste, new evocations of cosmopolitan culture are produced
and emotional attachments to multicultural locales are forged.

To understand how the senses work within the production of cosmopolitan
forms of sociality and how emotional attachments to multiculture are fashioned, it
serves to turn attention from racially codified cultural quarters. Instead, we should
consider some of the city's more everyday locations in which a preponderance of
cultural heterogeneity is a defining trait. Street markets such as the one in which
we met Marcia in the opening vignette are exemplary. In distinction to the master-
planned cultural quarter, these sites have a very different relationship to cosmopolitan existence. Far from facilitating the mimetic reproduction of the ethnic enclave's
'sensory order' (Vannini et al. 2011: 145), or even being a site for the gluttonous
ingestion of the other, London's street markets are important sites of cosmopolitan
sociality and ones which, while facilitating sensuous connections to elsewhere, also
generate strong emotional attachment to the local.

Getting the right ingredients

As has been argued elsewhere (Watson 2009; Rhys-Taylor 2013) inner-city street
markets can be important sites of social encounter, often across ethnic difference.
As such they might be one of the contemporary city's most important sites of what
Paul Gilroy refers to as an unruly form of 'convivial multiculture'. Conviviality, as
Gilroy describes it, is

> a social pattern in which different metropolitan groups dwell in close prox-
> imity, but where their racial, linguistic and religious particularities do not – as
> the logic of ethnic absolutism suggests they must – add up to discontinuities
> of experience or insuperable problems of communication. In these condi-
> tions, a degree of differentiation can be combined with a large measure of
> overlapping.
>
> *(Gilroy 2006: 40)*

Such social patterns are surely resources for our inevitably global future. They
are, however, far from given and, as I have discussed, exist alongside enduringly
xenophobic sentiment. If we are to fully grasp, and ideally reproduce, the con-
tingencies of these cosmopolitan forms of existence it serves to look in detail at
the spaces in which they emerge. This means following not only the political historian's attention to past struggles against racism in inner-city London (Macklin
2007: 41–4), nor merely the urbanist's impulse to look at the spatial arrangement
of convivial street markets. It also means moving beyond focused ethnographic
attention on the skill-sets of the market's multi-linguistic vendors (Hall 2012;
Lyon and Back 2012; Rhys-Taylor 2013). In addition to all these modes of attention it is imperative that we remember to pay attention to the precise ingredients
that fill the space, and the 'social life' of these 'things' (Appadurai 1986). It is here
that we find perhaps the most abundant sites of 'overlap' around which convivii-
ality swirls, and an abundance of moorings through which attachment to local
culture is secured. To illustrate the point, let us return to Marcia's procurement
of mangoes.

As Marcia ambles towards her mangoes, she passes a large swathe of sensoria derived from across the tropical locations to which the British Empire once
extended its reach. Scotch bonnet chilli peppers from Jamaica sit alongside mangoes from Pakistan and Ghana, spices from Sri Lanka and rice from Bangladesh.
The presence of these ingredients in contemporary London is the result of a well-
recognised northward movement of bodies, culture and commodities, from erst-
while colonies in the tropics, into the temperate markets of Europe. Some of this
movement, as is the case with the drier and more easily exported spices (pepper, cinnamon, nutmeg) started as part of a European 'spice-orgy' (Braudel 1981:
221) over four centuries ago, by way of Venetian, Portuguese and Dutch traders
(Schivelbusch 1993; Freedman et al. 2008). Hardy vegetables like potatoes arrived
not much later (Reader 2009) while more tender ingredients – mangoes, papayas
and fresh chillies – only arrived in notable numbers in the later part of the twentieth
century, facilitated by industrial agriculture, refrigeration and radically affordable air
travel. In distinction to the sixteenth-century spices, which were savoured by elite
'native' Londoners, the more recently arrived morsels have tended to initially sup-
ply the demands of migrant groups looking to reconstruct a sense of home. However, the ingredients that fill Marcia's basket are a part of a social process that results
in something much more than a metropolitan mosaic of relocated ethnicities. They
are nutrients that sustain local forms of convivial multiculture.

Fruits and spices are not merely the backdrop to, or superficial surface of, multicultural existence. Rather, they are part of its foundations. Part of this foundational role is related to histories of the ingredients, histories that suffuse them with a potential for involvement in transcultural processes. It is worth recalling that before they were carried on the colonial conveyor belts longitudinally from the tropics to temperate zones, the same spices, fruits and herbs that are associated with the distinct regional cuisines of Asia, Africa and the Americas embarked on an array of latitudinal journeys. For years before arriving in London, a wide range of trees, shrubs, seeds, vines and tubers were hauled – along with slaves and indentured labourers – around the Earth's tropical girdle. Churning around the tropics, they became embroiled in a range of culinary and cultural exchanges. Today both the contemporary taste of, and a taste for, many of the market's most abundant groceries can be traced to these exchanges.

Consider one of the most abundant items across London today, the chilli pepper. Like their cousins in the nightshade family – tomatoes and potatoes – the chilli peppers that fill one pound bowls throughout London's markets were first pulled up from the lower slopes of the Andes by early conquistadors before being planted into the soil of India and South East Asia. Adapted to new terrains and cultivated into new varieties, these deeply affective sources of heat became central to a wide array of 'authentic' Asian cuisines, from Thailand through Mongolia to India and Pakistan (Collingham 2010: 47–81) before becoming a regular feature in mainstream twenty-first century British cuisine. In each location they became both an important source of nutrition and flavour, but also an object of emotional cultural attachment.

Moving in the opposite direction, having been uprooted by Portuguese traders from somewhere in the forested foothills between north eastern India, Burma and Bangladesh (Bompard in Litz 2009: 19–42), the perfumed flesh of Marcia's mango was folded, with blood and sweat, into local cultures all along the return leg from Asia, through Africa and over the Atlantic. First it was planted, with little initial success, in Brazil, before finding its feet in the West Indies (Lyer and Schnell in Litz 2009: 69). With their roots established, the mango's ever-diversifying cultivars became icons of regions from Burma through Cameroon and Senegal to St Vincent, Monserrat, Malaysia, Vietnam and Samoa. As extensive anthropologies and histories of food, taste and desire have demonstrated (Mintz 1986; Schivelbusch 1993; Ortiz 1995; Okihiro 2009), many of the cuisines that are reconstituted in European and North American cities emerge out of prior sensory collisions. The result in post-colonial British cities like London is a remarkable array of overlap between the 'sensory orders' (Vaninni et al. 2011) of migrant groups. Consequently, where bodies followed sticky fruits, berries and spices northward – from the tropics into the impoverished urban centres of post-colonial Europe – histories of colonial rule seem to partly prefigure the sites for interaction between seemingly discrete traditions, by providing the material culture of post-colonial multiculture.

Intersemiotic fruits

In no way should gustatory analogies between discrete post-colonial cultures be taken to imply that distinct cultural traditions converge through the meanings they ascribe to these artefacts. Rather, these sensoria can be thought of simply as points of material overlap while the meaning that each consumer ascribes to them remain determined by the sensibility of each individual and the culture they inhabit. Yet despite divergence in their signification, such polyvalent artefacts remain important for the production of convivial multiculture in that they create the *potential* for intercultural exchange, dialogue and translation, as well as the spaces in which this could happen. In this sense we might think of many of the ingredients Marcia passes on her weekly shopping trip as 'intersemiotic signs' (Case 2001: 40–3). As Frederick Ivor Case argues of his study of the creole religion of Kali Mai in Guyana, the distinct cultural traditions of Guyanese people from African and South East Asian backgrounds meet at particular 'intersemiotic' signs – in his case the fragrant coconut. For Case each practitioner in the island's local religion, whether of Asian or African heritage, recognise the same symbols. However, each ascribes the religious artefacts with their own signification. Yet despite these differences in interpretation, the rituals that the practitioners of Kali Mai perform together contribute to the creation of a new dynamic belief system and a culture peculiar to the nation (Case 2001: 40–53).

Consider now the queue of shoppers waiting with Marcia to bag a box of bargain mangoes. It would be fair to say that there is a degree of overlap between everybody arrested by the scent (and sight) of the fruit in terms of the object it indexes (Peirce 1998: 306). However, the scent and flavour also triggers, as was the case with Marcia, more 'arbitrary' forms of association. That is, the smell and flavour connote specific meanings derived from both the individual's own biography and the wider cultural milieus in which the fruit and individual are embedded. In the case of the mango, there is notable cultural variation in its significance. For Hindus across Asia, for instance, the mango has – for millennia – carried religious significance as a transformation of Prajapati, Lord of Creatures (Popenoe 1920: 84) as well as being used in a range of folk rituals across the subcontinent (Kostermans 1993: 19; Mukherjee and Litz in Litz 2009: 9). For a certain generation of Chinese migrants the fruit carries strong associations with the Cultural Revolution and Chairman Mao who handed out fruits – donated to him by Pakistani farmers – to workers as symbolic gifts (Dutton 2004). For Marcia, the scent and texture of the fruit rekindle specific biographical memories of a childhood in the shade of the gnarled village mango tree in the mountain fringes of St Lucia (Rhys-Taylor 2007). For Chi, a Vietnamese woman, the mango is also a precious reminder of home, one of the few notoriously fragile fruits from her childhood that is readily available. She prefers lychees and rambutans but the season is much shorter. A mile south of the market in a small neighbourhood grocer Sham, a Bengali shopkeeper, speaks proudly of his mango selection. The mango is his favoured fruit to follow the dates with which he breaks his fasts during Ramadan: 'refreshing and sweet . . . but not so sweet' so as to satisfy both his thirst and hunger. He tries to stock as many different types of the fruit as he can for the holy month so as to appease the diversity of tastes amongst his devout customers – mainly, he says, from Somalia, Nigeria and Bangladesh. He rarely sells single fruit during Ramadan, instead vending whole boxes to customers who, like Marcia, share the fruits with their neighbours and family – an important, and highly affective aspect of the Iftar – once the sun has set.

While it might be seen to prohibit the emergence of common culture, the convergence of diverse meanings and emotional cadences around the scent and flavour of one artefact is not insignificant in terms of production of local forms of multiculture. Certainly, the presence of such fruits enables discrete cultural identities to be partially reconstituted. However, at another level, the presence of such fruits in spaces like the street market or grocers creates spaces of sensory 'overlapping' (Gilroy 2006) between different cultures. While this is an overlap in terms of sensoria, and not necessarily sensibility, it is an overlap that nevertheless affords social interaction and through it, the production of convivial multiculture.

London's street markets and grocers can be identified as important sites of cross-cultural encounter (Watson 2009) and as breeding grounds of convivial multi-culture (Hall 2012: 66–7). However, they are only so, in part, because of the presence of specific artefacts. Contrary to discourse weighted towards discussions of assimilation and acculturation, it is not just established artefacts of definitively British culture – Highland shortbread, or the Arsenal football team (Gilroy 2006) – that can perform that loosely integrative 'overlapping' role. After centuries of intermingling in the tropics, specific imports into the post-colonial city create sites at which conjoined colonial histories re-converge, and from which post-colonial futures unfurl. While being signifiers of distinct and partly disparate cultures, many of the city's morsels also, by virtue of their 'intertwined histories' (Said 1993: 1) signify something more. Alongside the jerk chicken bagels and halal hotdogs sold in the same markets, these fruits are becoming symbols of a distinctly local, yet nevertheless cosmopolitan, inner-city culture. And people's affections for them, as much they are affections that once germinated elsewhere, are also inevitably entangled with affection for the diverse and delectable neighbourhoods across which they share fruit.

Conclusion

There is a cornucopia of ingredients available on the shelves of world cities, arrived of a network of shipping containers, contrails, highways and white vans. Therein they move through a range of urban spaces, inflecting the social in a multitude of different ways. The smells and flavours of the world city's food hall are, of course, central to the reconstitution of dislocated identities and culture. They enable those swept up by the winds of late modernity to remake homes away from home and give pleasurable pain to the homesick. The global shopping basket also represents considerable economic opportunities for new migrants to the world city, alongside sources of anxiety and fear. The rekindling of hermetic forms of difference alongside xenophobia and cosmopolitan cannibalism are, however, but one aspect of the social life of the city's larder. Amidst intertwined histories of colonialism, local anti-racist struggles and the cramped confines of inner-city living, various forms of multiculture are potentialised by specific ingredients themselves. Offered for the delectation of a diverse public, mangoes are amongst an important myriad of 'intersemiotic' flavours (Case 2001: 40) at which difference converges, across which translation takes place and through which multicultural conviviality lives. Even more significantly, while sustaining a cosmopolitan social milieu, these ingredients also make up the materiality of a very local culture, to which people inevitably become attached.

Similar things might once have been said about the Franco-Sephardic fusion food that was recoded as iconic British fish and chips, as well as more recently, chicken tikka masala, both quintessentially British dishes precisely because of their mongrel origins (Cook 2002). As it is elsewhere, the mango and her cousins could also be icons of contemporary culture in London equal to fish and chips. Like many of the items mentioned here, they carry with them stories that help make far more sense of today's assortment of urban cultures and identities than the crude histories in which nationalist discourse scuffles to find footholds. They offer a testament of the maritime metropolis and its inhabitants' enduring connections to elsewhere, a reminder of how those connections were forged, but also an 'intersemiotic' anchor for convivial multiculture. While London is a gourmand's paradise, it is much more than a playground of omnivorous post-modern consumers. Rather it is one in which deeply affective relationships with everyday items, forged on the taste buds and in the guts of its citizens, give rise to social forms redolent with resources for a global existence.

References

Anderson, K.J. (1987) 'The idea of Chinatown: The power of place and institutional practice in the making of a racial category', *Annals of the Association of American Geographers*, 77(4): 580–98.

Appadurai, A. (1986) *The Social Life of Things: Commodities in Cultural Perspective*, Cambridge: Cambridge University Press.

Bauman, Z. (1998) *Globalization: The Human Consequences*, New York: Columbia University Press.

Beebeejaun, Y. (2004) 'What's in a nation? Constructing ethnicity in the British planning system', *Planning Theory & Practice*, 5: 437–51.

Benedetta, M. (1936) *Street Markets of London*, London: John Miles Ltd.

Braudel, F. (1981) *The Structures of Everyday Life: The Limits of the Possible*, Berkley, CA: University of California Press.

Caplan, P. (1992) *Feasts, Fasts and Famine*, London: Goldsmiths College.

Case, I.F. (2001) 'The Intersemiotics of Obeah and Kali Mai in Guyana' in Taylor, P. (ed.) *Nation Dance: Religion, Identity, and Cultural Difference in the Caribbean*, Bloomington, IN: Indiana University Press, 40–53.

Classen, C. (1990) 'Sweet colors, fragrant songs: Sensory models of the Andes and the Amazon', *American Ethnologist*, 17(4): 722–35.

—— (1992) 'The odor of the other: Olfactory symbolism and cultural categories', *Ethos* 20: 133–66.

—— (1997) 'Foundations for an anthropology of the senses', *International Social Science Journal*, 49(153): 401–12.

Classen, C., Howes, D. and Synnott, A. (1994) *Aroma*, London: Routledge.

Collingham, L. (2010) *Curry: A Tale of Cooks and Conquerors*, London: Random House.

Cook, I. and Harrison, M. (2003) 'Cross over food: Re-materializing postcolonial geographies', *Transactions of the Institute of British Geographers*, 28: 296–317.

Cook, R. (2002) 'Chicken tikka masala speech', *The Guardian*. Available at www.theguardian.com/world/2001/apr/19/race.britishidentity (accessed 30 July 2013).

Dutton, M.R. (2004) 'Mango Mao: Infections of the sacred', *Public Culture*, 16: 161–87.

Edensor, T. (2006) 'Sensing Tourist Spaces' in Minca, C. and Oakes, T. (eds) *Travels in Paradox: Remapping Tourism*, London: Rowman & Littlefield, 23–45.

Freedman, P.H., Frey, B.S. and Stutzer, A. (2008) *Out of the East: Spices and the Medieval Imagination*, New Haven, CT: Yale University Press.

Gilroy, P. (2005) 'Multiculture, double consciousness and the "war on terror"', *Patterns of Prejudice*, 39(4): 431–43.

—— (2006) 'Multiculture in times of war: An inaugural lecture given at the London School of Economics', *Critical Quarterly*, 48: 27–45.

Hall, S. (2012) *City, Street and Citizen: The Measure of the Ordinary*, London: Routledge.

Holmes, K. and Beebeejaun, Y. (2007) 'City centre masterplanning and cultural spaces: A case study of Sheffield', *Journal of Retail & Leisure Property*, 6: 29–46.

Howes, D. (1987) 'Olfaction and transition: An essay on the ritual uses of smell', *Canadian Review of Sociology/Revue canadienne de sociologie*, 24(3): 398–416.

Kim, Y.Y. (2001) *Becoming Intercultural: An Integrative Theory of Communication and Cross-Cultural Adaptation*, London: Sage.

Kloosterman, R. and Rath, J. (2001) 'Immigrant entrepreneurs in advanced economies: Mixed embeddedness further explored', *Journal of Ethnic and Migration Studies*, 27(2): 189–201.

Korsmeyer, C. (2002) *Making Sense of Taste: Food & Philosophy*, Ithaca, NY: Cornell University Press.

Kostermans, A.J.G.H. (1993) *The Mangoes: Their Botany, Nomenclature, Horticulture and Utilization*, London: Academic Press Inc.

Law, L. (2001) 'Home cooking: Filipino women and geographies of the senses in Hong Kong', *Cultural Geographies*, 8(3): 264–83.

Leong, C.-H. and Ward, C. (2000) 'Identity conflict in sojourners', *International Journal of Intercultural Relations*, 24(6): 763–76.

Litz, R.E. (2009) *The Mango: Botany, Production and Uses*, Wallingford: CABI.

Lyon, D. and Back, L. (2012) 'Fishmongers in a global economy: Craft and social relations on a London market', *Sociological Research Online*, 17(2): 23. Available at www.socresonline.org.uk/17/2/23.html (accessed 1 October 2013).

Macklin, G. (2007) *Very Deeply Dyed in Black: Sir Oswald Mosley and the Postwar Reconstruction of British Fascism*, London: I.B. Tauris.

Manalansan, M. (2006) 'Immigrant Lives and the Politics of Olfaction in the Global City' in Drobnick, J. (ed.) *The Smell Culture Reader*, Oxford: Berg, 41–52.

Mason, J. and Muir, S. (2013) 'Conjuring up traditions: Atmospheres, eras and family Christmases', *The Sociological Review*, 61(3): 607–29.

Mintz, S.W. (1986) *Sweetness and Power: The Place of Sugar in Modern History*, London: Penguin Books.

O'Reilly, K. (2002) *The British on the Costa del Sol*, London: Routledge.

Okihiro, G.Y. (2009) *Pineapple Culture: A History of the Tropical and Temperate Zones*, Berkeley, CA: University of California Press.

Ortiz, F. (1995) *Cuban Counterpoint: Tobacco and Sugar*, Durham, NC: Duke University Press Books.

Peirce, C.S. (1998) *The Essential Peirce: Selected Philosophical Writings. 1893–1913*. Vol. 2. Bloomington, IN: Indiana University Press.

Popenoe, W. (1920) *Manual of Tropical and Subtropical Fruits: Excluding the Banana, Coconut, Pineapple, Citrus Fruits, Olive, and Fig*, London: The Macmillan Company.

Reader, J. (2009) *Potato: A History of the Propitious Esculent*, New Haven, CT: Yale University Press.

Rhys-Taylor, A. (2007) 'The Irrepressibility of Mangifera', *Eurozine*. Available at: www.eurozine.com/articles/2007–04–23-rhystaylor-en.html (accessed 16 July 2009).

Rhys-Taylor, A. (2013) 'The essences of multiculture: A sensory exploration of an inner-city street market', *Identities: Global Studies in Culture and Power*, 20(4): 393–406.

Said, E.W. (1993) *Culture and Imperialism*, London: Vintage Books.

Schivelbusch, W. (1993) *Tastes of Paradise*, London: Vintage Books.

Seremetakis, C.N. (1996) *The Senses Still*, Chicago, IL: University of Chicago Press.

Sutton, D.E. (2001) *Remembrance of Repasts*, Oxford: Berg.

Tacchi, J. (2003) 'Nostalgia and Radio Sounds' in Bull, M. and Back, L. (eds) *The Auditory Culture Reader*, Oxford: Berg, 281–9.

Valenta, M. (2009) 'Immigrants' identity negotiations and coping with stigma in different relational frames', *Symbolic Interaction*, 32(4): 351–71.

Vannini, P., Waskul, D. and Gottschalk, S. (2011) *The Senses in Self, Society, and Culture: A Sociology of the Senses*, London: Routledge.

Waskul, D., Vannini, P. and Wilson, J. (2009) 'The aroma of recollection: Olfaction, nostalgia, and the shaping of the sensuous Self', *The Senses and Society*, 4(1): 5–22.

Watson, S. (2009) 'The magic of the marketplace: Sociality in a neglected public space', *Urban Studies*, 46: 1577–91.

3

THE PIGEON AND THE WEAVE

The middle classes, dis/comfort and the multicultural city[1]

Emma Jackson

Weave hair in the road/Pigeons, cats in the car park/Still, Choumert is home
Runner-up in the Peckham haiku competition (2010)

Two cups of tea in Peckham

Tea 1: Dr Huang

We sit in Dr Huang's dining room, the first room you walk into in her ground floor flat. The walls are covered in drawers and cupboards. She says that I can relax and that she knows all about the university where I work and asks me if a certain doctor is still there. She makes me jasmine tea and offers a box of mini-Toblerone. Dr Huang is retired and originally came to the UK as a refugee from Vietnam. When she moved here in the 1980s, people warned her against the neighbourhood but she has never had any trouble. She has seen changes since then, more 'Caucasians', young white couples, moving in. She likes living in an ethnically mixed neighbourhood; she says as a refugee you have to live in the big city where you don't stick out. Besides, here she can get the food that she needs; being able to get the ingredients for Vietnamese food in Peckham saves her going to Chinatown. She has a couple of friends in London but she says coming to the country when she was a bit older and as a refugee meant that it was difficult to make friends. Unlike many of the other interviewees, North Peckham figures in her account of the neighbourhood as she used to work there. Although she doesn't use the new local restaurants she is glad that they have opened as it means that there are more people around on the street in the evening.

Tea 2: Fiona

Fiona apologises for the cold: 'I don't have the heating on in the day.' The interview takes place in the kitchen which looks out onto the back garden. She makes me a cup of tea. She is in her thirties and isn't currently working but is in the process of setting up as a self-employed consultant. She describes the area as 'family oriented' and is keen to stress the proximity to East Dulwich. She makes sense of the neighbourhood as being between 'two worlds' ('I've lived in Brixton, so Rye Lane doesn't surprise me. You know I like it. And equally Lordship Lane . . . two worlds, completely two worlds . . . two minutes down the road you've got very posh shops and lots of, you know, middle-class people and then a few more roads down the other way you've got Africa!') While not exactly guarded, I get the impression that Fiona isn't entirely comfortable. She answers the questions concisely and afterwards I realise I have missed out some questions, due to the dynamic of the interview. The big issue of this interview is schools. After failing to get her children into her school of choice, they went to the local primary. The school is, she says, the only place where the different groups in Peckham mix. Fiona knows her neighbours; she says they are mainly 'people like us, middle-class people'. School choice has become a rather fraught issue among these neighbours, as some have made the decision to send their children to private school. When asked about secondary school she says that she hopes she will send them to the local school but would not rule out moving in order to be close to a better school.

While working on a project about the relationship between the middle classes and the city, I spent a lot of time sat at kitchen tables drinking tea (the project was interview-based and these always took place in people's homes unless a public place was requested). Going into this research project, having previously worked on young homeless people's relationship to city space, I had not considered the kinds of emotion that sitting across kitchen tables and asking middle-class people about place and biography might conjure up.

In the two interviews described above, emotions manifested themselves in narrations of place and of the past (including loss, dislocation, loneliness, anger, comfort) and were also present in this interaction between two people (unease, humour, enjoyment, anxiety). Here my focus is on the former, more specifically on the relationship between multiculture, dis/comfort and the production of middle-class space and subjectivities which are hinted at in the above field notes. Particularly, on what stories of spectacular and ordinary diversity, both dispassionate and full of emotion, can tell us about classed and racialised formations of identity and spaces in the post-colonial city.

Mapping an enclave

This chapter focuses on one of ten neighbourhoods studied as part of a research project on the middle classes in Paris and London (see Bacqué et al. forthcoming), Peckham in south east London. The project was particularly interested in residents' relationships to their local area and those who lived there. The area that we studied in Peckham was described by the interviewees as an enclave within a wider diverse area and roughly mapped onto the area targeted for the Bellenden Renewal Scheme (1997–2007), a scheme where funds were made available by Southwark Council for business and home-owners to apply for grants to improve the outside buildings (see London Borough of Southwark, 2005). The interviewees (n = 42) were all white apart from Dr Huang and one other, and ranged in age from their twenties to their eighties.

Within the UK, Peckham is a well-known urban reference. It has been shaped by various waves of immigration (most recently immigration from west Africa) and economic fortunes and interventions. It has been associated variously with the white working class (via the market trader/jack-of-all-trades Del Boy of the television series *Only Fools and Horses*), problem estates (see Hall, this volume) and gun and knife crime. As Paul Goodwin (2007: 9) argues:

> Peckham has emerged in the last few years as an undeconstructed, mythical symbol of all the ills of urban society: gun crime, feral youth, sink estates, moral and family breakdown etc. This almost metaphysical image of Peckham's urban pathology has remained unchallenged despite the arrival in the area of a huge regeneration programme and new public spaces such as the Library and town square.

In recent years Peckham has also become a fashionable location for young middle-class people (and had the dubious honour of being hymned as 'the new Dalston' – a gentrified trendy neighbourhood in east London – in *Vice* magazine (Martin 2013)).

The resonance of Peckham as representing a 'metaphysical image of urban pathology' (Goodwin 2007: 9) figured in many stories about moving to Peckham. The horrified reaction of friends and relations at the news of the move to Peckham was a recurring motif within the interviews (Lucy: 'They were like "OH MY GOD! You're crazy!" But it's gorgeous!' (see Benson and Jackson 2013)). These stories, predicated on the notoriousness of Peckham, describe a strong emotional reaction against it from others. In these arrival stories, Peckham is evoked as pathological through the voices of others and then this portrayal is quashed (see also the discussion of Hackney in Jones 2013). Most interviewees were keen to stress how their area of Peckham was different to the wider area and would confound these expectations of others once they experienced it for themselves (John: 'Peckham's had this nasty reputation, and then when it comes to Peckham Rye . . . They see a leafy, gentle, sort of suburban area, where quality food is on offer, and this is top end'). In the process of presenting their slice of Peckham as different, the inter-viewees not only disputed the reality of Peckham as deserving these reactions but also drew boundaries around their immediate area in order to distinguish it from the rest of Peckham.

The two clear boundaries that repeatedly emerged from the interviews were the shopping streets of Peckham High Road and Rye Lane. The other edges of this neighbourhood were given as more blurred, with nearby East Dulwich character-ised by the interviewees as a more mainstream, less bohemian, whiter, middle-class area (Jackson and Benson forthcoming). But Rye Lane in particular was repeatedly cast as a boundary between a middle-class enclave and the rest of Peckham and also as a place of exotic difference.

Of all the London neighbourhoods studied for the 'Middle classes and the city' project, Peckham was the one in which middle-class residents expressed the strong-est affiliation to place, strong forms of what Savage et al. term 'elective belonging' (2005). Part of the narrative about why it is good to live in Peckham was a com-mitment to living in a multicultural and socially mixed neighbourhood. Interviewees co-opted narratives of difference into the stories they told about themselves, often drawing on previous places of residence and experience of travel, in order to explain why they could value this aspect of Peckham. Alongside this celebratory account of living with diversity, we found visceral stories of difference focused on one street in particular, Rye Lane, which invoked 'orientalist' discourses (Said 1995). Others talked about living with difference in far more mundane and less emotionally charged ways. In the rest of this chapter, I will explore these accounts in order to argue that a range of feelings about difference are central to how middle-class people relate to and make claims to space in this London neighbourhood. First, I will consider how 'border talk', concerning Rye Lane and boundary-crossers, carves out a particular niche in the neighbourhood for the middle classes. I will then examine the ways in which difference is rendered acceptable or else discussed as plain ordinary.

Borders part 1: Rye Lane, dis/comfort and 'anxious vitality'

> The nineteenth century imperial project most clearly, but not exclusively, depended upon racialised notions of Self and Other . . . Such racialised constructs were never stable and were always threatened not only by the unpredictability of the Other but also the uncertain homogeneity and bound-edness of the Self. Indeed, the vitality of such binary constructs is most likely a result of their being anxiously reinscribed in the face of their contested or uncontainable certainty. It is, in part, this *anxious vitality* that gives racial-ised categorisations elaborated under colonialism such a long life and allows them to remain cogent features even of those contemporary societies that are formally 'beyond' colonialism.
>
> *(Jacobs 1996: 3; emphasis added)*

Borders need to be threatened in order to be maintained . . . and part of the process of 'maintenance through transgression' is the appearance of border objects. Border objects are hence disgusting, while disgust engenders border objects.

(Ahmed 2004: 87)

From the beginning of the Peckham field work it was striking how symbolically important Rye Lane seemed to be to our interviewees' stories of place. Whether praised as exotic and exciting, or disparaged as dirty and 'other', there was some of the 'anxious vitality' that Jacobs describes in our respondents' accounts and pre-occupation with Rye Lane. So, for example, when asked about local issues, Lisa replies: '[O]ne thing we always do end up talking about, I think with the neighbours . . . is Rye Lane.' In order to probe this fascination with Rye Lane further, let us take three differing accounts that range from the ambivalent to the negative to the ordinary.

Fiona, who we met in the introduction, refers to Rye Lane simply as 'Africa'. She described using Rye Lane to buy cheap vegetables, as her household was trying to economise. She also described enjoying the experience, but for her this pleasure could also slip over into being 'too much':

> There's shops full of . . . vegetables that you literally, that I couldn't name. Um . . . you know, the other day we were walking down and there were big buckets full of giant snails, that size [gestures] the size of a coconut, just sort of crawling out of the bucket above my head and I was like 'oh my god' that's a bit too much!

At the end of the interview Fiona returned to the question of the troublesome snails in order to give a more positive account of Rye Lane and living with diversity:

> I think [husband] and I are one of these classic people who really do genu-inely feel that life is good when there's a diverse community . . . we just really appreciate, although Peckham can be dirty and a bit crazy, it's also 'wow' what an amazing place to live where you got snails crawling out of buckets on the high street.

Now the snails are reincorporated into Fiona's story. They become part of making her and her husband the kind of people who can appreciate diversity. They move from being 'too much' to being part of what makes Peckham amazing. Fiona is typical of the interviewees in finding both pleasure and squeamishness (see Rhys-Taylor 2013 on 'the squirm') in this experience.

However, other accounts of Rye Lane were infused with less ambivalent feel-ings. For example, Marjory described the African-ness of Rye Lane: 'Nigerians when they come here say, quite honestly and genuinely, it's like coming home to Lagos. Well I mean I don't want to live, and a lot of people round here don't want to live, in the grime of Lagos.' As Peckham becomes understood by Marjory as a home for another group of people, for her it becomes uncomfortable and un-homely and she equates this with dirt. This visceral reaction towards Rye Lane was also found in other interviews (Richard: 'I personally think it's disgusting, most of Rye Lane'). The otherness of Peckham, more specifically Peckham's perceived blackness, is central to the descriptions of both Marjory and Fiona. While both accounts can be read as echoing an 'orientalist' (Said 1995) discourse, in Fiona's account there is pleasure and value to be found in this experience whereas for Mar-jory difference is merely reduced to grime. While Fiona expresses mixed feelings, Marjory is wholly negative. However, both of these stories of Rye Lane fix it as an 'other', African place.

These characterisations of Rye Lane imbued with disgust – and sometimes an element of pleasure – play an important role here in defining neighbourhood. As Ahmed (2004) argues, to designate something as disgusting is to expel it. Expressing the opinion that Rye Lane is disgusting both expels Rye Lane from the neighbour-hood and also creates it as a boundary. This can be read as a form of 'practical ori-entalism' (Simonsen 2008) as what is 'other' is both exoticised and excluded from the Bellenden residential area. This talk of Rye Lane as 'Africa' also homogenises Rye Lane, pointing to how difference is illegible to some of our interviewees. When Rye Lane is just read as 'Africa', variety is lost: the Vietnamese market that Dr Huang uses, the Irish butchers, Primark, the Ghanaian supermarket, the Asian barbers.

Such discourses of strangeness and disgust are used not only to describe Rye Lane but also slip over into discourses of morality about dirty and disorderly behav-iour and disregard for rules and regulations of the people who use it. The affective landscape of Rye Lane is important not only in the construction of the idea of white middle-class neighbourhood but as a basis for mobilisation within the local area. Rye Lane was constructed as a troublesome place requiring intervention in many local renovation campaigns (Benson and Jackson 2013).

However, some accounts of Rye Lane, and Peckham in general, were alto-gether less fraught. Dr Huang did not read Rye Lane as 'African'; rather, she related how it provided her with the food that she needed to feel at home and a measure of invisibility:

> I feel OK here, to tell you the truth . . . I can use things around here . . . the food and things is comfortable . . . I can use the facilities like train, bus, swim-ming, library. I don't think that I move outside. *And outside of London is no good for foreigners like me. Unless you live in a big town, being a foreigner sometimes is kind of . . . [sticking out] like a sore thumb?* If you go outside everybody is Caucasian and things, what am I going to do there? [emphasis added]

Dr Huang describes a degree of comfort and necessity, being able to get the right food, being unnoticed, not sticking out. She describes being cautious as a refugee, about who she talks to, as when she came to the country 'not too many people were very happy about [it]'. Her ethnicity and immigration status shape her experience of Peckham, in a way that is radically different to the other middle-class Peckham interviewees. She was forced to leave her country, has had to move around England in order to find work, and eventually selected Peckham as an 'OK' place.

There is a difference between this everyday necessity of ordinary cosmopolitanism and the giant snails with the 'wow' factor. Where Fiona finds remarkable difference, Dr Huang finds a place where the mix on the street and the available food make things 'OK' for her, more liveable. Perhaps some of the foods that Dr Huang buys that provide a sense of home are the same vegetables that Fiona can't name. For Marjory though there is neither a 'wow' factor, nor comfort to be found in Rye Lane, rather a sense of unease at what she sees as the neighbourhood becoming more like Lagos. Such accounts foreground how difference is talked about through place, more specifically about forms of emotion, multiculture and the drawing, and transgression, of borders. Not only is experience of multiculture expressed through different forms of emotion (disgust, fascination, comfort) but there is also a difference in the intensity of the expression, from the intense 'wow', or the recoil, to the flatter 'OK'.

Borders part 2: Disgust and boundary-crossers

> The black false hair, comes out, wraps itself around pigeon legs. That annoys an awful lot of people. And who, we can't get anybody to control the false hair that comes out into the streets . . . The dirt, the filth, it wraps around the general run-down appearance.
>
> *(Marjory)*

In our interviewees' descriptions of Rye Lane, certain places and objects reoccur as reference points. A concern with a proliferation of butchers, fishmongers and hair and nail bars is repeatedly voiced and imbued with disgust (Becky: 'Going down Rye Lane with guys with Morrison's trolleys with bits of goat hanging out, and blood covered overalls was a bit different to Elephant, or Islington, or Mile End where I lived before, and very different to where I'm from up in Lancashire.' Lisa: 'I cycle past in the morning and they've got this big wagon with just half a cow laying in it, makes me feel a bit sick'). The lack of containment of these businesses is a common complaint from our respondents: the hair, notably black hair, that gets brushed out into the streets, the smell of the butchers. Hair and nails being classic examples of what Mary Douglas terms 'matter out of place' (1966) and meat and fish fitting Kristeva's argument that 'Food loathing is perhaps the most archaic and the most elemental form of abjection' (1982: 2). Food is particularly 'elemental' as it is something that is consumed, crossing the boundary from outside to inside the body.

Kristeva argues that what is disturbing is ambiguity, that which 'disturbs identity, systems, order. What does not respect borders, positions, rules. The in-between, the ambiguous, the composite' (1982: 4). These objects (hair, smelly meat) and places (a butchers, a beauty parlour, Rye Lane itself) threaten to cross between what is perceived as two worlds. Fixating on boundary-crossers, the fish and meat, hair and nails, anxiously re-inscribes a binary division of place, yet also points towards the leakiness of multiculture, the smell, the noise.

It is precisely this leakiness that can be seen in the example of the hair from beauty parlours getting wrapped around pigeons' legs described by Marjory, above and in the opening haiku. Marjory's description of the pigeon and the weave is about things leaking over, refusing to stay in their proper place and creating a mess. The pigeon is right on the border of *unheimlich* and *heimlich* representing an idea of indigineity, of Englishness as well as urban grime (see Jerolmack (2008) for a discussion of pigeons as troublesome boundary-crossers). The black hair swept into the street becomes 'matter out of place'; there is a slippage between her disgust at general 'filth' and what she perceives as an Africanisation of space ('black hair' and 'the grime of Lagos') that she finds threatening.

This image of the pigeon and the weave is also drawn on by fiction writer Evie Wyld in an autobiographical essay about growing up in Peckham. She recalls: 'I remember the fug of fish, and vegetables and goat and spices every time I come out of the train station and turn left, past the tumbleweeds of discarded weave blowing under the arches, catching the mangled feet of pigeons . . .' (Wyld 2011: 2). A rather different kind of emotion is tied up with this second, almost romantic, rendering: nostalgia. The blowing weave here is described as tumbleweed, a natural part of the multicultural street ambience. In the haiku and in the extract from Evie Wyld, the weave in the street, hair from the hairdressers, and the pigeon are both dirt and somehow accepted as part of home ('Still Choumert [Choumert Road] is home').

Resourcing the cosmopolitan middle-class self or ordinary multiculture?

> [R]acial, ethnic and cultural relationships are not only negotiated and 'managed' in literal spatial form . . . but imagined through specific emotional and ethical injunctions, such as 'embracing the other' and loving thy neighbour.
>
> *(Fortier 2007: 107)*

As we have already seen with Fiona and the snails, Evie Wyld and the pigeon, the relationship between the interviewees and Rye Lane is not one of plain disgust but is often expressed in more ambivalent or positive ways. Valuing diversity is given by many as a reason for choosing to live in Peckham. There are two interlinked positive discourses about difference that emerge here. The first is the ability to live with Rye Lane and what it represents as an 'other' space. The second, and slightly different, is a general subscription to the idea that multiculture is good. Such accounts seem to be less about troubling objects and more about people, especially neighbours, or are more concerned with accounting autobiographically (Giddens 1991) for the developing of a cosmopolitan outlook. In the rest of this section I will explore how 'other' becomes homely or just plain ordinary in the stories of our interviewees. Is this merely a case of the middle classes absorbing multiculture as cultural capital or are other forms of cosmopolitanism hinted at here?

Embracing the other part 1: Neighbours and curried goat

> It's very mixed, it's quite a complicated mix of people I think . . . they're Pentecostal Church next door because you hear the organ going which is fantastic . . . and then this side I think is white social housing . . . estate agents would love to get their hands on these properties . . . but it just seems you've got quite a mixed area, and obviously you've got different nationalities in Peckham. Which is good.
>
> *(Sarah)*

Being able to live with difference was often told through stories about the mixedness of the residential area (often the area was talked of as both an enclave and mixed) and particularly through stories of encounters with neighbours, often older black Caribbean or white working-class people. Descriptions of interactions with neighbours came as part of a wider story of general neighbourhood change, a typical gentrification story of the older generation of white and black Caribbean working-class people leaving or dying and being replaced by white couples or white couples with young children. Thus, those older white and black Caribbean working-class people who remained provided reassurance for the new arrivals of the multi-ethnic and socially mixed character of the neighbourhood. It should also be noted that in Peckham, compared to the other London neighbourhoods in our study, we found the most positive descriptions of relations with neighbours, with many people describing talking to their neighbours, even socialising with them. Patricia, for example, after having a dispute with her neighbours about trees on the border between their houses, had become quite close to them:

> My Pakistani neighbours, we know each other very well. Quite a traffic of food between us. And their son, he's a very lively 14 year old boy. And he comes in and out regularly . . . they have a large number of daughters who always have to be married. And I get invited to the wedding.

Moreover, some of the interviewees (including Patricia) who were concerned about their own role in the gentrification of the area saw the preservation of ethnic and social mix within their immediate residential area as key to what they valued about Peckham. These sorts of neighbourhood relations were described rather matter-of-factly and contrast with the lurid, more emotionally charged, accounts of Rye Lane. They seem more in line with what Stuart Hall has described as 'multicultural drift' (Hall 1999; see also Watson and Saha 2012; Saha and Watson, this volume).

However, neighbours as the acceptable face of multiculturalism were also contrasted with the non-acceptable 'African' space of Rye Lane. Adrian, a lawyer, expressed a great deal of anxiety about Peckham while also being very attached to the immediate Bellenden area. He said in his interview that he thought all people were 'inherently racist' and his fears about the neighbourhood seemed to be about the presence of black people. He repeatedly referred to the 'goats hanging in the window' in Rye Lane. However, he also talked about living in a very multicultural street and having dinners with his neighbours who include people from India, the Caribbean and various other 'others'. Here he describes a dinner in the home of a neighbour from the Caribbean:

> [S]he made, like you know, curried goat, you know, and we had dinner there and stayed and had a drink. So *that* is multicultural, and the people on my street are multicultural, but other than that if you basically walked out on Peckham High Street, or Rye Lane which is the main shopping street, I would say at least two thirds to three quarters if not more of those people are black. And . . . you are the minority as a white person.

What was 'other' and off-putting elsewhere in the interview ('the goats hanging in the window') gets turned into something palatable, made homely through the neighbour serving them up in a curry. It is not the goat that in itself is the object of disgust but rather its place in the context of a window in Rye Lane.

Here being able to eat goat with a neighbour is co-opted into the white middle-class self as a form of cultural capital (May 1996; Skeggs 2004) and then used as an example to prove being open to multiculture. This is then contrasted with a portrayal of a predominantly black shopping street, the implication being that this is not truly multicultural because there are not enough white people. This acceptance of an element of multiculture, the goat, but only in a controlled environment fits with Hage's characterisation of the 'cosmo-multiculturalist' (2000) where the 'ethnic element is included and even welcomed into the world of the white multiculturalist . . . but for only as long as it knows and keeps to its place as a function for the white multiculturalist' (2000: 202).

Embracing the other part 2: 'Oh, this is just like Africa'

In order to explain why they like Peckham, other respondents hark back to their experiences of other places. Peter, who regaled me with a story of buying half a circus in Cairo in the 1970s, had travelled around the world throughout his working life and drew on this experience to explain why he was attracted to Peckham:

> I'm very happy because of course, I love um . . . it's rather like being back in Yemen or Afghanistan! Countries that I love! And, I'm so happy to see the Mosque here and, I can read the Quran in Arabic and discuss . . . things [with] the clergy! So yeah, it um, suits me very well.

He goes on to say, 'I love walking up and down Rye Lane [laughing], it amuses me. But, um, it's not everyone's cup of tea.'

Elsewhere in the interview he talked about the things he missed from living abroad, the open spaces and stars at night. Moving between his little house in Peckham and a cottage in the country, he manages to create a home for himself. The English country village, which mirrors his upbringing where he can experience open spaces as he did on his travels, and also Peckham where he can enjoy the street life and discussing the Quran.

Peter was in his seventies, but more often we found it was younger people who drew on their experiences of travel in order to explain Rye Lane:

> I'd never lived in London, I didn't have any preconceptions, I'd spent . . . a year living out in Africa . . . so for me it was quite entertaining to come here and go 'oh this is just like Africa!'
>
> *(Geoff)*

> Rye Lane which is, incredibly kind of, lively . . . day and night, and feels quite African – which I really like because I spent a couple of years living in Africa so I, I, kind of, it makes me feel quite at home, there's a lot of African people and there's quite, it's got quite an African feel to it.
>
> *(Sophie)*

Across these three cosmopolitan accounts there are varying expressions of rather detached entertainment ('I find it amusing', 'it was quite entertaining') and also of home attachment. Finding Rye Lane amusing evokes Butler and Robson's idea of 'social tectonics' where others constitute 'social wallpaper' (2001). However, Peter's relishing of being able to discuss the Quran and Sophie's 'at home' feeling seem to go beyond this and hint at genuine exchange and involvement rather than standing back as a spectator.

Others had not travelled as far as Africa but instead drew on their experience of living previously in other London neighbourhoods, particularly Brixton, in order to describe why they could live in Peckham. Conversely, there were those who reflected that this ambience was far removed from their previous experience. In these cases a taste for this kind of neighbourhood had to be learned. For some of these interviewees, the things that they had initially found alarming about Peckham had just become ordinary over time. For example, Linda, who had previously lived in Camberwell and had reservations about moving down the hill, recalled her arrival in Peckham and her horror at Rye Lane (she particularly hated the chicken shops) but she concludes: 'I have been very surprised by how I have now turned my way of thinking completely around.' She recalled:

> [T]here are a lot of men who hang around, they're African men and they are hanging around . . . and that's absolutely fine, and they are . . . and I just realised it's just sort of, in a way, you know, it's just ordinary people having a nice time.

She was keen to draw a distinction between the person she was on her arrival, saying she was a 'snob' then, and herself today. She thus presents living in Peckham as a transformative experience, coming in part from living in close proximity to difference.

This could be read as merely another example of white middle-class people absorbing multiculture in order to make a claim to being cosmopolitan, but perhaps this account points to something else. This is unlike the descriptions of bloodied goats or spectacular snails but is about a creeping sense of the ordinary. In this account, the space has become both more legible and mundane over time (see Saha and Watson, this volume, for further discussion of 'mundane multiculturalism'). Linda's attitude towards Peckham is gradually mellowing as her idea of what is 'normal' is gently reconfigured:

> Peckham has surprised me, I mean it's no more dodgy than anywhere else actually. In fact, it's not dodgy at all, I mean everyone's just going about their normal business getting on with their lives, it's very easy to be judgemental, but um . . . you know . . . err, it's actually, it's fine, and even the chicken shops I've grown to . . . just ignore!

As Linda's account of how her feelings had changed demonstrates, as people do work to, and on, places so do places work on people. This is important as it shows the ways in which space is experienced in affectual (feeling sick) and emotional (feeling out of place) ways are not automatic or fixed but can evolve into something else, not through a major rupture or moment but through everyday life.

Conclusions

Discussions of multiculture and living with diversity were central to middle-class Peckhamites' descriptions of their neighbourhood. Such stories were infused with a range of emotions (disgust, comfort, fear, fascination) of varying intensities and with stories of other places. The 'elsewheres' drawn on to make sense of Peckham (Lagos, Vietnam, Brixton, a village in Lancashire) came from experience and imagination. These other places are drawn upon to link places together and can imbue place with emotion. Such accounts tell us about how difference is made sense of through a relational sense of the spatial, at an interpersonal level and also through modes of 'thinking autobiographically' (Giddens 1991).

Across all of the accounts examined here there are at least three discourses present. The first is an almost classic 'orientalist' (Said 1995) approach to difference, characterised by extreme distaste, and sometimes fascination, with what is perceived as exotic or 'other'. Such accounts are often tied up with boundary talk, particularly about Rye Lane or boundary-crossers (pigeons and weaves, meat). These descriptions attempt to map clear divisions onto space in a way that preserves spaces of white middle-class identity. The second is a banal everyday cosmopolitanism. These descriptions of neighbourhood are lacking in emotion, and are characterised by either a non-spectacular sense of 'multicultural drift' (Hall 1999) or as being related to one's own background or travels. The third is less straightforward and involves a fraught ambivalence, a combination of praising diversity as valued but combined with a concern for the preservation of control over place. This has most in common with the 'cosmo-multiculturalist' (2000) identified by Hage. The distinctions between these discourses are not always clear cut, with some interviewees combining elements of all three.

These expressions of feeling are not merely narrated but are performed in and produce neighbourhood, in the performative practices of everyday life, the avoidance of some streets and the using of particular shops and in more concerted interventions, such as campaigning for a restoration that wipes out what is already there. Thus, these emotional accounts of place need to be understood as being part of power relations. Who gets to define what is disgusting? When do individual emotional stories come together into collective narratives that form the basis for mobilisation? Which accounts are heard, accepted and acted upon by official bodies, such as the local council?

There is a danger, however, that the most highly charged emotional accounts of difference are the ones which leap out at both researcher and reader. Despite these sensationalised accounts of Rye Lane there are other more everyday practices described which take place across boundaries (doing the shopping, neighbours popping by) which perhaps point to other parallel (and more optimistic) unfoldings of place, emotion and multiculture. The nuances in these different stories of pigeons and weaves demonstrate the importance of being attentive to emotional stories of place. One person's uncanny boundary-crosser evokes nostalgia in another.

Finally, these descriptions were given as part of an interview-based project and are therefore snapshots of the attitudes and feelings that people expressed on one particular day in their lives. In Linda's interview, our hour long discussion in her kitchen provided space for reflection on her changing relationship with place, but this reflection is always from the point of the here and now. Linda's story raises a methodological question about how to capture this shifting over time, this multicultural drift, in people's experiences of emotion, location and the formation of cosmopolitan sensibilities.

Note

1   The interviews in this chapter took place in London between September 2010 and January 2012.

References

Ahmed, S. (2004) *The Cultural Politics of Emotion*, New York: Routledge.
Bacqué, M., Bridge, G., Butler, T., Benson, M., Jackson, E., Launay, L., Fijalkow, Y. and Vermeersch, S. (forthcoming) *The Middle Classes in Paris and London*, London: Palgrave Macmillan.

Benson, M. and Jackson, E. (2013) 'Place-making and place maintenance: Performativity, place and belonging among the middle classes', *Sociology*, 47(4): 793–809.

Butler, T. and Robson, G. (2001) 'Social capital, gentrification and neighbourhood change in London: A comparison of three south London neighbourhoods', *Urban Studies*, 38(12): 2145–62.

Douglas, M. (1966) *Purity and Danger: An Analysis of Concepts of Pollution and Taboo*, London: Routledge & Kegan Paul.

Fortier, A.M. (2007) 'Too close for comfort: Loving thy neighbour and the management of multicultural intimacies', *Environment and Planning D: Society and Space*, 25: 104–19.

Giddens, A. (1991) *Modernity and Self-Identity: Self and Society in the Late Modern Age*, Stanford, CA: Stanford University Press.

Goodwin, P. (2007) *Peckham Rising*. ebook. Available at http://diffusion.org.uk/?p=144 (accessed 1 October 2013).

Hage, G. (2000) *White Nation*, New York and London: Routledge.

Hall, S. (1999) 'From Scarman to Stephen Lawrence', *History Workshop Journal*, 48: 187–97.

Jackson, E. and Benson, M. (forthcoming) 'Neither "deepest darkest Peckham", nor "run-of-the-mill" East Dulwich: The middle classes and their "others" in an inner London neighbourhood', *International Journal of Urban and Regional Research*.

Jacobs, J.M. (1996) *Edge of Empire*, London: Routledge.

Jerolmack, C. (2008) 'How pigeons became rats: The cultural-spatial logic of problem animals', *Social Problems*, 55(1): 72–94.

Jones, H. (2013) *Negotiating Cohesion, Inequality and Change: Uncomfortable Positions in Local Government*, Bristol: Policy Press.

Kristeva, J. (1982) *Powers of Horror: An Essay on Abjection*, New York: Columbia University Press.

London Borough of Southwark (2005) *Bellenden Renewal Scheme Final Report*, London: London Borough of Southwark.

Martin, C. (2013) 'We went on a quest to find the new Dalston'. Available at www.vice.com/en_uk/read/we-went-on-a-quest-to-find-the-new-dalston (accessed 28 August 2013).

May, J. (1996) 'Globalization and the politics of place: Place and identity in an inner London neighbourhood', *Transactions of the Institute of British Geographers*, 21(1): 194–215.

Rhys-Taylor, A. (2013) 'Disgust and distinction: The case of the jellied eel', *The Sociological Review*, 61(2): 227–46.

Said, E. (1995) *Orientalism*, London: Penguin.

Savage, M., Bagnall, G. and Longhurst, B. (2005) *Globalization and Belonging*, London: SAGE.

Simonsen, K. (2008) 'Practice, narrative and the "multicultural city": A Copenhagen case', *European Urban and Regional Studies*, 15(2): 145–58.

Skeggs, B. (2004) *Class, Self, Culture*, London and New York: Routledge.

Watson, S. and Saha, A. (2012) 'Suburban drifts: Mundane multiculturalism in outer London', *Ethnic and Racial Studies*, OnlineFirst, 1–19.

Wyld, E. (2011) *Writing Home: Peckham*. Available at www.granta.com/New-Writing/Home-Peckham (accessed 1 October 2013).

PART II

Places that don't exist
England(s) and elsewheres

4

UNCOMFORTABLE FEELINGS

How local belonging works on local policy makers[1]

Hannah Jones

What can we learn about how government works on feelings of belonging by treating policy practitioners as embedded, situated social subjects? What can this tell us about the operation of power and emotion in governing work? Increasingly, critics are analysing the ways that citizens are governed through emotional mechanisms. But this often treats the people doing the governing as invisible, or as somehow outside the sociality of emotional reactions to policy and place. In this chapter I will use in-depth interviews extracted from a wider empirical study, to consider how two people working in local government in England negotiated their own senses of belonging, and their personal political, ethical and professional commitments, while working as part of projects of governance that explicitly focused on developing attachments to place and local identities among local people.

Too often, critical engagements with policies of national and local belonging treat policy documents, speeches and legislation as demonstrating the intentions, practices and likely outcomes of policy decisions. Yet these documents are not end-points. It is easy to critique language as vague or lacking nuance, but this does not take into account that such rhetoric can be a tactic for negotiating political and ethical choices, leaving possibilities for their mediation off the page. This is particularly the case with policies dealing with contentious subjects like belonging and local identity, where agreement even within institutions can be hard to reach except on the very blandest level. The policies I have been researching are just such a case. Even the term which brings them together, 'community cohesion', is one whose meaning shifted constantly throughout the decade or so it has been prominent in British policy debates (Robinson 2005; Cantle 2012).

One way to think about the set of ideas that coalesced as 'community cohesion policy' is as a form of crisis management emerging from and shaped by reactions to events including riots in northern English cities and towns with a large proportion of South Asian heritage residents in 2001; growing migration to the UK following expansion of EU membership and freedom of movement through the 2000s; and terrorist bombings in London in 2005 in the name of Islamic extremism. Such 'moments' were treated as crises needing a policy reaction that would increase connections between people of 'different backgrounds'. To this end various agencies of government produced local community cohesion strategies, statutory duties on schools to promote community cohesion, and interventions such as cultural festivals, twinning of schools and youth clubs with significantly different ethnic populations, setting up of interfaith networks, and 'myth-busting' communication strategies. In almost every case, there has been a focus on shared local identity, alongside (to varying degrees) 'British values'.

Alternatively, we could view community cohesion policy as part of a chain of related interventions aimed at 'dealing with' tensions arising from Britain becoming a more multicultural society, parallel with similar developments elsewhere in the world (e.g. see Vertovec and Wessendorf 2010). Britain has never had an official programme of 'state multiculturalism' dubbed as such, though one would not think so from the attacks on this straw man from politicians and thinkers across the political spectrum (e.g. Phillips 2005; Cameron 2011; Goodhart 2013). As the scale of immigration to Britain from around the world increased significantly following the Second World War, successive governments since the 1960s have produced laws and policies to limit immigration, which we might see as an attempt to halt what Stuart Hall has described as 'multicultural drift' (Hall 2000; see also Saha and Watson in this volume). Alongside this, legislation to counter racist discrimination within national borders has made specific behaviours and actions illegal (Solomos 2003), while more policy- and practice-focused interventions have worked directly on feelings of belonging and equality, whether such interventions have been called community relations, community development, social regeneration or community cohesion. As Hall notes, 'multicultural drift' has been a slow change over time, ebbing and flowing, but is not something that can be 'turned back'. Policies like community cohesion (along with legislation on discrimination) are attempts to manage potential discomforts and crisis seen to arise from this 'drift', but also part of the drift itself as they reconfigure public imaginations about what it means to be and feel both part of Britain, and part of a shared local community.

Anne-Marie Fortier's explorations of political and policy discourses on community cohesion and related subjects demonstrate the requirement placed on racialised 'others' to *feel like* part of the nation, while being constantly reminded of one's exclusion from it (Fortier 2008). Meanwhile, Sara Ahmed's work on 'happy multiculturalism' asks us to consider what it means to be required to represent the uncomplaining 'other' who constitutes the success of post-colonial 'diversity' settlements (2010; see also Berlant 2011 on 'cruel optimism'). Expressing empathy or compassion can work to exclude consideration of power inequalities, when the idea that 'we all feel similar things' can ignore that some people have more opportunity than others to narrate their feelings as matters for consideration, and to work on those feelings (Berlant 2004; Skeggs 2004; Pedwell 2012).

Sarita Srivastava has shown how claims of empathy can function through her studies of exchanges in feminist, anti-racist organisations in Canada when white women have been confronted with accusations of racism (Srivastava 2005). She argues that 'The struggle by some white feminists and feminist organisations to maintain an ethical nonracist feminist identity can then become an impediment to meaningful anti-racist analysis and change' (ibid.: 42), where the reaction 'You're calling me a racist?', accompanied by anger, tears and shaming, demonstrates how being accused of racism has seemingly become equated with, or worse than, experiencing racism (see also Ahmed 2005). Srivastava's interviews with both white and minoritised women show how the emotional reaction felt as an attack on a person's anti-racist identity prevents any meaningful discussion of the charges of racist behaviour which have been raised, and can reinforce the power relations around who (and whose emotions) gets to be heard (similar dynamics can be seen in accounts of Racism Awareness Training in 1980s British local government, e.g. Ouseley 1990).

In this chapter, I will discuss just two interview encounters from a much broader study of how policy practitioners understood and practised 'community cohesion policy' – peaceful 'living together with difference' – as a responsibility of government, inculcating appropriate emotions (respect, belonging, trust) as well as addressing material inequalities (of housing, education, discrimination) (Jones 2013). Alongside participant observations from working as a local government practitioner, I conducted over 80 semi-structured in-depth interviews with senior and middle managers in local and central government in four areas of England (Barking and Dagenham, Peterborough, Oldham and Hackney). In my research, the work done by practitioners to understand themselves as politically progressive or sympathetic was striking, and has parallels with Srivastava's discussion of emotional reactions to inequality. For some, the 'work' being done to this end was mainly in the structuring of accounts within the interview, the 'telling of the reflexive self' (Skeggs 2002) in the interview situation. However, many others gave examples of their actions or thought processes within the practice of policy and governance which suggested some of this 'work' went on in everyday processes, as they made ongoing negotiations about how to reconcile their own political and ethical views within professional and organisational settings. After the first six 'pilot' interviews for my study, I realised that my initial questions (How do you understand community cohesion policy? How has it affected your work? How do you think it will develop in the future?) had provoked much reference to the interviewees' own personal experiences, beyond the 'professional' realm, as it is usually understood, so I added a further broad question: 'How do your own background and experiences affect how you think about community cohesion policy?' It is the answers to this question, from two of my participants, which I now want to discuss, arguing that they provide valuable insight into the deeply felt consequences of the mundane reality of Britain's everyday cosmopolitanism, and into how local governing and place-making is constituted by emotional, political, ethical subjects.

Michael: Fear, loss, anxiety

Michael had worked in roles linking police officers with local authorities in the most ethnically diverse boroughs of inner London, and talked elsewhere in the interview about how in these contexts he saw ethnic diversity as 'almost a non-issue, because it's so diverse'. Michael drew on his experience of living in Barking, an area notorious for political mobilisation of extreme racist politics, to express his distance from those politics ('I hate those bastards as much as anyone'). When I asked directly about any relationship between his biography and his work practice, he gave an impassioned response.

Hannah: So I just wondered if your own background and identity and experience affect how you approach these issues?

Michael: Totally, 110 per cent. And it affects the way I think about it, every day, when I think about community cohesion, I can honestly say I challenge myself and I'll – so this is why, people tell you all the time, that they're not racists, people will tell you, I'm not a racist. Now I've just got one question for those people and that's how do you know? How do you know you're not a racist cos how the hell do you tell that?

When you talk about communities, so, I live in Barking. I've always lived in Barking except for when I was at University of Essex, I am a Barking boy. My whole town has completely and utterly and totally changed. Doesn't look the same, smell the same, feel the same. Completely different. This afternoon, I will put my house on the market to sell it to move. So then when you think about that in terms of your own personal experience and think about well, what's that all about? Why do I wanna do that, why do I wanna move? And I suppose it's about, for me, and my experiences of community cohesion, my community no longer exists. My community in Barking doesn't exist any more, there isn't one. The community that I grew up in isn't there, it's gone. Cos they've all moved out. They're all part of the white flight, bang, they've all gone. Everyone lives in Leigh-on-Sea, Brentwood, Shenfield. Everyone lives there. So all my friends have gone, I'm the last man standing, that's what they say . . . The only people that buy houses where I live, and this is a given, all the estate agents will tell you, are Muslim families, essentially large families that buy the larger houses to bring in large families, that's what happens. What that has is that has a disproportionate effect on the schools. So the schools, my children are now a significant minority in their schools. So they are, I think my little boy, is one of four white kids in his class that he's going into. And my little girl in her [nursery class of] 50, I think there are six white kids, and of those white kids I think two are eastern European, so in terms of, we talk about understanding of and engagement with Muslim communities. Well, I'm a minority aren't I, where is the understanding and engagement with my community?

I think that it came home to me really really hard to me, really really hard, when one day my little boy came home from school at Christmas and said, oh, I've been doing about Christmas at school. Oh alright, so I went, that's nice, so what's Christmas all about then? And what he said was, he said CHRISTIANS believe. That's what he said. And for me that's like – that's a real check-up. That's a real, oh, hang on a minute. What's that? And on the other hand, it's right to say that the school, like all the other schools, they just go through the year, and they just pick out the religious events that are on the calendar. But for me and for my background, I have to say well . . . that's hard. That is really hard for me to accept that. Not because I don't understand the fact that there are differ-ent faiths and different religions, but I expected, unconsciously, that my kids would be brought up in the same tradition that I was brought up in. Collective acts of worship, this, that, and then when my son comes home, well Christians believe, so oh my god, don't say that when your nan's here because that will be it, that will be uproar over that, so [sighs] yeah my whole background has been challenged by a complete and utter change in demographic of where I live, which has forced me to consider very strongly the way I interact and meet with other communities and other people.

Cos the question is, so why do I need to move? So what? Why don't I just accept it, and live there? And that's the question that I ask myself, and it's really hard to quantify that, and give that a tangible answer isn't it? And I keep asking myself the same time, 'Mick, are you racist, is that what this is, are you actually a racist?' and you think, hang on a minute, I suppose the Asian community are coming together cos they wanna be together, why should it be any different for me? Why should I not want that as well. You know, why should I not want my kids to grow up in the tradition that I've grown up in, and the only way I can't secure that where I am. They can't have that because where I lived doesn't exist any more except geographically.

Hannah: And does that kind of help you understand how other communities are – or is it making you feel . . .

Michael: No I think it makes me feel how communities may feel under threat. And that might sound really bizarre, you could say how can this white feller that's from Barking possibly sit there and say that, that

> you think you understand how a community under threat feels, how can I possibly say that?
>
> Well you know what? My children are a massive minority in their school, that is how they f- how it is, my children are coming home at Christmas and they're not being told the nativity is the nativity, they're being told, this is what Christians believe. So all the things about where I live have completely changed, so I think it does give me a way to think about how communities might feel if they feel under threat. And attacked. And it's a terrible way to say it isn't it, that I feel under threat and attacked, but actually my – way – of – living, my existence, is under threat, is under attack, it has been threatened. It has changed. The shops where I live have changed. They're not the same any more. Ha! There you go.
>
> **Hannah:** Okay. Thank you.
>
> **Michael:** I bet no one's been that honest have they?

There is much to reflect upon in Michael's response. The key things I want to highlight are his deeply felt sense of abandonment and isolation where he lives; his sense that because the ethnicity of the people living in his area has changed, the place itself no longer exists – and that this means a profound loss; and the ways that Michael relates these feelings to the work that he does on community, belonging and living with difference.

Apparently, I was interviewing Michael on the very day that his feelings of isolation in the place where he had lived his whole life had come to a head, and he was about to advertise his house for sale with a view to moving away. But he did not really feel that he was moving away, rather that the place had moved away from him: 'my community in Barking doesn't exist any more, there isn't one . . . they've all gone.' He did not understand the frame of reference that his children were learning in school, where Christianity was just one faith among many, rather than a reassuring default background ('the nativity is the nativity'). This was not expressed as a fear that his children were learning the wrong faiths; he expected them to learn about other cultures. But he 'expected, unconsciously', that within any multiculturalism, unmarked white Englishness would remain the dominant norm. That Michael felt this viscerally was clear from his language.

Michael's loss was not just in time – that history had changed his home – but he felt like the place itself had gone. It 'doesn't exist any more, except geographically' – it was still on the map but this no longer seemed to be the place he recognised, in even its basic facets – it 'doesn't smell the same'. And this was because his friends had moved away – significantly, his white friends. The population had not disappeared; his friends had been replaced by new residents, but he saw them as fundamentally different from himself. This is not to say that they were not British; many were simply moving out of central London to larger affordable housing. He found it almost impossible to contemplate staying and adapting to the minoritised status of his children in school and the new sights and smells of Barking; they were a 'threat', an 'attack', and something he had courageously been 'the last man standing' amongst, now joining the rest of his friends and family in retreat out of London.

Michael recognised some structural factors in his account; that the departure of his friends, his 'community' was 'part of the white flight'; the changing demographic of Barking in terms of the housing stock appealing to people with bigger families. He worried, because he knew that his reaction of wanting to leave might be problematic – 'am I a racist?' In Michael's account, this had all happened *to* him – the world had shifted around him, rather than him being part of that change. What springs to mind is Paul Gilroy's diagnosis of 'post-colonial melancholia' as the condition of early twenty-first century Britain (Gilroy 2004), where those raised with an expectation of imperial greatness become unable to place themselves in a post-colonial world where losses become blamed on racialised others and the reality of mundane multiculture is viewed as a threat and associated with a sense of nostalgic loss. At the same time, Michael was desperately trying to reconcile these feelings of loss, detachment and fear with a desire not to 'be a racist' and a reflexive (and fraught) questioning of his own attitudes.

Amrit: Commitment, anger, pride

Amrit worked in a race equality organisation in Peterborough, a small city in the east of England. He was in his fifties and an experienced professional familiar with the fluctuations, commonalities and contradictions of changing approaches to ethnic diversity and racism within British social policy – anti-racism, race equality, community relations, community cohesion. Through the major part of the interview, he drew on national events, familial experiences and professional encounters to answer and counter my questions about how he understood 'community cohesion' as a policy formation. And when I came to my final question which addressed biography and professional understandings directly, like Michael he answered affirmatively and at length.

> *Hannah:* I just wondered if you think – your own background and experiences affect how you think about some of these issues?
>
> *Amrit:* Of course they do. Because . . . I'm a father of three young children, I'm married to an English woman, I'm married to a Christian, I'm a practising Muslim, I have a shared heritance, [*sic*] in the sense that my father came from Karachi, my mother came from Bombay so I'm an Indo-Pakistani if you want to – in today's terms, and I am inherently also somebody who had an African culture in him because I spent most of the first 18, 19 years of my life in Uganda,

okay? And it's a fact that I am a practising Muslim, but my surname is still a Hindu surname, okay?

And so, everything about me in terms of where I am today and the job I do and the way I speak and how I speak it, has been moulded by – not only my ethnicity, not only by my nationality, not only by my and my wife's faith, but also the fact that my son in fact, has been assaulted on three occasions, twice by Asians, once by whites, and so I actually have to live that, sort of, you know, well it's more than just leading a double life, okay?

I'm instinctively a political animal, and yet in my job I have to be very careful that I'm not seen to be political in any way. I have a responsibility to the people who pay me, who are also my clients, to the people that I am doing the casework for, who are also my clients, and so, I don't actually only live a double life, I sort of live a multifaceted life, and all that then is modified and influenced by where I come from, and where I'm going.

If you had said to me, when I first came into this country, was I British, I would say of course I'm bloody not British! Okay? I'm a Ugandan Asian! If you for instance were to ask me that question now, I would say yes I'm British! And my wife jokes me a bit to sort of say, yeah, but are we prepared to have you now? Okay?

And so, there are all those sort of things, that basically influence where I come from, and what I do. And I actually quite like where I am, in the sense that I can actually listen to Bach, and I can listen to Bruch's violin concerto, and then I can also listen to Bob Marley and Pink Floyd, and Indian music, and Qawwalis, and so all that also influences the way that I in fact do my work, or try to do my job, the way that I sort of liaise with people, the way I do my job, the way I talk to my executive, the sort of things that we raise, and how I have real ambitions about what we really need to do about community development, in this city, and what we really need to do and how we can work with agencies, to move forward, and all that very much is influenced by the fact that I am who I am, that I have the benefit of in fact getting a Master's, funded by the SSRC, that my wife is a teacher, that my children have gone to university, etc., etc. And that one of my sisters, in fact, several of my sisters – I have six sisters – were not only mothers to their children, but fathers to their children as well, and how you know, when we came into this country, in 1972, penniless, with 50 quid on the table and another 50 quid sort of stuffed in my knickers, and how, we have not done too badly.

So, the fact that, I came here used to a life as a minority, and the fact that whether I was in India or in Pakistan. If I was in Pakistan, I

> would have had a surname that was Hindu, if I was in India, I would be in a country where Muslims formed roughly 20 per cent of the country, and so, I've developed this sort of, happy fatalism as well, which influences what I do and what I say. And in all that, I also have a lot to celebrate, because my background, together with the culture and identity that marrying a white person has given me, sort of has widened my horizons, so, I would like to believe that most of the time, I am a happy bunny.
>
> *Hannah:* [laughs] Good. [laughs]
>
> *Amrit:* Community cohesion, or no community cohesion.

Again, I want to draw out some key themes to think about further in the way Amrit answered this question. First, his account of himself as embedded in a complex network of identity, experience and connection, including a pride in his city and anger at those who would undermine the place; second, the way he related this embeddedness to his work.

It is notable that both men immediately reacted to my question by agreeing strongly that their background, identity and experiences affected how they approached issues related to community cohesion policy. But where Michael's initial reaction was to give a lengthy account of his personal experience of feeling threatened, and only came back to how this related to his work after additional prompting, Amrit's account made more direct links. He began with an autobiographical sketch of his family relationships and their transnational routes, but described these as shaping 'everything I do'. He made a point that it was not simply ethnicity, or ethnic difference, that did this 'shaping', but other experiences – like being the father of a son who had been the victim of apparently racially motivated attacks; being a brother to women who had been single mothers; having a university education; being a migrant. His migrant story is not just about arrival in Britain, but about the changing places he and his parents grew up – Uganda, India – which, in Michael's words, could be said to 'no longer exist', as a result of the imperial legacy of political redrawing of boundaries, bloody warfare and displacement.

Amrit's account was less explicitly emotional than Michael's, but it was given with an equal, if differently nuanced, passion.[2] And his 'ambitions' for Peterborough were, he said, driven by his awareness not just of complexity in his own life, but by what he had learnt from and valued from each 'facet'. Earlier in the same interview, Amrit talked even more explicitly about how his fierce pride and belonging to the city he had chosen to make his home related to his work when confronted with people proclaiming hatred against others:

> [B]ecause this is my city, my children were born here, I'm going to be around here for a while, if not til the day I die, and I feel that anybody who is going to then muck up, or have a negative impact, on community relations, basically needs to be told that there is no place here for you.

Here, rather than claiming empathy or feelings-in-common, Amrit argued for a more political solidarity which can be threatened by people resisting connection (in this case, he was talking about someone advocating violent action against non-Muslims). By never quite fitting with the norm, in all the ways he outlined, Amrit's account recalls Du Bois' conception of the double consciousness, which originally showed how black Americans in a majority white society experienced 'constantly measuring oneself through the eyes of others' (Du Bois 1994 [1903]: 2). Besides feeling somehow 'split', the double consciousness Du Bois described was a way of understanding the world as differently experienced by those in different relations of power. Amrit said he lived 'more than just a double life', but a 'multifaceted life'. The intersections of his experience, of both exclusion and privilege, of knowledge of differing perspectives, 'influences the way' he 'does his work', the 'set of issues that we raise'. This was a sensibility and motivation, rather than a claim to know how others feel.

Amrit and Michael: Belonging and (dis-)connection

Amrit and Michael had many things in common – both were men, married with children, university educated, professionals working in the same field. Both were being interviewed by me for academic research, and neither knew me beforehand yet both seemed extremely frank and candid in what they shared. Beyond this, the two men were differently positioned in relation to many axes of power. Amrit described himself as a migrant with a complex set of cosmopolitan belongings, allegiances and hybridities which he was used to having to account for, while Michael saw himself as having a firmly situated anchor in one place – but a place that had 'disappeared' as a result of other people's local and transnational migrations. Amrit's professional career had long been focused on equalities work; Michael was newer to this having specialised from a policing career. Michael felt that his children were threatened by the multicultural drift around them; Amrit's son had been physically attacked several times in, he implied, racialised attacks. Amrit was working in a city he had chosen as his home and where he had strong attachments and intended to stay. Michael worked in a location not far from, but distinct from his home, and his home was somewhere he struggled to see in the same terms as the multicultural settlement he accepted at work.

Michael's yearning for a place (or privilege within it) that had 'disappeared' – his post-colonial melancholia – was deeply felt. Yet he wanted to retain the identity of a good, ethical self, in the way that Srivastava (2005) describes; he did not want to 'be a racist'. So he tried to reconcile his alienation in his life-long home with the languages of inclusiveness, diversity and anti-racism he used at work (see also Hunter 2010; Ahmed 2012). Michael's suggestion that feeling 'under attack' allowed him to understand the feelings of marginalised people was his way of connecting his ethical and professional commitments with his visceral feelings of alienation and fear.

This move relies on an interpretation of Michael's feelings as both personal and universal. Yet his raced, classed and gendered privilege remained – he was highly qualified, owned his own home, was able to move to an area where he expected to feel more comfortable and not be reminded daily that his own outlook and behaviours were particular. He was not required to measure himself 'through the eyes of others' (Du Bois 1994 [1903]: 2) as structurally minoritised people are. And so the empathy Michael expressed is more like an expectation that his fear of not being 'the norm' will be the same feeling others have; and that he could 'empathise' because his feelings of exclusion must be the same as others who are excluded.

As Amrit's account showed, being outside the dominant norm (in multiple ways) does not necessarily mean experiencing fear, anger and nostalgia. Amrit's account focused on relationships between people and within institutions, rather than on a retreat into the self and the nuclear family, into sameness. Indeed, there would be no comfort of ethnic 'sameness' for Amrit in doing so, with each of his parents, wife and children being of different ethnicities, nationalities and/or religions from him. This complexity of raced, classed, gendered, transnational power relations is a given in Amrit's life as he recounted it, and not something he could flee from even if he wanted to. Rather than a reaction of sympathy or empathy, a dealing with emotion in and for itself, he treated his feelings of connection, disconnection, anger and pride as social processes – as political phenomena in themselves, not simply reactions to politics and history (while also feeling that he may be 'too political' for his role).

These accounts together suggest that belonging somewhere – feeling like somewhere belongs to you – is not just about an association with a particular location (or space) but about the ability to imagine it as a *place* that is inclusive (or exclusive) of certain other people, behaviours or ethics. For Michael, place change was materialised in who lived in Barking, what was taught in school, the shops, the smells. His feeling that things had changed in a way he found uncomfortable led him to decide that he should leave. For Amrit, place was constituted through his living (and working) in Peterborough, especially his family life, and his expectation of staying. He expected the same ethos of others – those who did not respect other people should 'be told there is no place here for you'. Amrit saw himself as belonging to his current place despite or because of coming from elsewhere – his belonging was accrued and created over time and use, not inherited. Michael saw his belonging as having been inherited but eroded by the presence of others.

What does this mean for the practice, translation and implementation of local policy about belonging and cohesion? Let us move away from these two individuals, and think more broadly about the ways of recognising and using emotion in policy and political practice. With very little prompting, both interviewees described embodied, emotional and biographical contexts that they felt were intimately connected with how they worked to make communities more cohesive. With these two interviews (and many others in my wider study) it was not necessary to dig very hard to find some form of reflexive practice almost as a reflex action in the way that local and national policy people talked about their work. What is notable, though, is that for some this reflexivity remained at a personal, individualised level, seemingly reinforced by discussion of emotion. Feeling angry, scared and so on is understandably uncomfortable and unpleasant, and most people will seek to avoid these feelings where they are able. Once those feelings have been made to go away – by moving house, by avoiding confrontational situations, by finding bland policy language that erases the hard edges of conflict and inequality – understanding them as having been personal and internal, and no longer at issue – not an ongoing political issue – makes sense.

For some people it is not as easy to make uncomfortable feelings go away. They might not be, or be allowed to feel like, an invisible, comfortable norm anywhere. Even if there were such a comfortable space available, there may be all sorts of barriers – financial, physical, political – to getting there. In this case, uncomfortable feelings persist. And rather than seeing this as a trauma in need of psychological treatment (though in many cases it may lead to that) I want to suggest that this persistence of discomfort can make it clearer to those affected that feelings are intimately intertwined with material, political and social relations of power. Thus for Amrit, his feelings about who he was, what he had experienced and who he interacted with all influenced his understanding of his work as being 'multifaceted', about challenge and change rather than closure.

Does this mean that someone privileged by their raced, classed, gendered or other identities or positions can never have the 'right emotions'; is doomed to defensively reify difference in feeling, thinking and practice? Far from it. But to remain open to the political weight of emotions, it is necessary not to flee from uncomfortable feelings, but to inhabit them (like Sara Ahmed's 'feminist killjoy' (2010)). To recognise one's privilege and question one's discomfort and the discomfort of others. We need to ask practitioners not 'how they feel', or what these feelings might mean about them personally ('am I a racist?'). The question is where these feelings come from in circuits of power, place and history; and what these feelings mean for ongoing relations of power and belonging. By seeking political and social causes and consequences of the feelings at the centre of so much governing practice – whether the feelings of practitioners or those of their publics – the power of emotional reactions can be harnessed to make political connections rather than reify social difference.

Note

1   The interviews in this chapter took place in London and Peterborough in 2009.
2   As can also be seen from the fact that neither man needed additional prompting during these long accounts.

References

Ahmed, S. (2005) 'The non-performativity of anti-racism', *Borderlands e-journal* 5 (3). Available at www.borderlands.net.au/vol5no3_2006/ahmed_nonperform.htm (accessed 10 February 2014).
—— (2010) *The Promise of Happiness*, Durham, NC, and London: Duke University Press.
—— (2012) *On Being Included: Racism and Diversity in Institutional Life*, Durham, NC: Duke University Press.

Berlant, L. (ed.) (2004) *Compassion: The Culture and Politics of an Emotion*, New York and London: Routledge.

—— (2011) *Cruel Optimism*, Durham, NC: Duke University Press.

Cameron, D. (2011) 'PM's Speech at Munich Security Conference', Number 10 website, 5 February. Available at www.number10.gov.uk/news/pms-speech-at-munich-security-conference (accessed 1 October 2013).

Cantle, T. (2012) *Interculturalism: The New Era of Cohesion and Diversity*, Basingstoke: Palgrave.

Du Bois, W.E.B. (1994 [1903]) *The Souls of Black Folk*, New York: Dover Publications, Inc.

Fortier, A.-M. (2008) *Multicultural Horizons: Diversity and the Limits of the Civil Nation*, Abingdon: Routledge.

Gilroy, P. (2004) *After Empire: Melancholia or Convivial Culture?*, London: Routledge.

Goodhart, D. (2013) *The British Dream: Successes and Failures of Post-War Immigration*, London: Atlantic Books.

Hall, S. (2000) 'Conclusion: The Multi-Cultural Question', in B. Hesse (ed.) *Un/Settled Multiculturalisms: Diasporas, Entanglements, Transruptions*, London and New York: Zed Books.

Hunter, S. (2010) 'What a white shame: Race, gender and white shame in the relational economy of primary health care organizations in England', *Social Politics* 17 (4): 450–76.

Jones, H. (2013) *Negotiating Cohesion, Inequality and Change: Uncomfortable Positions in Local Government*, Bristol: The Policy Press.

Ouseley, H. (1990) 'Resisting Institutional Change', in W. Ball and J. Solomos (eds) *Race and Local Politics*, Hampshire: Macmillan.

Pedwell, C. (2012) 'Economies of empathy: Obama, neoliberalism, and social justice', *Environment and Planning D: Society and Space* 30 (2): 280–97.

Phillips, T. (2005) 'After 7/7: Sleepwalking to segregation', speech to the Manchester Council for Community Relations, CRE, Manchester.

Robinson, D. (2005) 'The search for community cohesion: Key themes and dominant concepts of the public policy agenda', *Urban Studies* 42 (8): 1411–27.

Skeggs, B. (2002) 'Techniques for Telling the Reflexive Self', in T. May (ed.) *Qualitative Research in Action*, London: Sage.

—— (2004) *Class, Self, Culture*, London: Routledge.

Solomos, J. (2003) *Race and Racism in Britain*, Basingstoke and New York: Palgrave Macmillan.

Srivastava, S. (2005) '"You're calling me a racist?" The moral and emotional regulation of antiracism and feminism', *Signs: Journal of Women in Culture and Society* 31 (1): 29–62.

Vertovec, S. and Wessendorf, S. (eds) (2010) *The Multiculturalism Backlash: European Discourses, Policies and Practices*, Abingdon: Routledge.

5

DREAD CULTURE

Music and identity in a British inner city

Kieran Connell

Introduction

In 1978, the Handsworth-based reggae band Steel Pulse released their debut album, *Handsworth Revolution*. The band was heavily influenced by Rastafarianism and the album's artwork was indicative of the growing importance of Africa to a young black generation in Britain. The cover of the album depicts a scene from urban Britain – presumably Handsworth – being fused with, even taken over by, African imagery. High rise flats and slabs of concrete make way for green shrubbery and plants. In the background are mountains, onto which are etched the band's logo; in the foreground, highlighted by a beam of light, a group of children stand in African-style robes, with one beating a drum next to an abandoned car.

Drawing predominantly on interviews conducted in Handsworth, Birmingham, as well as existing oral history projects like the Trinity Arts Oral History Project – undertaken during the 1980s at the Trinity Arts Centre in Birmingham – this chapter unpicks the significance of Africa for a young black generation in Britain.[1] It takes as its case study Handsworth, an inner-city area to the north of Birmingham's city centre, during the 1970s and 1980s, a key period of community formation.

The aims of this volume are partly to foreground the way in which people feel everyday life in urban spaces, often in relation to the structural inequalities that form part of the daily reality of such spaces. Elsewhere in this book, the work of Holgersson and Grünenberg, for instance, shows how people from a range of backgrounds come to terms with distinct forms of displacement in two Scandinavian cities. In different ways, displacement was also an issue for black communities in 1980s Britain. In the context of a culturally insensitive education system, widespread racial discrimination, scapegoating in the media and the disproportionate targeting of black communities by the police, anger, disillusionment and a desire for new, positive definitions of 'black' were all prominent feelings in Handsworth and places like it. This is made apparent – whether explicitly or implicitly – in the words of the musicians, fans, poets and ordinary residents of Handsworth quoted in this chapter.

As the editors of the volume argue, localised feelings about a particular space are often connected with global notions of belonging. The chapter shows how perceptions of the global – in this case, perceptions of Africa – also impact on how people feel in the local. Africa was used as a way of coming to terms with the anger and disillusionment that people felt on the one hand, and on the other, as a way of meeting a profound need for a reclamation of the meaning of 'black'. The chapter documents what Stuart Hall calls a young black generation's 'renegotiation' and 'rediscovery' of Africa (Hall 1995: 9), through reggae music and sound systems. But this was not Africa in any literal sense. Rather it was, as Hall put it – following Benedict Anderson – an 'imagined community' (Hall 1995: 4), an example of what the historian Eric Hobsbawm called the 'invention of tradition', the real effects of which were firmly rooted in the Handsworth locale.

Hobsbawm argues that traditions are often 'invented' when particular communities require the establishment of certain values or identities (Hobsbawm 1983: 12). As Hall elaborates, the turn to conceptions of the past for legitimisation in the present is critical when it comes to the construction of identities. 'The discourse of identity', Hall argues, suggests there is always the need to try to find a 'kind of ground for our identities, something to which we can return, something stabilized, around which we can organize our identities and our sense of belongingness' (Hall 1995: 4). For Avtar Brah, this 'something stabilised' is often manifest within diasporic identities in an emphasis on the home, what Brah calls the 'homing desire' (Brah 1996: 180). This desire, as Hobsbawm recognised in a different context, can be met through the invention of traditions, rituals and the 'conscious manipulation of symbols' (Hobsbawm 1983: 9). This chapter documents some of the traditions, rituals and symbols that were deployed in Handsworth in the 1980s. In so doing, it marks the moment Africa became a critical source of identity amongst a young black generation in Britain.

Reggae

It was reggae music – both the British reggae of bands such as Steel Pulse, and that which was imported predominantly from Jamaica in the 1970s – that facilitated the turn towards Africa in Handsworth. And this was achieved primarily because of the way in which reggae brought younger generations into contact with the ideas of Rastafarianism. Reggae popularised Rastafarianism in Britain in the 1970s and 1980s. And in the context of the racism that permeated British society in the period, it was Rastafarianism, Stuart Hall argues, that 'saved the second generation of young black people in [British] society' (Hall 1995: 14).

Hall sees the Rastafarian embrace of Africa as resulting in a new form of language through which history could be 'retold' and the 'aspirations of liberation and freedom can for the first time be expressed' by a younger generation. For Hall, this was nothing short of a 'cultural revolution' (Hall 1995: 12–13). But the importance of Rastafarianism also illustrates the nature of the turn to Africa in Handsworth as an 'invented tradition'. By engaging with Rastafarianism younger generations were in fact following a movement that was Caribbean in origin, having first emerged in Jamaica in the 1930s and been revived in part by the music of Bob Marley and other Jamaican artists in the 1970s (Campbell 1980: 13). In many ways, therefore, Africa was being viewed from Handsworth through the prism of what it looked like from Jamaica. This was Africa as a concept or an idea that had little connection to the physical nature of the continent itself. It was used by a young black generation as a means of channelling the feelings of anger and powerlessness many felt in order to construct a new identity specifically in the British context.

In its original form, Rastafarianism emerged in Jamaica following the accession of Ras Tafari – who became known as Haile Selassie – to the Ethiopian throne in 1930. Rastafarians believed this represented the fulfilment of biblical prophecies regarding the deliverance of the black race. For Rastafarians, Tafari – or 'Jah' – was 'the Lion – the One True God of the prophecy, not merely God's vicar, like the Pope, or even an immaculate son – but the Living God' (Plummer 1978: 12). Rastafarians identified the contemporary and historical sufferings of black people as the 'reincarnation' of the plight of the ancient tribes of Israel, whose people had been enslaved by the kingdom of Babylon (Hiro 1991: 72). The biblical notions of Judgement Day, Zion and the Promised Land provided for Rastafarians answers to the suffering of black people living in contemporary 'Babylon'. Rastafarians were also influenced by the Pan-African philosophies of Marcus Garvey, and believed that salvation for black people would be found in their 'return' to their true home of Ethiopia and Africa, where all black people would one day live as 'free and dignified human beings' (Hiro 1991: 72).

For Dick Hebdige, 'somewhere between Trenchtown and Ladbroke Grove, the cult of Rastafari had become a "style"' (Hebdige 1979: 36). It was this, Hebdige argues, that enabled a young black generation to positively assert their 'blackness' by visually expressing an association with Africa. Rastas in England began to wear the national colours of Ethiopia (red, gold and green) and grow their hair into 'dreadlocks' in order to 'cultivate a more obviously African "natural" style' (Hebdige 1979: 43). Many dressed in surplus army uniforms (onto which were often sewn the Ethiopian colours), a 'sinister guerrilla chic' designed to show commitment to the onward march 'back to Africa' (Hebdige 1979).

In 1930s Jamaica, it is thought that Rastafarians began growing dreadlocks in order to emulate the 'long, plaited hairstyles of the East African Somali, Masai and Galla tribesmen who were appearing regularly in magazine photographs at the time' (Hebdige 1974: 14).

In places like Handsworth in the 1980s, however, the Rastafarian style was, as Hebdige puts it, 'borrowed from the sleeves of imported reggae albums' (Hebdige 1979: 43). For many, reggae provided their only point of contact with pan-Africanist ideas. 'I'm not into Marcus Garvey's concepts as much as I'd like to be', one black teenager from Handsworth mused in the 1980s, 'But Bob Marley had nice concepts. That's what I'm for . . . his music was an inspiration' (Trinity Arts Oral History Project 1984).

As Jaffe argues elsewhere in this volume, images of reggae music in films like the classic *The Harder They Come* (1972) were an important part of negative representations of the Caribbean that centred on the stereotypes of violence and deviance. Yet for a young black generation in Britain, the music of artists like Bob Marley was a way of overcoming the alienation many felt in British society. As one fan reflected, Marley's music 'was giving us a different spin on our cultural identity to what we saw on TV – things like Tarzan. Bob Marley was representing us in a positive way' (Brown, personal interview 2010). Marley's *Catch a Fire* album was released in 1973, and both Marley and the music were marketed with overtly Rastafarian imagery specifically in order to appeal to overseas audiences (Hebdige 1987: 79). The front cover of the album, for example, showed a close up Marley – his trademark dreadlocks in full view – smoking a spliff. 'I heard *Catch a Fire* when I was about fourteen', remembers Basil Gabbidon, co-founder of Steel Pulse. 'I just played it to death. I must have gone through about three copies of that album. It was at that point that I decided I had to form my own band' (Gabbidon, personal interview 2009).

By the mid-1970s, just as Bob Marley was urging his listeners to 'never forget who you are, and where you stand in the struggle' (Marley 1977), bands such as Aswad and Matumbi in London, and Beshara and Steel Pulse in Birmingham, were applying aspects of Rastafarianism explicitly to the lives and experiences of those who were brought up in Handsworth and places like it. Steel Pulse was formed in 1975 by Gabbidon and David Hinds, who went to school together at Handsworth Wood Boys School. From the beginning, the band adopted a Rastafarian aesthetic, placing African symbolism at the heart of their performances. Hinds, for example, who was the band's lead singer, wore particularly large dreadlocks that he further emphasised by often tying them up vertically above his head. The band regularly appeared on stage dressed in uniforms, including the prominent display of the Ethiopian national colours, red, gold and green. The idea, according to Michael Riley, a backing vocalist with the band, was to challenge the expectations of audiences, and make a 'mockery of the regimentation of this society' (cited in May 1978). Band members also appeared on stage dressed as bankers or priests, with the latter forming a visualisation of Rastafarianism's re-appropriation of mainstream, 'white' Christianity (Hebdige 1974: 12). A 'lot of what we sing about is corruption, the "civilised" world', Riley elaborated, 'so we dress up accordingly' (cited in May 1978).

Africa helped a young black generation form a re-appraisal of their position in contemporary British society. This is something embedded in Rastafarianism, and it was elaborated by bands such as Steel Pulse in terms that were explicitly relevant to people in the British context. As Horace Campbell (1980) and Paul Gilroy (1981, 1987) have argued, although Rastafarianism focuses on Africa as the true home of all black people, somewhat paradoxically, it is also a movement concerned with the inequalities of the immediate historical moment, 'a movement organised around a political and philosophical critique of oppressive social relations' (Gilroy

1981: 216). Rastafarianism was characterised by 'a culture of resistance', in particular to 'white society, white racist values, white education' (Campbell 1980: 20). As William 'Lez' Henry elaborates, Rastafarianism's emphasis on Africa is 'not about escapism' (Henry 2006: 75). Rather, it is about 'learning why as Afrikans we are in this situation, and using that knowledge to determine what can be done on our own terms to transcend a system that is, by its very nature, anti-Afrikan' (Henry 2006: 75). Fundamentally, Rastafarianism is a 'distinct expression of the contradiction between black people and the power block' (Gilroy 1981: 216); rather than focus on abstracts, Gilroy argues, quoting Marx, Rastafarianism is very much concerned with the 'concrete': the 'criticism of heaven turns into the criticism of earth, the criticism of religion into the criticism of law, and the criticism of theology into the criticism of politics' (Marx 1844 in Gilroy 1981: 217).

Such themes are well illustrated by the poetry of Benjamin Zephaniah, who was born in Handsworth in 1958. Handsworth in the 1970s and 1980s was described by Zephaniah as the 'Rasta capital of Britain' (Zephaniah, personal interview 2009), and Rastafarianism became one of the central influences on Zephaniah's work.

Zephaniah's early poetry is indicative of the appeal of Rastafarianism amongst his generation. *The Dread Affair* (1985) is Zephaniah's second collection of poetry, and it is based in large part on his experiences in Handsworth. Many of the poems were originally released in 'dub' form on Zephaniah's debut album, *Rasta* (1982). On the one hand, *The Dread Affair* illustrates the way in which Africa helped those of Zephaniah's generation articulate a positive definition of 'black'. England 'did reject me / I must cling to my tree', Zephaniah writes.

> Africa, Africa
> reaching out
> Africa
> very black
> very proud
> shouting loud
> AFRICA.

This was about Zephaniah getting 'me back me real true culture', and for him, was 'a matter of survival' (1985: 47, 57). Zephaniah urges his readers to 'listen to the drum' and to hear 'Africa calling . . . African history, African culture' (1985: 92).

Yet on the other hand, Zephaniah's work also demonstrates the way in which Rastafarianism helped facilitate an engagement with conditions in the present. 'One ting I know if you deal with de dead', Zephaniah writes, 'den you dead already like I said', and Zephaniah urged his readers to 'come reason with living stuff' (1985: 40). *The Dread Affair* thus also forms a gritty and often satirical engagement with 'living stuff' – his experiences living as a Rastafarian in Handsworth and later in Brixton, where he moved at the age of 22. His poems speak of the anger he felt as a young black man living in urban Britain, made clear in one of his best known poems, 'Dis policeman keeps on kicking me to death'.

> Dis policeman keeps on hitting me and pulling out my locks
> he keeps on feeding me unlimited broc-lacs
> dis policeman is a coward he gets me from behind
> he can jail my body but he cannot jail my mind.[2]

Zephaniah provides a commentary on the nature of the conditions around him, but places this in the context of a desire for change firmly grounded in the here and now. 'I turn around and took myself to see dis preacher guy', Zephaniah continues in 'Dis policeman keeps on kicking me to death', who told 'me 'bout some heaven/dat was in the bloody sky . . . I don't think I'm free/if I'm free den why does he/keep fucking kicking me' (1985: 96).

The Rastafarian critique of the present was something shared by British reggae bands such as Steel Pulse. As Basil Gabbidon recalled, 'that's basically why we started – we thought we had something to say' (Gabbidon cited in Velk 2010). Part of the engagement with the present included a growing awareness of events in Africa. 'When I got together with David, there was a lot of stuff going on TV about starvation in Africa, and that kind of woke us up to a consciousness. We thought the best way to spread the message of unity and awareness was through music' (Gabbidon cited in Velk 2010). However, as the title of Steel Pulse's debut album makes clear, *Handsworth Revolution* was primarily concerned with themes in their own lives in Handsworth. As Gabbidon surmised, 'you get your creativity, your strength, from your environment, and we got ours from Handsworth' (Gabbidon, personal interview 2009). *Handsworth Revolution* was 'a commentary on things that were going on in the community'. It was about 'the blues [dances], the police, the Rastas, everything. All that fed into the music'. One song, for example, entitled 'Macka Splaff', talks about 'feeling high' in 'ganja smoke tonight', while 'Sound Check' depicts a Handsworth 'blues dance' (Steel Pulse, 1978).

Handsworth Revolution thereby highlighted themes that could be immediately referenced by black youth in Handsworth and places like it across Britain. Like Zephaniah, this included being the victim of racist attacks. 'Ku Klux Klan', for example, 'tackled British racism indirectly' by referring to the American racist organisation (Hebdige 1987: 95), but its first person perspective makes it clear that it is the situation in Britain that is being addressed. The band performed the song in Ku Klux Klan hoods 'should anyone fail to grasp the meaning of the lyrics' (Hebdige 1987: 95). Yet the overriding tone of the album is fundamentally not one of victimhood. Steel Pulse predicted that 'Babylon is falling', but that 'Handsworth shall stand firm, like Jah rock, fighting back'.

> We once beggars are now choosers
> No intention to be losers
> Striving forward with ambition . . .
> We rebel in Handsworth revolution

(Steel Pulse 1978)

Ultimately, at the heart of *Handsworth Revolution* was a desire to reclaim Handsworth from the stigmatisation to which both it and those who lived there were subject. 'We called the album "Handsworth Revolution" because [if] I wasn't in the band and came from Handsworth, and a group called their album that, it would make me feel good and give me something to aim for', stated Michael Riley. 'We are trying to clean the name up' (cited in Silverton 1978).

Steel Pulse were the most successful of a number of groups from Handsworth who performed this particularly British brand of Rastafarian-inspired reggae in venues such as the Rialto in Handsworth or the Hummingbird in Birmingham city centre. Just as Bob Marley had been for Basil Gabbidon, Steel Pulse became an inspiration for reggae bands in Birmingham, precisely because of their dual emphasis on Rastafarianism and on events and themes in the local context. Amlak Tafari, for example, was born in Handsworth in 1965 and was the founding member of Amlak Band. 'I used to keep a scrapbook with pictures of Steel Pulse in there', he remembers (personal interview 2009). 'Songs like "Handsworth Revolution" and "Ku Klux Klan" made it big in Handsworth because they were about the lives we were leading. I was going through exactly the same things they had been through. They glorified Handsworth, just as I myself was proud to come from Handsworth. As a young reggae musician, a young Rasta man, a young man from Handsworth, I looked up to them.'[3] Jacko Melody was the lead singer of Eclipse, a band from the nearby Winson Green area of Birmingham, and recalled that 'everyone was a Rasta [at that time]. Even if you didn't have the locks, you were still a Rasta. The back to Africa thing, Garvey, it was like a teaching. I didn't know anything about Rasta until I joined [the band], and they taught me who Emperor Selassie was, who Garvey was, all those things' (personal interview 2011).

Sound systems

Perhaps because of the near-impossibility of emulating the success of Steel Pulse, who to date have released 11 studio albums and won a Grammy award, there were during the 1980s more active participants in 'sound systems' (Hebdige 1987: 125). A sound system can be defined as a 'large mobile hi-fi or disco' (Gilroy 1987: 164). Rather than writing music or playing musical instruments, the object in a sound system is to obtain an extensive collection of music and to play it with the highest possible quality at various social events. The concept has its origins in Jamaica, where sound systems appeared in order to cater for a growing demand to hear first American R&B and then ska and reggae played competently at large dance halls or in slum yards (Wood 2008: 165). The sound system was thus brought to Britain by the first generation of immigrants from the Caribbean, and was often played at 'blues dances' – organised parties generally held in people's homes at which an entrance fee would be charged.

This concept, however, was re-appropriated by a younger generation to suit its own specific needs and tastes. This generation moved away from the domesticated, house party style of their parents' generation – in part, to get away from their parents – and replaced it with a culture of dances held in youth clubs, church halls, garages or warehouses. Sounds 'represented' the particular area in which they were from, and fans that came from the same area would follow the sound wherever they went to play. A whole network of promoters sprung up to facilitate 'clashes', events that pitted one sound system and their followers against another, and posters advertising them were commonly 'plastered over the pillars under the Hockley flyover' in Birmingham (Bishton and Reardon 1984: 37). A flyer dated 28 May 1979, for example, advertises one such clash, taking place on Whit Monday at Digbeth Civic Hall in Birmingham:

> This is the Real thing, the Biggest Show [between] Jah Tubby representing London Tape control, Jah Mafia, representing Birmingham [and] Jah Tippertone, a skilful move up to Division 1. Jah Tubby believes no one can play him on music, he says first to go down will be Jah Tippertone but first to fall Jah Mafia no bells to save you this time . . . Did you hear what happened to the mighty Coxon? So shall it be to you says Jah Mafia [*sic*].

The event was one of many marketed as 'the show everyone is waiting to see!'[4]

A critical difference between the sound systems of younger generations and that of their parents is that whereas older sounds would largely play Caribbean 'festival music' such as calypso and ska (Brown, personal interview 2010), the focus of the great majority of younger generations' sound systems was specifically reggae. For Michael La Rose, sound systems 'helped to shape a new black identity' for younger generations in Britain (cited in Harris and White 1999: 136). As it was with the British reggae bands, Rastafarian and African imagery was central to this identity. Sound systems called themselves names such as 'Jah Shaka' that explicitly referenced Rastafarian ideas. Many dressed in the Ethiopian red, gold and green.[5]

From the late 1970s to the mid-1980s, 'Jungleman' was the biggest sound system in Handsworth. For Brian Bennett, who at the time ran 'Rootsman', a rival sound system in Birmingham, Jungleman was 'revolutionary' (personal interview 2009). Julian Henriques has written about the importance of the quality and volume of a sound system's sound in expressing ownership of a particular space (Henriques 2003: 453), and this was clearly a critical part of the Jungleman act. The group's sound was like a 'killing machine', remembers Bennett. 'All of a sudden, a needle would go on the record', he said, 'and a piece of earthquake would hit the room':

> Boom! Even your eyeballs would start to shake with the bass. The whole place would shake. You know when thunder hits? It was like that, if the thunder was right outside your front door. It had a way of speaking to you and saying, 'man is nothing'. Jungleman were like that.
>
> *(Bennett, personal interview 2009)*

Ras Tread was Jungleman's photographer and engineer throughout the group's existence, and he summed up the group's sound. 'We were a very raw talent', he said. 'Our Deejay, Speedy, was very up front, very to the point. If it wasn't going well, we would literally turn up on them; turn the volume up on them. We were one of the first sounds to have thousands of watts in our amp. We had one of the heaviest sounds going.' It was as a result of this that at their height in the early 1980s it was claimed that Jungleman had a following of 'thousands' in Handsworth (Tread, personal interview 2009).

However, as Bennett makes clear, Jungleman's popularity was not only the result of their quality of sound, what Henriques calls a sound system's 'sonic dominance' (Henriques 2003: 431). Jungleman also 'had this energy, like an aura' (Bennett, personal interview 2009), Bennett remembered. As it was in Steel Pulse, Rastafarian imagery was a central part of Jungleman's act. The Jungleman 'aura', then, came from their Rastafarian image and the way this met the desire for a positive black identity in Handsworth. Each member adopted names such as Pharaoh, Ras and Boa that were loosely meant to reference Rastafarianism and Africa, and many members also grew thick dreadlocks. 'We just tried to be as natural as possible', Tread commented (Tread, personal interview 2009). Jungleman wore uniforms of khaki suits and tunics, and hats specifically designed to incorporate particularly large dreadlocks:

> We were trying to follow Haile Selassie and Garvey's teaching. When we saw images of them looking impeccable in suits, we thought well, why not us? At that time a lot of Rastas looked like real vagabonds, but we thought having smart tunics was important – it was a militant style that showed we were serious about what we were doing.
>
> *(Tread, personal interview 2009)*

For Tread, such uniforms occupied a central part of what Jungleman was about. 'It was about our image and how we were going to portray ourselves. We wanted to look immaculate.' The uniforms, like the decision by Steel Pulse to call their debut album *Handsworth Revolution*, was about a desire to reclaim the Handsworth locale. It was, Tread recalled, an attempt to 'say to Handsworth: "if we can make ourselves better, so can you"'.

For Jungleman, Rastafarianism provided a way out of some of the problems in their everyday lives in Handsworth. Tread recalled how prior to their formation many in the group were 'what you call disenfranchised youth'. Jungleman's members were in their 'teens or early twenties . . . we didn't have jobs, weren't qualified . . . we weren't happy with the way we were being treated by the police'. Rastafarianism helped those in Jungleman to come to terms with this situation, particularly with its emphasis on self-help. 'A lot of sociologists came to Handsworth and wanted to know why we were turning to the Rasta "cult" as they called it', Tread reflected. 'Well the Rasta vibe was important because it let us take a different road. It was that Rasta ethos of self-help. We wanted to do something good with our lives – self-help, self-reliance.' Jungleman set up their own tailors that made the uniforms they wore on stage, and a photography venture, which sold photographs of reggae acts performing in Birmingham. The umbrella group for each of these projects was called 'Exodus' – named after the title of Bob Marley's seminal

1977 album. The idea, according to Tread, was simply to 'do what we can to help ourselves and the youth'.

Jungleman, however, did not see the turn towards Africa as being for use solely in Handsworth. Africa was of more than a symbolic significance to the group. As Tread recalled, 'we had this militancy thing about a return to Africa – that was central to what Jungleman were about. We saw ourselves as righteous soldiers, soldiers from God.' In 1982, Jungleman obtained funds from the Cadbury Trust to make a trip to Africa. The idea was to emigrate permanently, and 'set up a clothing industry with the tailors, set up a radio station, and continue with the sound. That was the intention.' Before making the trip, Jungleman sent some of its members, including Tread, over to Africa to check whether permanent emigration would be feasible. Tread and two others made the trip from Handsworth to Ghana, Nigeria, Togo and the Ivory Coast, and according to Tread, the 'feedback was all really positive. We began to believe that this could actually happen.'

Yet the planned migration to Africa was a failure. Whilst Tread was in Africa, other members of Jungleman in Handsworth were having second thoughts. 'There was all these stupid arguments about cars', Tread recalled. '"What are we going to do with the cars?" The most stupidest excuses I ever heard. The other members didn't have the courage to come, they said we were rushing ahead too quick. It's so saddening because we left a lot of equipment in Africa, really believing that we were going to go, and when we got back, there was just all this shock and fear. I was so pissed off.' Unlike Benjamin Zephaniah and Steel Pulse, Jungleman had mixed the concept of Africa garnered from reggae music and Rastafarianism with a desire to physically follow through with Garvey's 'back to Africa' mantra. Tread recalled that he felt 'let down. We had a set of bredrin, saying we're going to do this collectively, and then . . . it just made me question my faith in man.'

The point of the turn to Africa in Handsworth was that it enabled the channelling of the anger and alienation many felt into the articulation of a positive black identity, specifically in Handsworth. It was an 'invention' of a tradition for use in the present. Jungleman, however, mistook it for something more literal. In the event, the group were forced to return the grant they had received for the African trip to the Cadbury Trust and within two years, Jungleman had disbanded. For Tread, 'the dream had gone out the window'.

Conclusion

By the beginning of the 1990s, many of the acts discussed in this chapter had changed almost beyond all recognition. Following the release of *Handsworth Revolution* and three, less successful follow-up albums,[6] for example, Basil Gabbidon had left Steel Pulse, the group that he himself had co-founded. 'I couldn't handle it anymore', he remarked. 'I was tired and worn out, angry and depressed' (cited in Brouwer 2002). The band's core market increasingly became the United States and following their Grammy for *Babylon the Bandit*, Steel Pulse performed at President

Bill Clinton's 1993 inauguration party. By this time, Steel Pulse had already moved to America, with only two remaining members from their original Handsworth line-up.

This chapter has shown how the African 'tradition' functioned as a source for identity amongst a young black generation in Britain. Feelings of anger, disillusionment and a desire for a new, positive definition of 'black' were clearly widespread in 1980s Handsworth. It was the concept of Africa that helped a young black generation come to terms with these feelings. Of all the acts that have been discussed, it is perhaps Steel Pulse and *Handsworth Revolution* that best encapsulate this process. 'As soon as you leave school', David Hinds reflected in the late 1970s, 'you find that all the things you were promised – a job, a future and so on – it's all different. When you realise that, all you've got to turn to is your own culture and yourself. There's nowhere else to look' (cited in Plummer 1978: 48). As reggae fanatics such as Brian Bennett or Amlak Tafari made clear, Steel Pulse were popular in Handsworth not only because of the quality of their music, but also, through their focus on Rastafarianism, because they emphasised an African identity that was specifically for use in Handsworth, something made apparent by the front cover of *Handsworth Revolution*. There was, as another youth put it in the mid-1980s, a desire to 'rebel' because parents 'never told us about the racism' (Sealy, Trinity Arts Oral History Project 1984). The turn to Africa evolved out of this situation. As one person put it, Africa was 'something unique to us West Indian kids'; it provided 'something to hang on to' (Cameron, personal interview 2006).

The turn to Africa in Handsworth did not mean Africa in any literal sense. Whereas Benjamin Zephaniah and Steel Pulse were content to 'return' to Africa metaphorically, Jungleman attempted to physically migrate there. For Ras Tread, Jungleman was 'not just a dream of going to Africa and waiting for something mysterious to take us away. We felt we had realistic dreams' (Tread, personal interview 2009). With the arguments over cars the dream had, for Ras Tread, 'crashed'.

It is important to recognise that for many Rastafarians such as Tread, the 'return' to Africa was both realistic and the ultimate objective. However as this chapter has attempted to show, whilst the African tradition may have been 'invented', this did not stop it from having important effects in Handsworth. As Stuart Hall argued:

> [T]he point was not that some people, a few, could only live with themselves and discover their identities by literally going back to Africa – though some did, not often with great success – but that . . . people re-engaged with an experience which enabled them to find a language in which they could re-tell and appropriate their own histories.
>
> *(Hall 1995: 13)*

The 1970s and 1980s was the moment in which the search for that 'kind of ground for our identities', that 'something stabilised', was found by younger generations in the shape of Africa, and for the majority, this was for use not in Africa but in Handsworth. As Steel Pulse simply put it, this was a 'Handsworth revolution'.

Oral histories consulted

Existing collections:
Trinity Arts Oral History Project, Trinity Arts Centre, Small Heath, 1984. Shared with the author by John Dalton, former employee of Trinity Arts Centre.

Conducted by the author:
Brian Bennett, 22 May 2009
Mykal Brown, 22 February 2010
Eric Cameron, 28 September 2006
Basil Gabbidon, 15 July 2009
Jacko Melody, 9 June 2011
Amlak Tafari, 12 June 2009
Ras Tread, 12 June 2009
Benjamin Zephaniah, 20 May 2009

Notes

1   For a history of the 'community arts' movement in an area of London, see Wetherall (2013).
2   In 2003, the issue of police brutality became even more personal for Zephaniah when his cousin, Michael Powell, died whilst in police custody at Thornhill Road police station, Handsworth.
3   Tafari would eventually fulfil a lifelong ambition of playing with Steel Pulse, and is currently a touring member of the band.
4   These flyers were obtained by the author from John Dalton, former director of Trinity Arts Centre in Small Heath, Birmingham.
5   For a dramatisation of sound system culture in 1980s Britain, see *Babylon* (1981), a film set in Brixton and directed by the Italian Franco Rosso.
6   The albums were *Tribute to the Martyrs* (Mango Records: 1979), *Caught You* (Mango Records: 1980) and *True Democracy* (Elektra: 1982).

References

Bishton, D. and Reardon, J. (1984) *Home Front*, London: Jonathan Cape.
Bob Marley and the Wailers (1973) *Catch A Fire*, Island Records.
—— (1977) *Exodus*, Island Records.
Brah, A. (1996) *Cartographies of Diaspora: Contesting Identities*, London: Routledge.
Brouwer, A. (2002) 'The Basil Gabbidon Story', Online. Available at http://andybrouwer. co.uk/basil.html (accessed 27 September 2013).
Campbell, H. (1980) 'Rastafari: Culture of resistance', *Race and Class*, 22 (1): 1–22.
Gilroy, P. (1981) 'You can't fool the youths . . . race and class formation in the 1980s', *Race and Class*, 23: 207–22.
—— (1987) *There Ain't No Black in the Union Jack*, London: Unwin Hyman.
Hall, S. (1995) 'Negotiating Caribbean identities', *New Left Review*, 209: 3–14.
Harris, R. and White, S. (eds) (1999) *Changing Britannia: Life Experience with Britain*, London: New Beacon Books.
Hebdige, D. (1974) *Reggae, Rastas and Rudies: Style and the Subversion of Form*, Birmingham: University of Birmingham; Centre for Contemporary Cultural Studies.
—— (1979) *Subculture: The Meaning of Style*, London/New York: Methuen.

—— (1987) *Cut 'n' Mix: Culture, Identity and Caribbean Music*, London: Routledge.

Henriques, J.F. (2003) 'Sonic Dominance and the Reggae Sound System Session', in M. Bull and L. Back (eds) *The Auditory Culture Reader*, Oxford: Berg, 451–80.

Henry, W. (2006) *What the Deejay Said: A Critique from the Street!* London: Nu-Beyond.

Henzell, P. (dir.) (1972) *The Harder They Come*. Film.

Hiro, D. (1991) *Black British, White British: A History of Race Relations in Britain*, London: Paladin.

Hobsbawm, E. (1983) 'Inventing Traditions', in E. Hobsbawm and T. Ranger (eds) *The Invention of Tradition*, Cambridge: Cambridge University Press.

May, C. (1978) 'Rocking against racism', *Black Music*, February. Online. Available at http:// andybrouwer.co.uk/art0278.html (accessed 27 September 2013).

Plummer, J. (1978) *Movement of Jah People: The Growth of the Rastafarians*, Handsworth: Press Gang.

Rosso, F. (dir.) (1981) *Babylon*. Film.

Silverton, P. (1978) 'No Jah-bubble in-a Birmingham', *Sounds*, 22 April. Online. Available at http://andybrouwer.co.uk/art0478b.html (accessed 27 September 2013).

Steel Pulse (1978) *Handsworth Revolution*, Island Records.

—— (1979) *A Tribute to the Martyrs*, Mango Records.

—— (1980) *Caught You*, Mango Records.

—— (1982) *True Democracy*, Elektra.

—— (1986) *Babylon the Bandit*, Mango Records.

Velk, R. (2010) *Handsworth Evolution*, Birmingham Music Heritage radio documentary. Available from http://radiotogo.blogspot.com/2010/10/handsworth-evolution-documentary.html (accessed 1 October 2013).

Wetherall, S. (2013) 'Present at their own unmaking: Community arts and the white working class in Tower Hamlets', conference paper given at the *New Times Revisited* conference, University of Birmingham, 28–9 June.

Wood, A. (2008) '"A Design for Social Living": Sound System Culture from JA to UK', in P. Macpherson, C. Murray, G. Spark and K. Corstorphine (eds) *Sub/Versions: Cultural Status, Genre and Critique*, Newcastle: Cambridge Scholars Publishing.

Zephaniah, B. (1982) *Rasta*, Upright. LP.

—— (1985) *The Dread Affair*, London: Arena Books.

PLATE 1 *The Temptation of Christ on the Mountain*, Duccio di Buoninsegna (*c*.1255–*c*.1319). Reproduced with kind permission of the Frick Collection

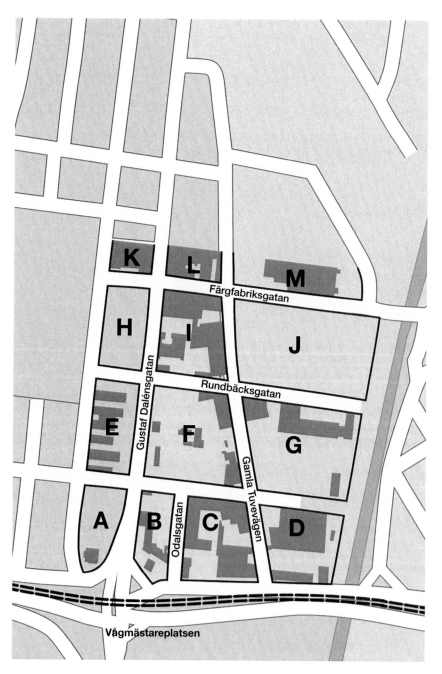

PLATE 2 Map of the Gustaf Dahlén area, 2001

BUSINESSES AND ASSOCIATIONS LOCATED IN THE NOW REDEVELOPED AREA, 2001

A

1. Kebab shop *

B

2. Butcher shop/grocery shop/gift shop **
3. Travel agency ****
4. Corrosion protection shop *
5. Petrol station *

C

6. Tyre shop ***
7. Construction company *****
8. Roofing company *
9. Balkan association *
10. Turkish association and mosque ***
11. Motorcycle shop ****
12. Café *
13. Garage ***
14. Christian second-hand shop *
15. Furniture shop *
16. Moving company *
17. Car junkyard ****

D

18. Appliances store ***
19. Auto company *
20. Clothing shop *
21. Paint store ****
22. Paint store ****
23. Clothing shop *****
24. Garden furniture shop *

E

25. Garage ****
26. Garage *
27. Petrol station *

F

28. Trailer rental company ****
29. Car wash *
30. Sex shop ***
31. Indian spice and grocery shop *
32. Grocery import & export company *
33. Garage *
34. Turkish Islamic funeral fund *
35. Residence *
36. Somali association and mosque *
37. Turkish association *
38. Bosnian association *
39. Café *
40. Auto company ***
41. Auto company *

G

42. Swedish Rescue Services Agency depot *
43. Alarm system company *
44. Turkish association and mosque ***

H

–

I

45. Second-hand furniture shop *
46. Christian second-hand shop ***
47. Art studio and storage *****
48. Second-hand furniture shop ***
49. Second-hand furniture shop *
50. Grocery shop ***
51. Second-hand furniture shop ***
52. Glaziers ****

J

–

BUSINESSES AND ASSOCIATIONS LOCATED JUST NORTH OF THE NOW REDEVELOPED AREA, 2001

K

53. Paint store
54. Chinese restaurant
55. Manicure studio
56. Occupational health centre

L

57. Motorcycle club
58. Novelty shop + bus travel agency
59. Finnish association
60. Indian restaurant
61. Restaurant
62. Gambian association and mosque
63. Second-hand furniture shop

M

64. Electronics shop
65. Furniture shop
66. Sweet shop
67. Furniture accessories shop
68. Electronics shop

---

*　　　　Closed or no information
**　　　Still in the area after redevelopment
***　　Moved to nearby area, soon up for redevelopment
****　Moved further out on Hisingen
*****Moved to other part of Gothenburg

1　Based on the 2001 real-estate survey *Östra Kvillebäcken: Fastighetsinventering* (*Stadsbyggnads-kontoret – Distrikt Norr*). This has been complemented with information from a 2012 survey (conducted as part of our research project) of where these businesses and organizations are located today.

PLATE 3　Key for map of the Gustaf Dahlén area

PLATE 4 Residents watch a street demonstration against demolition from the sidewalk across the entrance of Las Gladiolas. Photo by Melissa Fernández Arrigoitia

PLATE 5 Children play in the common courtyard of Las Gladiolas. Photo by Melissa Fernández Arrigoitia

PLATE 6   Panopticon–like view of the courtyard from a Tower B stairwell opening. Photo by Melissa Fernández Arrigoitia

PLATE 7   Poster for the 61st anniversary celebrations for the CUPA in 2010. The central image is an aerial view of the CUPA in 1949. Photo by Adam Kaasa

PLATE 8 Detail of the north-east block and stairwell of the CUPA. Visible are the exterior corridors every three floors and the landscaped gardens in full bloom. Photo by Adam Kaasa

PLATE 9 Sign for the Multilava, the laundrette on the site of the CUPA still in operation. Photo by Adam Kaasa

6

AMBIVALENT AFFECT/EMOTION

Conflicted discourses of multicultural belonging[1]

Anamik Saha and Sophie Watson

> I think that's another thing that is going downhill there's so much building going on, all the life and soul has gone out of it, all the traditional stuff.
>
> *(Waheed, 33)*

> I think it's gone downhill. It's just got a bit dirtier and then people who have moved into the area they're different . . . there's no sense of pride any more, though there was when I moved here all those years ago.
>
> *(Sharmila, 35)*

Where emotions have emerged in discussions of race/ethnicity, multiculturalism and the city they invariably tend to be of a particular hue – negative in the form of an exploration of racism (Back and Nayak 1999; Dwyer and Bressey 2008). There has been a particular focus on attachments to and detachments from place, on the part of migrants, and on the emotional responses of 'indigenous' communities or residents to the 'strangers' in their midst. But very little research has considered the reaction of migrants to other migrants – even those belonging to the same ethnic group. How to interpret and explain those difficult and troubling moments of daily feeling that migrants sometimes express towards what they themselves see as the less palatable residues of contemporary multiculture? What power relations do these negative emotional responses of migrant groups to the material practices of other (or indeed, the same) migrant groups reflect, reinforce or undermine?

The quotes that open this piece were taken from interviews with a sample of 30-something British South Asians, living in the London Borough of Redbridge, a suburb located on the boundary of east London and Essex, that consists of a very large Asian community (Redbridge is the fourth most diverse local authority in England and Wales).[2] The sample formed part of a larger research project that examined the sense of attachment to place expressed by three generations of the South Asian communities in Redbridge. While the older and younger generation were very clear in the attachment they feel towards the area where they live (see Watson and Saha 2012), the group of 30-somethings were almost universal in their dislike of the area, and more specifically what they perceived as a decline in the physical look of Redbridge, which was seen as going 'downhill'. What was striking was how they attributed this decline to the particular material practices of the expanding Asian community, which had almost doubled in size within the previous ten years.[3] The aim of this chapter is to explore the nature of this emotional response, and to consider what it reveals about the state of contemporary multiculture.

In research on the multicultural city, with the growing influence of psychoanalytic geography and the cultural turn more generally, there has been an extensive body of work mapping emotions in different contexts from anger to joy, anxiety to happiness and fear (Bannister and Fyfe 2001) to desire. These are often explored through notions of attachments or lack of attachments. One lens for understanding the complexities inherent here are the different ways in which global and local processes intersect to produce for many migrants an attachment to both places of origin and arrival at one and the same time, made possible by the increasing speed and ease of communication across space. These transnational lives and identifications with two places and peoples can produce emotional complexities that are difficult to maintain, as many researchers have shown (Glick-Schiller 2011). Other research has explored the myriad ways in which migrants attach themselves to their new surroundings. Svasek (2010), for example, has investigated the ways in which migrant organisations and institutions frame migrant experiences and increase the experience of belonging, while Burrell (2008) points to the importance of objects brought from home to create a sense of belonging. As the introduction to a special issue of the *Journal of Ethnic and Migration Studies* on emotions and human mobility emphasises (Svasek 2010: 877), personal attachments to people and places are multiple and changing and the type and strength of emotional connectivity of migrants to place at one time clearly depends on a plethora of factors. The responses of the people in place, what Hage (2000) refers to as the 'white nation' in the Australian context, to new migrants are also unstable and changing, ranging from fear, resentment (Watson and Wells 2005) and expressed hostility or racism to acceptance, joy or public tolerance albeit from a position of power (Hage 2000). In her study of belonging in a multicultural suburb in Sydney, Wise (2005) suggests the notion of 'hopeful intercultural encounters' as a way of reflecting on the social possibilities of new forms of integration of diverse cultures, notwithstanding the negative reactions she found amongst the local elderly population to the incoming Chinese who they saw as culturally different and disruptive of their sense of community and place.

This very brief excursion into the literature on migrants' sense of belonging and attachment to place can only scratch the surface of a now growing literature exploring the complex emotions in play in a world of increasing mobility of populations across space which has changed the face of cities across the world, such that the diversity and heterogeneity of urban populations is now the norm. That said, writing on emotions in geography and in relation to migrant populations more specifically has focused on some emotions more than others, and on some practices, institutions and spaces more than others.

Our argument here is that the emotion of ambivalence from migrants towards the practices of other migrants within their community has been little explored. We see three reasons for this. The first reason, we suggest, lies in the research process itself. Where researchers are of a different ethnicity to the subjects of their research, the expression of negative or ambivalent emotions to 'kindred others' (not necessarily those of a similar ethnicity but subject nevertheless to racist discourses) would be seen as disloyal and even wrong. Arguably these emotions emerged in our interviews because one of us shared ethnicity (as well as 'regional' identity) with the respondents. Second, practices of attachment, with some exceptions have tended to look more at cultural practices rather than at material practices. Material practices of attachment have been considered most frequently in relation to religion, in particular, the buildings and sites, such as mosques and temples, which have provoked resistance and contestation from local populations (Dodsworth et al. 2013). Material practices in domestic and private spaces have received less attention. Third, the sites of multicultural diversity, where questions of emotion and affect have been explored, have tended to be the more visible and central parts of cities, particular the inner city areas of London, New York and other global cities. Less attention has been paid to the quiet everyday suburbs which have only recently been recognised for the radical shift in populations that have taken place, as white residents have moved further out, leaving the traditional white suburbs to a diversity of migrant households, both first and second generation (Wise and Veluyatham 2009; Butler and Hamnett 2010).

This chapter thus aims to address these lacunae by looking at the ambivalences, often unspoken, expressed by the children of South Asian migrants (i.e. second generation) in Redbridge, towards the material practices of people in their own community in the domestic landscape that they inhabit. Such a move brings with it its own ambivalence for the authors in different ways. For Saha this involves revealing tensions within his own community (that is, the British Asian community in Redbridge where he too grew up) that may have only been revealed in the research because of his presence as a researcher. For Watson, there is the discomfort of speaking about 'other communities' in what could be conceived in negative terms. Certainly it was felt that belonging to the same community and growing up in the same area immediately created a rapport between the respondents and Saha (who conducted this particular set of interviews). That is not to say that the responses they gave were more 'truthful', but it certainly appeared to give respondents freedom, or *confidence* to express ideas about racial and ethnic difference in a way that might have been different if the interviewer was, for instance, white. That said, the research was conducted with due process and regard to ethical procedures, and represents an intervention which hopefully destabilises normative assumptions and paradigms concerning emotions in a world of mobility and change.

The research project

The aim of this research was to explore the ways in which three generations of Asian communities (60+, 30–40 year olds and 16–18 year olds) express belonging and attachment to the London suburbs where they live. This chapter focuses on the accounts of the older second generation: a group of 30-something British-born South Asians who grew up in the London Borough of Redbridge, from the 1980s onwards. Redbridge was selected as it has a large South Asian community and is illustrative of what has been described as the *ethnicisation* of British suburbs (Huq 2008; Nayak 2010; Butler and Hamnett 2011). Whether real or imagined, the suburbs have long been considered homogeneous, white, middle-class enclaves, representing social success and aspiration, and on the reverse side, banality and boredom (Silverstone 1997). Yet this image of a monocultural, cultureless desert is finding itself increasingly at odds with the growing diversity of suburban spaces. Six of the ten boroughs with the highest proportion of non-white residents nationally are located in outer London – an issue virtually overlooked in the London Councils' report on suburbs (Local Futures 2007). According to the 2011 census, as stated, Redbridge was rated the fourth most ethnically diverse local authority in the country, with a higher number of people stating their ethnic group as black and minority ethnic (about 60 per cent) than the average for London, and 34.5 per cent of people stating their ethnic group as white British, compared to 45 per cent for London and 83.35 per cent for England and Wales. In numerical terms, of the total Redbridge population of 278,970, 96,253 were white English, 116,503 were Asian or Asian British, and 24,845 identified as black or black British.[4]

For this part of the project we conducted ten in-depth interviews with a mix of Asian ethnicities (including Gujaratis, Bengalis and Pakistanis) and religions (including Christian, Hindu, Muslim and Sikh). While we aimed to reflect the diversity of British Asian communities, we were acutely aware of the dangers of using the term 'British Asian', and reifying the very ethnic and racial categories which we in fact seek to trouble and problematise (Alexander 2006; Nayak 2006). Alexander points out that while this is an inevitable risk, it is not an easy one to resolve, and is indeed the paradox of researching racialised communities in the first place. For the purposes of this study, we want to stress that we use the term 'Asian'[5] for pragmatic reasons alone – and in a strictly anti-essentialist sense, to describe a diverse and constantly evolving set of overlapping communities, but nonetheless defined by the shared experience of racism and (post) colonial histories.

We anchor the analysis that follows with an interview with Jean,[6] a worker at the Redbridge Museum, located in Ilford, the borough's administrative centre and its main shopping destination. We visited Redbridge Museum to get a sense of the official narratives of local (and national) heritage in Redbridge. At the time of our fieldwork the museum was showing an exhibition entitled 'Pieces of Ilford' described as 'a (very brief) journey through the history of Ilford'. The main portion of the exhibition consisted of displays based around Ilford residents from history, both famous and not-so-famous. This included Sylvia Pankhurst, the famed suffragette, who moved to Redbridge after the First World War, Mary Davis, a worker at Ilford Ltd, the photographic equipment company based in Redbridge from 1879 to 1976, and Tahera Khan, a Pakistani woman born in Zimbabwe, who moved to Ilford in the 1980s after getting married. The glass display based on Mrs Khan's life was centred on her wedding, containing the dress she wore, the wedding album, a box of henna, and a globe symbolising her journey across three continents. Jean was working on the main information desk when we visited the museum, and an informal chat turned quickly into a very interesting interview (with her permission the interview was recorded), and provided a useful introduction into the experience of living in Redbridge and feelings of attachment and belonging.

Jean was a 51-year-old black woman of Caribbean descent who had lived in Redbridge all her life. And from her accounts it was clear that she had a very strong attachment to the area. When we asked her about the way in which Ilford had changed she talked about it predominantly in terms of the increasing multicultural make-up of the area.

Interviewer:	What have been the key things that have changed in Ilford in the 50 years you have lived here?
Jean:	The different uses [of buildings] for example, churches. We obviously had Church of England, Anglican, Roman Catholic. Now we're seeing mosques and Sikh temples – things like that. Types of foods that were available . . . As a child if my mum wanted to cook something traditional she would have to travel quite a distance to purchase those things. Now you can go to Tescos, Sainsbury's, Waitrose, things like that. The music we listen to . . . you have greater access to the different styles, you see the different fusions in terms of music. The types of clothing that we wear . . . If I saw someone walking down the high street down my road in African dress or in a sari when I was five years old I would have just stood there and stared. Now I just go round the corner to Ilford Lane and the shops reflect the culture and the types of foods relating to those particular communities. Languages that we hear . . . as a child, English, cockney. In the 70s we had the east African Asians coming over and I remember quite distinctly my class teacher saying *oh, I'm leaving Shabina with you because you're the same.* In what ways? She's Ugandan Asian, we don't speak the same language we don't eat the same food, our cultures are so different but it's the mere fact that we are two people of colour. The street that I grew up . . . there were maybe half a dozen black families from different Caribbean islands . . . now there are probably three or four of those families still around. The neighbours are no longer English and German, they are Pakistani and Chinese, and over the road we have a lady from Saudi Arabia . . .

In this whirlwind tour of Ilford life Jean describes the shift from a predominantly white area (with accompanying racism, such as the way Jean and Shabina were partnered at school on account of both being non-white) to one that is increasingly diverse. There are references to changing demographics, but also to popular culture, as well as the visual markers of contemporary multiculture (clothes, food, places of worship, etc.). But as the interview developed what became apparent in Jean's story was a slight lament for the way things used to be. In particular Jean described a deterioration in the physical environment, and a concurrent decline in community relations.

Interviewer: How has the look of your street changed?

Jean: Right, well we no longer have those pretty front gardens with rose bushes, the shrub in the middle. All of those front gardens tend to be paved over and we have three or four cars.

Interviewer: Why is that? When did it start happening?

Jean: Probably the 80s and 90s . . . people wanted to be mobile. They got relatively good jobs and one way of showing their upward mobility would be the display of their wealth on the front driveway.

Interviewer: What other markers of change have you seen in every day spaces that people use?

Jean: In terms of the way streets look . . . I know from the types of railings that are put up outside the house to enclose their living space, the type of family who would live there. There are a lot of houses with porches that are additions to the general fabric of the house, and in that space, before you enter the house, you have all the shoes piled up outside. Sometimes people would buy houses next door to each other, and enclose the two properties in those black railings with the gold tips.

Interviewer: What kind of families are we talking about?

Jean: Mostly Asian. And sometimes they are very friendly, other times they . . . they'll speak to you on the path, but once they are in within the confines of their gated community there's not much interaction.

We could not help but notice a slight discomfort or embarrassment when Jean was pressed to admit that the 'type of family' to which she was referring is 'mostly Asian'. But for Jean the incoming Asian communities had changed the look of the area, with the removal of front gardens for off-street parking, porches for family members and visitors to remove their shoes before entering the house, and the erection of 'black railings with gold tips', which, it was implicitly suggested, comes across as slightly vulgar or ostentatious. In this comment, the visual markers – porches, driveways and gold-tipped railings – connote cultural difference (and in particular the association of Asians with big families, and status symbols), underpinned by discourses of class and respectability. It was particularly revealing when Jean referred to how these Asian families effectively live in 'gated communities'. These are not gated communities in the strictest sense, but Jean is referring here to the perceived inwardness of Asian communities, who might say hello on the path but that is the extent of any interaction.

Jean's last quote echoes the findings of Butler and Hamnett's (2010: 87) study of east London and its outer boroughs where they found that white residents in Redbridge complained about the negative impact of the extensions and conversions that Asian families tended to build onto their homes. But what was interesting to us, and the reason we open with this narrative, was how Jean's account was almost exactly replicated in our interviews with second-generation 30+ Asians. Compared to the members of the older generation and school pupils that we interviewed who described a clear attachment to the area where they live (see Watson and Saha 2012), the group of ten older second-generation British Asians in our study expressed feelings of ambivalence about Redbridge. The group of respondents found it noticeably more difficult to describe their favourite places in Redbridge, and was more likely to highlight the banality and blandness of the area. Except for the leafy environ of Wanstead, with its cafes, boutiques and gastro pubs, which was often mentioned as the most pleasant part of Redbridge (all the respondents were university educated, and nearly all of them professional, perhaps explaining their affinity for this more middle-class area), the respondents were quick to express their dislike of Redbridge – the lack of things to do and places to go, but in particular the increasing physical decline of the area. But while this would suggest little emotional attachment to the area, we argue their narratives and the feelings that are expressed are revealing in a different way.

Like Jean, the respondents lamented the way that Redbridge was physically changing. Perhaps because of a shared ethnic and racial background with one of us also, the respondents felt no misgivings about explaining what they also perceived as a deterioration in the visual look of Redbridge explicitly in terms of the increasing numbers of Asians in the area:

> One of the things I am quite conscious of and feel quite strongly about is the character being ripped out of the area. Not that there was a lot of character in the first place but it was a typical 1930s suburb. You could tell in the way that it was built. And it used to be part of an orchard hence why we had so many trees. But unfortunately I am seeing less of these trees because [Asian] people are moving in, buying houses and knocking down these trees and building houses in their backyard or building extensions. Before it was a really green area but I think it's been taken away.
>
> *(Sharmila, 35)*

In terms of housing people have more cars, three, four cars stuffed in their driveways! People get rid of their front gardens, and I know that's across the board and not necessarily to do with ethnicity, but you tend to find that Asians as they become more successful, it means more cars, bigger houses, let's add every single conversion, extension possible on the house. They just don't [have] you know, the typical English country feel which a lot of the houses here have, like the Woods Estate [an area in Clayhall, a particularly leafy and desirable part of Redbridge]. It's not gone totally downhill but I've seen our road change quite a lot and you know that the houses that are left behind – in terms of [those that keep] the original features – are owned by the locals, the English, who have been here a long time, have a bit more regard for this stuff.

(Naila, 35)

In the first quote Sharmila expresses her feeling that the supposedly Asian tendency towards building extensions onto their houses has little regard for the aesthetics of the area. In the second quote Naila attempts to explain why Asians carry out this practice (though she wants to stress that it is not unique to Asians) – bigger families, concern with status and signifiers of upward mobility. There is additionally a reference to how older white residents have a greater respect for Redbridge's heritage. Indeed, it is interesting to note in both quotes the reference to the decline in greenery. Another respondent develops this further:

There are so many main roads around here . . . we're next to the M11, the A406. We definitely need that green. So it's a shame that so many trees have been cut down. Do you remember those cherry blossom trees? It's a shame that's gone. It would look nicer, more healthy, more attractive.

(Reshmin, 36)

Reshmin is describing the implication of Redbridge as the main thoroughfare connecting London and Essex. But what is of interest in all these quotes is the underlying nostalgia for Redbridge's past. In the description of the destruction of trees and front gardens there is a lament for Redbridge's fading heritage as a former orchard and as a quintessential 1930s London suburb. It may appear surprising for children of immigrants to be so sentimental for a very particular English past, but nonetheless nostalgia was the key theme that came out the most in our interviews with this group (see also Watson and Wells 2005 for a similar nostalgia expressed by the old established white residents in an inner London borough).

During the time these respondents were attending school in the 1980s and 1990s, Redbridge felt more mixed. In addition to the majority white/Christian community, there was a significant Jewish community who, like the Asian communities, had left the east end of London, to settle in suburbs like Redbridge. Yet since the turn of the century, as more Asian people – particularly Pakistanis, Bangladeshis and South Indians – moved into Redbridge, the white and Jewish communities have moved further out to Essex. And what was evident in the respondents' complaints about the decline in the physical appearance of Redbridge was a sentimental longing for a time when the area was more ethnically diverse and multicultural:

> I like it when there's bit of a mix. When it goes to one ethnic minority, the character of places changes. And I'm into nostalgia and I quite like original buildings and I think you had more consistency in the facades of houses and stuff and now you have seen so much change and I don't think it's that great . . . people just putting up gates.
>
> *(Jas, 35)*

According to this respondent, as particular neighbourhoods become more monocultural, there is a loss in heritage (through the changing facades of houses), which in turn has a negative effect upon neighbourhoods and communal relations, where more inviting front gardens are replaced by inhospitable driveways and gates. Thus, emotional attachment to an area is expressed through a perception of how the physical area has changed, which in turn, expresses a certain ideal about multiculturalism and community.

Such a theme is exemplified in relation to the pedestrianisation around the Ilford Exchange – Redbridge's main shopping centre:

> I think the original Ilford had a lot of life and soul before it got pedestrianised. It had a good vibe to it. Because it was a lot more mixed, a lot more white folk, a lot of Asian folk; melting point-wise it was a lot better. But it all changed . . . there was a period when it was okay but then it got progressively worse, because the population increased with all the Asians and the white folk were pushed out to more leafy areas such as Chigwell. But even Chigwell is changing and becoming much more Asian.
>
> *(Waheed, 33)*

Again there is a lament for a time when Redbridge was more ethnically mixed. In the above quote the pedestrianisation is seen to be somehow symbolic of the negative effect of the movement of Asians into the area, as the paving over of Redbridge's old heritage (its high streets, and front gardens), driving the white residents further out to leafy areas more reminiscent of the old Redbridge. In fact this account from a British-born Pakistani man seems almost forgiving of the white flight, as though this was the natural, inevitable response to the influx of newly arrived Asians.

Gilroy's (2005) important concepts of postcolonial melancholia and conviviality in his account of Britain's uncomfortable relationship with contemporary multiculture have some purchase here. In our interviews with the oldest generation of respondents (Watson and Saha 2012) we found evidence that illustrates how 'racial differences appear ordinary and banal . . . (how) urban conviviality has taken hold' (Gilroy 2005: 438). But more troublingly we find that the younger generation appear to have internalised a particular bourgeois, nationalist view of the effects of multicultural diversity on their communities. The following quote for instance, would appear typical of a particular nationalist discourse on the negative impact of demographic change and the 'influx' of immigrants on community, particularly its depiction of a prior, almost quaint local neighbourhood:

> I think you can see it in terms of the main road Redbridge Lane East. When we first moved here, I remember there was a little bakery, a café, and I think you saw people out and about a lot more. I think there was more of a sense of community. You got the impression that people knew each other even from school. That people knew each other's parents. And now I don't think there is that sense of community.
>
> *(Joyti, 37)*

A similar narrative appears in the following quote:

> I think [Redbridge has] gone downhill. It's just got a bit dirtier and then people who have moved into the area, they're different . . . there's no sense of pride any more, though there was when I moved here all those years ago . . . I'm Asian myself, but it has become more predominantly Asian, and that's fine. But I just find that for some reason regardless of what their backgrounds are, some of these people who have moved in . . . people don't talk to each other, and when I'm walking down the street I do notice that I get a bit of agro from the local boys, and there's more joy riders and there's not much respect for the elders of the community.
>
> *(Sharmila, 35)*

Here, the references to cleanliness, anti-social behaviour, people who are 'different' (even though they share the same 'race' as the respondent) has a more explicit racialised discourse running through it. There is an underlying discourse of class too; as mentioned the respondents are aspiring middle class and many of the newer Asian communities to which they refer to are working class or at least do not share the same cultural capital. The nostalgia for the way things were (despite the fact that the respondents almost certainly experienced more racism in the 1980s than they do now), a time where according to Sharmila there was more 'pride', evokes emotionally the postcolonial melancholia Gilroy describes as a 'malaise', as 'anxieties about identity' which 'are an unwelcome product of the particular historical circumstances' which mobilise the 'contemporary fears that globalization has emptied England of its distinctiveness' (2005: 433–5).

The troubling aspect of this narrative, on the loss of pride, the loss of heritage and how this is a reflection of the failure of newer arrivals to Redbridge to integrate themselves properly into the community (whatever that community might be), is how it appears to dovetail with Prime Minister David Cameron's assertion of 'failure of multiculturalism'. But we argue that this describes in fact something much more *ambivalent*. Within these narratives there is a lament not just for the way things were but for a more convivial time when Redbridge was an evenly distributed multicultural community. This is captured in the following reminiscences:

> I have to say the thing about this area when I moved into it was that it was . . . Redbridge Junior School where I went to, at the time it was Jewish, black, Christian and Asian – it was really well mixed. We had a school play about Lord Nelson, and the girl who played the lead part – remember this was 1985 in a mixed school, mixed boys and girls – the person who got picked to play the part of Lord Nelson was an Asian girl. Which was really powerful for that time. Which just goes to show that we were brought up in a way where we never distinguished each other by our skin colour or religion.
>
> (Sharmila, 35)

There is certainly something very evocative about the image of a young Asian girl cast to play a central character in England's imperial past. Jean expressed a similar emotion when we asked her to reflect on the 'Pieces of Ilford' exhibition.

Interviewer: How do you relate to all this kind of history [pointing to the exhibit].

Jean: I love it. This is my history. Just sitting here, I have childhood friends reflected here. The story of Tahira Khan reminds me of my friend Shabina. The [display of the] teacher's story, reminds me of my Jewish teachers and classmates – we sort of fell into a clique because we were a little bit different.

Jean's fond memories of her friend Shabina – who her teacher partnered with her on account of them both being 'non-white' – and also the Jewish classmates with whom she bonded because they were all a 'little bit different', similarly reflect the ordinariness of schoolyard relationships and the 'urban conviviality' of which Gilroy speaks. Les Back's (1996) valuable concept of 'cultural intermezzo' too has some resonance here. Similarly, the final note in Sharmila's quote, where she and her peers never distinguished each other by race or religion, illustrates a mundane multiculturalism, where, as Gilroy again puts it, racial differences appear ordinary and banal.

Conclusion

In conclusion, in what appears as a fairly conservative and troubling narrative on the influx of Asians into Redbridge and the perceived decline in the aesthetic beauty of the area that has resulted (and in turn, the negative impact this has on

a sense of community) there is a sadness expressed not for a (mythical) culturally stable yet homogeneous, post-war Britain, but for a relatively brief period
in Redbridge's past, spanning just two decades, when the borough felt more
racially and ethnically mixed and integrated. This, we suggest, demonstrates the
ambivalence of what Stuart Hall (1999) calls 'multicultural drift'. What could be
diagnosed as postcolonial melancholia regarding the decline of a London suburb
is actually a lament for a particularly convivial time in the borough's past. Even if
it was not experienced exactly in this way, this is how it is remembered and how
the moment has been idealised.

This excursion into the reflections of a particular generation of Asian residents
on the local aesthetics of domestic spaces and the streets of Redbridge has demonstrated a complexity of emotions/affect in relation to senses of attachment to place
which disturbs some of the more normative accounts of processes of belonging. As
Gilroy, Watson and Wells and others have found, nostalgia operates in complex
ways not just within the longer established white urban populations, but also within
more recent migrants' experiences, to produce complex accounts of attachment, or
lack of attachment, to place.

What was striking throughout all our interviews was how feelings of belonging to place, to nation, were expressed through nostalgia – and through *lament*.
Even in the more pointed responses given by interviewees, there was no expression of anger, fear or disgust. The more sorrowful tone that characterised the
responses of this group of second-generation Asians is precisely what demonstrates the ambivalence of multicultural drift. It certainly can be read as a form of
melancholia, but the almost humdrum emotional tone of the narratives also jars
against what various political leaders proclaim as the failure of multiculturalism.
As we have suggested, it is difficult to explore these emotions, given their potentially damaging effects, but this research nevertheless has pointed to the importance of exploring the ambivalent emotions that many urban dwellers express,
whatever their ethnicity, in order to make sense of the complexity of experience
in the multicultural city.

Notes

1   The interviews in this chapter took place in Redbridge between June and August 2010.
2   http://data.london.gov.uk/datastorefiles/documents/2011-census-snapshot-ethnic-
    diversity-indices.pdf
3   www2.redbridge.gov.uk/cms/the_council/about_the_council/about_redbridge/
    2011_census/diversity.aspx
4   www2.redbridge.gov.uk/cms/the_council/about_the_council/about_redbridge/
    2011_census/diversity.aspx
5   We also use 'Asian' in the British English sense, referring to those originating from
    the Indian sub-continent, including India, Pakistan, Bangladesh, Sri Lanka, sometimes
    via particular postcolonial routes (e.g. Kenya and Uganda). It should be noted as well
    that the use of 'Asian' in British English excludes East or South East Asians (who are
    defined by their country of origin or, more problematically, as 'Oriental') and central
    Asians.
6   For the purposes of confidentiality we have changed the names of all respondents.

References

Alexander, C. (2006) 'Introduction: Mapping the issues', *Ethnic and Racial Studies*, 29(3): 397–410.

Back, L. (1996) *New Ethnicities and Urban Cultures: Racisms and Multiculture in Young Lives*, London: UCL Press.

Back, L. and Nayak, A. (1999) 'Signs of the Times? Violence, Graffiti and Racism in the English Suburbs' in T. Allen and J. Eade (eds) *Divided Europeans: Understanding Ethnicity and Conflict*, The Hague: Kluwer Law International.

Bannister, J. and Fyfe, N. (2001) 'Introduction: Fear and the city', *Urban Studies*, 38(5–6): 807–13.

Burrell, K. (2008) 'Materialising the border: Spaces of mobility and material culture in migration from post-socialist Poland', *Mobilities*, 3(3): 353–73.

Butler, T. and Hamnett, C. (2010) *Ethnicity, Class and Aspiration*, Bristol: Policy Press.

Dodsworth, F., Vacchelli, E. and Watson, S. (2013) 'Shifting religions and cultures in London's East End', *Material Religion*, 9(1): 86–112.

Dwyer, C. and Bressey, C. (eds) (2008) *New Geographies of Race and Racism*, Aldershot: Ashgate.

Gilroy, P. (2005) 'Multiculture, double consciousness and the "war on terror"', *Patterns of Prejudice*, 39(4): 431–43.

Glick-Schiller, N. (2011) 'Transnationality and the City' in G. Bridge and S. Watson (eds) *The New Blackwell Companion to the City*, Oxford: Wiley Blackwell, 179–92.

Hage, G. (2000) *White Nation: Fantasies of White Supremacy in Multicultural Society*, New York: Routledge.

Hall, S. (1999) 'From Scarman to Stephen Lawrence', *History Workshop Journal*, 48 (Autumn): 187–97.

Huq, R. (2008) 'The Sound of the Suburbs: The Shaping of Englishness and the Socio-Cultural Landscape after New Labour' in M. Perryman (ed.) *Imagined Nation: England after Britain*, London: Lawrence and Wishart.

Local Futures (2007) *State of the Suburbs Local Futures*, Leadership Centre for Local Government.

Svasek, M. (2010) 'On the move: Emotions and human mobility', *Journal of Ethnic and Migration Studies*, 36(6): 865–80.

Watson, S. and Wells, K. (2005) 'Spaces of nostalgia: The hollowing out of a London market', *Journal of Social and Cultural Geography*, 6(1): 17–30.

Watson, S. and Saha, A. (2012) 'Suburban drifts: Mundane multiculturalism in outer London', *Ethnic and Racial Studies*. Available at doi:10.1080/01419870.2012.678875.

Wise, A. (2005) 'Hope and belonging in a multicultural suburb', *Journal of Intercultural Studies*, 26(1–2): 171–86.

Wise, A. and Velayutham, S. (eds) (2009) *Everyday Multiculturalism*, Basingstoke: Palgrave.

PART III

Displacement, its aftermaths and futures

Tracing connection to, from and through Europe

7

POST-POLITICAL NARRATIVES AND EMOTIONS

Dealing with discursive displacement in everyday life

Helena Holgersson

In the years 2010–2011 the past and the future overlapped – physically and mentally – in the old run-down and reused industrial area behind the shopping centre Backaplan on Hisingen, close to the harbour in Gothenburg. With the closing down of the small factories here in the 1970s, garages, mosques, flea-markets, import grocery stores, motorcycle associations and sex shops had found affordable premises in the old buildings. But now the southern part of the area was about to be demolished and transformed into a modern residential area – *New Kvillebäcken*. During the walking interviews I conducted here in this early stage of the redevelopment process, employees from the construction companies pointed at imaginary buildings planned to be erected within a few years while local people pointed at already demolished buildings, as if they were still there.[1] At each of the four corners of the site, huge posters were put up on construction containers. They were directed away from the area, addressing people passing by, and their message was that *with a bit of imagination you could* '. . . smell the scent of fresh coffee coming from the kitchen in your new three-room flat', '. . . see people having a crayfish party on their balcony', '. . . hear children laughing in the shady inner yards between the houses' and '. . . watch the setting sun as it sinks behind the rooftops'.

New Kvillebäcken ends abruptly in front of the old buildings at the northern edge of Färgfabriksgatan [Paint Factory Street]. From the premises of a Finnish association on the second floor of one of them (which once housed a textile factory), Arto has a front-row seat to watch the redevelopment process. Even though he was not invited, from the window he watched the public ground-breaking ceremony at which the chair of the Municipal Board 'dug the first spadeful of dirt'. By this time, the old paint factory across the street had been demolished. In the decades prior to the redevelopment, the building had housed a couple of flea-markets and an art studio, but in the 1960s when Arto migrated to Sweden from Finland with his parents, it was where he found one of his first jobs, putting labels on paint tins.

The big poster outside talks of smelling future coffee, but in the rooms of their Finnish association, Arto and the other seniors have been making coffee almost every day for over 15 years.

The writing of history is not a neutral task (e.g. Nora 1989; Puwar 2011), and drawing on writings on post-politics (e.g. Swyngedouw et al. 2002; Mouffe 2005; Mukhtar-Landgren 2012) and gentrification (e.g. Clark 2005; Checker 2011; Bridge et al. 2012) I argue that there is a discursive side to displacement that needs to be addressed. Future visions of transformed urban areas are often constructed with the past – and hence the former inhabitants – as an antipole (cf. Wilson and Grammenos 2005). Moreover, I find that the emotional and embodied aspects of displacement have not received enough attention in gentrification research (cf. Kern 2012). Consequently, this chapter focuses on how five inhabitants – Arto from the Finnish association, Lamin from the Gambian mosque, car mechanics Roland and Tore, and butcher-shop owner Tahere[2] – have dealt with the rapid territorial stigmatisation of the old run-down industrial area and their exclusion from the future vision of the new up-scale residential area.[3]

A story of industrialisation, immigration and redevelopment

In this chapter I analyse the construction of New Kvillebäcken against the backdrop of the industrial and immigration history of Gothenburg. The area is located in close proximity to the now closed-down shipyards on Hisingen, the big island north of the Göta Älv River that runs through Gothenburg. The buildings were constructed in the 1930s and 1940s for small-scale industry, but since the 1950s these companies were replaced – first by service and retail businesses and then also by migrant associations (Birgersson and Wrigglesworth 1984: 20ff; Olshammar 2002; Forsemalm 2007). For decades no political agreement was reached regarding the future of the area, and when architectural researcher Gabriella Olshammar (2002) studied it in the 1990s she characterised it as caught in a state of *permanent provisionality*; in the wait for an official plan the buildings were let out in their existing condition, often with short-term leases. The list of activities in the Gustaf Dalén area (see Plates 2 and 3) shows 52 small businesses and associations located in the southern part that is now being redeveloped, as well as a number of activities just north of the street Färgfabriksgatan. Together with the map, the list provides an image of the area's physical and social character ten years ago. It also includes information about where in Gothenburg the displaced activities are found today.

Kvillebäcken is a larger administrative area of Hisingen, of which New Kvillebäcken will make up only about one-fifth. The old industrial area did not have any commonly accepted name prior to the redevelopment, but in everyday language it seems to have been called things like 'behind Backaplan'. In my analysis I have to call it something and following Olshammar I have decided to use the term 'the Gustaf Dalén area', referring to Gustaf Dalénsgatan, the street that runs through it.

As a port city, Gothenburg has always been a multicultural node (Peterson 2010). However, the popular national and local narrative of immigration does not begin until after the Second World War (Schierup et al. 2006). This was when transnational industries such as Volvo invited workers from Finland and southern European countries such as Italy, Greece, Turkey and Yugoslavia (Dahlström 2004). If the canals in the original inner city tell the story of Dutch city planners, Hisingen is in large part a product of the post-war industrial expansion. In Kvillebäcken 40 per cent of the residents have 'foreign background', defined as people born outside Sweden or both of whose parents were born outside Sweden, compared to 31 per cent in Gothenburg as a whole (Gothenburg Municipal Government 2012: 6).

Up until the early 2000s, everyday life went on in the Gustaf Dalén area outside the media spotlight, but within a few years this completely changed. During 2003–2007 the media continuously reported on minor crimes such as assault, illegal gambling and drug dealing, but also a number of more serious violent crimes. In 2007 the situation escalated, with three brutal murders taking place there. Looking more closely at the reports you find that almost all the events were related to two illegal nightclubs in the area, one that was run by a member of the motorcycle club Hells Angels and attracted people from criminal circles, and one called the Balkan Club, most of whose members came from Kosovo. The three murders were all connected to the former, which was located north of the area now being redeveloped (e.g. Vikingsson 2007: 2). During this period the expression 'Gaza Strip' appeared in the press, and often was claimed to be what the area was called in popular speech (e.g. Micu 2006). This mostly seems to refer to the lawlessness and physical appearance of the area, but probably to some extent also to the multicultural character of the businesses and associations here; after having used the expression 'Gaza Strip', the free newspaper PunktSE received complaints from offended Palestinians (Fransson 2011).[4] Regardless of how the expression was interpreted, the image of the 'Gaza Strip' indisputably contributed to a rapid stigmatisation process.

In 2005, after decades of discussion, the municipal executive committee of Gothenburg decided to delegate the undertaking of a complete redevelopment of the Gustaf Dalén area to the municipal development company Riverbank Development [Älvstranden utveckling] (Adlers 2011).[5] Negotiations soon began with the many property owners, and six private construction companies were invited to join Riverbank Development and form the 'Kvillebäcken Consortium'. Later a public housing company also joined them. The project was officially opened in May 2010, and by 2018 2,000 flats will have been built in the area, 75 per cent being cooperative housing and 25 per cent rentals (Kvillebäcken Consortium 2013). As of this writing, in 2013, all but one of the activities listed on the map from 2001 have left the area.

Theoretical considerations

My research interest lies in how people, in their everyday lives, cope with what Loïc Wacquant (2008: 169) calls *territorial stigmatisation* in gentrification processes. This aspect of gentrification is often neglected in more abstract political–economy literature (Kern 2012). Physically speaking, the bodies of my interviewees were in the process of being removed from the Gustaf Dalén area, but there is also a *discursive* side to their displacement (cf. Wilson and Grammenos 2005). In the marketing of New Kvillebäcken, different bodies and social practices took over the area years before the last buildings were demolished. The main research question here is how people deal with being not just displaced, but also discredited and then excluded from the future vision of the city. I draw on Sara Ahmed's (2004: 28) writings on emotions coming from outside and moving inwards, connecting individuals and collectives, history and the present. She writes (39):

> How we feel about another – or a group of others – is not simply a matter of individual impressions, or impressions that are created anew in the present. Rather, feelings rehearse associations that are already in place, in the way in which they 'read' the proximity of others, at the same time as they establish the 'truth' of the reading.

Gentrification research has focused more on class than ethnicity, but I argue that one needs to look at how these two categories are intertwined, for instance by analysing the rhetoric of the developer and of both former and new residents.

When analysing ethnographic encounters arising from this transforming industrial area, I connect to theories of post-political urban planning from a growing literature on the neoliberalisation of local governance. Research shows that contemporary redevelopment projects are generally administrated in public–private partnerships – such as Kvillebäcken Consortium – which focus on technical solutions rather than political dilemmas (Swyngedouw et al. 2002). The aspect of this theoretical discussion that relates directly to the discursive side of displacement and emotions is how redevelopment projects are narrated within this logic. Policy has come to revolve around depoliticised concepts such as 'the good city' and 'social sustainability' (Bradley 2009; Tunström 2007; Mukhtar-Landgren 2012). And as Chantal Mouffe (2005) argues, such rhetoric undermines the possibility for people to politicise their exclusion. Critical gentrification research generally aims at challenging notions of win-win outcomes in urban planning (e.g. Slater 2006), but by focusing on how displaced people emotionally deal with being excluded from post-political future visions, I want to emphasise the need to further study what C. Wright Mills (2000 [1959]) famously described as the relation between public issues and private troubles.

Legitimising and marketing New Kvillebäcken

From criminality towards sustainability

'It felt like we had to communicate the journey from having hypodermic needles bobbing in the creek to being a modern, energy-efficient residential area', a woman from one of the construction companies in the Kvillebäcken Consortium told me. As David Wilson and Dennis Grammenos (2005: 295) argue, rhetoric is crucial to gentrification. Real-estate capital's greatest fear, they claim, is a situation where activists can depict a project as breaking up functioning neighbourhoods out of sheer greed. In their research on the redevelopment of Humboldt Park in Chicago, they point out how young minority bodies were used to create an image of a place and a community in irrevocable decay (ibid.: 305), and they suggest that 'confrontation and cleanup, rather than saving and salvaging, may be the new metaphors used to legitimate gentrification' (ibid.: 299). What I have come to consider the dominant, and typically post-political narrative of the redevelopment of the Gustaf Dalén area is the description of ten blocks that are beyond repair – in terms of both the physical structures and the social fabric – but will be transformed into a modern and sustainable residential area (see also Holgersson forthcoming).

Elements of the stigmatisation campaign appear in the marketing of New Kvillebäcken, in media reports, in political statements and in statements made during the walking interviews I conducted with employees of the Kvillebäcken Consortium. For instance, the marketing director of Riverbank Development told me that for a time there had been 'nearly a murder a week'. Interestingly enough, though, the decision to redevelop the area was made before the three murders occurred in 2007. My main example, however, of how the stigmatisation process is connected to the dominant narrative of the redevelopment is the speech that was given by the chair of the Municipal Board, Social Democrat Anneli Hulthén, at the public ground-breaking ceremony for New Kvillebäcken, on a cold morning in May 2010. Here she described how the chair of the Property Management Committee had locked the doors of their car when they drove through the industrial area six or seven years earlier. Afterwards they had concluded that: 'We can't let it remain this way!' Just before she entered the stage, a local singer-songwriter had sung a song about how the Danish army, referred to as the 'Danish pigs', had been chased off in the seventeenth century, and Hulthén stated that until recently 'other armies' had been found in the Gustaf Dalén area. She also mentioned that the area had been called the 'Gaza Strip' in popular speech. The formation of this part of the narrative can be described as a process whereby the signs 'Kvillebäcken', 'Gaza Strip' and 'criminality', as well as 'immigrants', I argue, came to 'stick together' – and to the former inhabitants (Ahmed 2004: 33; see also Hall's chapter in this volume).

A bright – and white – future

In a promotional film about New Kvillebäcken, produced by Riverbank Development as part of the marketing campaign, the speaker is a fictive future 'proud resident of Kvillebäcken'. After having described herself and her neighbours as 'pioneers', she talks about how the 'original spirit of old Kvillebäcken' will live on as a 'charming ingredient' in the future (Riverbank Development 2008). During my walk with two women working with the marketing blog, they each expressed a wish to refer to local history in their communications with potential buyers and tenants but, in an area that is in the process of being completely demolished, this is a delicate task. Stories of displacement were hardly considered likely to sell any flats. Nor, it appears, were the stories of the everyday multicultural life of the 1990s and early 2000s. As we stopped outside a building remaining from before, which at that time still housed a garage and a mosque, a man from a construction company told me that they might skip over the last 30 years in the marketing of New Kvillebäcken.

The promotional film is a clear case of what Sonia Lavadinho and Yves Winkin (2008) refer to as *enchantment engineering*, that is, how urban planners try to create not only a physical structure, but also a specific atmosphere. Throughout the film the fictive future resident refers to her neighbours as 'we', forming a warm community through shared social practices (Riverbank Development 2008, my italics):

> The park around *our* tranquil stream is marvellous and is full of life and activities all year round. *We* often jog along the bank down to the quays, and in spring, summer and autumn the park is *our* garden . . . Sometimes *we* order a food basket from one of the shops or local restaurants, filled with delicacies from every corner of the world, and then *we* have a picnic on the banks of the stream.

Multiculturalism is often described as a vision of the future, whether seen as desirable or otherwise, but in the narrative of this redevelopment project it appears to be a historical parenthesis. The people in the promotional film are white and appear to have been born in Sweden, or at least in northern Europe. A black marathon runner who passes by is one of the few exceptions. As gentrification researcher Mellissa Checker (2011: 216) notes, *greening* an area often also means *whitening* it (see also Bradley 2009).

Dealing with discursive displacement in everyday life

A Finnish association and a Gambian mosque

Moving on to how a group of former residents of the Gustaf Dalén area have dealt with the roles ascribed to them in the redevelopment narrative sketched out above, I will first return to Arto from the Finnish association, and then introduce Lamin from the Gambian mosque. As it turns out, these two associations had very similar reasons for renting in the Gustaf Dalén area – the need for large and affordable venues in a central location, close to public transport. They both had short-term leases, but since their block was located on the north side of the street Färgfabriks-gatan (block L) they have been able to renew their leases so far. Arto and Lamin tell the story of multicultural everyday life in the mental periphery of the city. Just north of the construction site the Finnish association continues to organise karaoke and tango nights, language classes, Zumba and senior lunches for its members. And right next door the Gambian mosque organises activities for young people, such as football and religious lectures. On Fridays people come here to pray, and on weekends for cultural parties. Lamin works as a prison officer and frequents the mosque. He ended up in Sweden after meeting his wife during a short holiday in Stockholm 20 years ago.

During our walk through the area Arto, slightly upset, stated: '[A]t least it's a vibrant neighbourhood, I'll tell you that! You find all sorts of things here', and then continued: 'And I don't think it's a major problem for the city either . . . the businesses and associations here.' I interpret these statements as responding to an accusation that has not been explicitly articulated and, most importantly, as examples of Arto's being aware of the dominant narrative of the redevelopment. Loïc Wacquant (2008: 238) describes territorial stigmatisation as the stigma Erving Goffman forgot. It is, Wacquant argues, something that people in deprived areas constantly have to deal with in their everyday lives (see also Fernández Arrigoitia's chapter in this volume). Arto and Lamin mostly appeared to contest the image of the area as run-down, outdated and criminal, and since their bodies were closely linked to the site, this was also a way for them to defend their own respectability. There had been a few incidents in the early 2000s, they admitted, but for most people in the Gustaf Dalén area, life had gone on as usual.

As Arto and I passed the block where the opening ceremony was held the year before, I asked how he felt about the speech by the chair of the Municipal Board in which she had referred to the industrial area as the 'Gaza Strip' and described it as dangerous. He told me that he had walked from Färgfabriksgatan to the tram stop at Vågmästareplatsen around midnight almost every Saturday for the last 12 years and never had any trouble. Lamin, for his part, liked Anneli Hulthén 'very much', and told me how the Gambian association had invited her to visit them before the last election. Showing me the rubbish-filled empty lot where she gave her speech he described how he found the uneasiness she felt driving through the area understandable. He was, however, a bit disappointed that she and others referred to the area as the 'Gaza Strip', and said: 'In Sweden we have this freedom of speech, and everyone is allowed to . . . say what they want. But you shouldn't . . . hurt other people . . . I don't think it's appropriate.' Taken together, their accounts illustrate how the stigmatising discourses that often appear as part of a gentrification process materialise and stick to certain bodies, and how the emotions that stem from this process – here for instance anger, worry, frustration and an ambition to resist – cannot be reduced to personal dispositions (cf. Ahmed 2004; Kern 2012).

Two displaced garages

To illustrate a very different strategy for dealing with territorial stigmatisation I will now turn to Tore and Roland, two Swedish-born automotive mechanics who had been in business in the Gustaf Dalén area since the 1960s and 1970s. At the time of my interview, they had already been forced to move their separate businesses, but before doing so they had each put up a fight, one against the municipality and the other against his landlord. Being displaced seems to have been a traumatic and quite unexpected experience for them. They were both over 60 years old, white, and most importantly here, seemingly accustomed to being treated as respectable citizens by public authorities. However, in the redevelopment process they had not been listened to. But a seemingly even more disturbing aspect of the process was how they had been bunched together with the rest of the inhabitants of the 'Gaza Strip', and thereby implicitly placed under suspicion. Taken together, their experiences of having been displaced seem to contain feelings of surprise, disappointment, betrayal and anger.

Unlike Arto's and Lamin's stories, Tore's and Roland's descriptions of the recent past of the Gustaf Dalén area for the most part resembled the dominant narrative discussed above. However, in contrast to its vague imagery of the multicultural character of the industrial area prior to the redevelopment, their stories were very explicit. They both explained the unrest in the area as a consequence of the small industries closing down in the 1980s. 'That's when it began: when those companies move away . . . Then it became . . . well, more and more places became these kinds of clubs for immigrants,' Roland said, and described how a mosque had been established across the street from his garage, in the very centre of the area (block F). Tore's garage was located west of Gustaf Dalénsgatan (block E), and he dissociated himself from the rest of the area – and some of its inhabitants. 'Well, we didn't need to get close to that clientele down there . . . And as we understood it, there were a lot of shady dealings with black money and things like that,' he explained.

In analysing Roland's and Tore's accounts, I wish to return to C. Wright Mills (2000 [1959]) and his appeal for sociologists to research the connections between private troubles and public issues. Their accounts of having been displaced from the Gustaf Dalén area must, I argue, be understood against the backdrop of how northern European industrial cities have had to adjust to new conditions by restructuring their economies and identities, ambitions which demand transformations of the urban landscape (Swyngedouw et al. 2002). Paul Gilroy has described the situation that the UK finds itself in today as *postcolonial melancholia*, and argues that in order to develop a habitable multiculture the country needs to work through its memories of empire (2006: 27). In Sweden, a similar condition might be characterised as *social democratic melancholia*. This could explain why the chapter on Scandinavia in Carl-Ulrich Schierup, Peo Hansen and Stephen Castles' book on European migration regimes has the title 'Paradise Lost?' (2006). What Sweden nostalgically looks back upon is not world domination, but the economic growth and welfare reforms of the post-war decades. In their analysis, Schierup, Hansen and Castles focus on the ambivalence between on the one hand the ideals of sustainable welfare, diversity and generous asylum policies, and on the other hand growing structural inequality due to both class and ethnicity (2006: 197). Tore and Roland seem to have dealt with the territorial stigma of the Gustaf Dalén area, which indisputably has racialised aspects, by interconnecting the parallel developments of economic restructuring and increasing immigration, explaining the latter with the former. Paradoxically, however, just as the immigrant tenants had to leave, so did Tore and Roland. Like their neighbours they were excluded from the future vision of New Kvillebäcken. This process turned out to have as much to do with class as with ethnicity.

From Iranian butcher shop to continental market hall

The people I met in the Gustaf Dalén area did not consider themselves such a clear-cut 'we' as do the fictive future residents in the promotional film about New Kvillebäcken, which is why I now turn to Tahere, a middle-aged woman who came to Sweden as a political refugee from Iran in 1983. Before the revolution she had worked as a secretary in the Royal Party. Of the 52 activities that were listed in the inventory from 2001, her and her husband's butcher shop is the only one that was able to negotiate its way into New Kvillebäcken, in the form of their managing the new market hall. This explains why her experience of the redevelopment project is dominated by pride. Before opening the butcher shop in the Gustaf Dalén area she had owned a number of businesses in Gothenburg, for instance a grocery store and a restaurant.

Tahere and her husband's shop was one of the first charcuteries in Gothenburg to focus on lamb, and this is still their speciality. For pragmatic reasons, because many of their customers are Muslim and Jewish, they do not sell pork in the shop. They do, however, deliver it to restaurants. Their butcher shop was located right next to the tram stop at Vågmästareplatsen, facing away from the rest of the industrial area (block B). Much like the two mechanics, Tahere had little good to say about the reused industrial area of the early 2000s – or about most of its inhabitants. As she showed me around the block she told me about the drunk and high party-goers who passed by their shop entrance early mornings on their way home from the illegal nightclub on Odalgatan. 'Every Saturday when we arrived . . . I swear, every Saturday, Friday, there was some kind of shooting, or someone who had shot someone, someone who had murdered someone,' she said. Like Tore and Roland, Tahere constructed a distinct opposition between 'us and them'. Yet, her 'them' did not include immigrants in general, but rather specific ethnic associations in the area and 'alcoholics and drug addicts' in general. Put differently, while the garage owners' division was based on ethnicity, Tahere's was just as much based on class. (See also Saha and Watson's chapter in this volume.)

Interestingly enough, while Tahere's story of the past resembles the dominant narrative, her story of the future is not as cheerful as one might expect. On the one hand, unlike many others in the area, she and her husband had the resources to make it into New Kvillebäcken. The market hall was their idea, she told us, and they managed to 'sell' it to the Kvillebäcken Consortium. On the other hand, however, she did not get in without a fight. An employee of one of the construction companies said the indoor market was their idea and that they had wanted it to specialise in organic and locally produced food, but Tahere had offered them a 'different' but 'safe' solution. And when it comes to Tahere and her husband, the market hall might not have been their ideal plan for the future either. They are both over 60 and had it been up to them, they might have chosen to stay in the shop that they had renovated so carefully until they retired, despite their qualms about the area behind it. However, when the plans for New Kvillebäcken were introduced, that future was made impossible.

Conclusion

When the marketing director of Riverbank Development was interviewed on local radio shortly before Christmas 2012, the reporter asked him what kind of people he thought would move into New Kvillebäcken. His answer was 'more modern people' (P4 Göteborg 2012), which implicitly portrays the now displaced inhabitants of the old industrial area as out of date. In this chapter, I have looked more closely at how people whose bodies are connected to places dismissed in post-political planning rhetoric as being dirty, unsustainable and criminal deal with this emotionally. As Sara Ahmed argues, it is on the surface of their skin that history is being written (2004: 39). In the Gustaf Dalén area of the early 2000s, Sweden's industrial as well as immigration history physically manifested, and this was articulated in different ways in my interviewees' accounts. While Finnish-born Arto embodies this, I suggest that Swedish-born Tore's and Roland's nostalgic backward-looking narratives can be described best as *social democratic melancholia* (cf. Gilroy 2006).

The Gustaf Dalén area was a difficult place to feel a sense of belonging to and my interviewees seemed to prefer to talk about their own spaces and activities than about the area as a whole. Even if the neglected buildings often made a shabby impression from the outside, many businesses and associations had invested a great deal of time and money in renovating their premises, and therefore naturally became attached to them. The complete absence of these efforts in the dominant narrative of the area's recent past caused some bitter feelings. Because the area was simply described as dangerous and in decay, there was no room in the narrative for any other former inhabitants than those few involved in criminal activities. What we can learn from this, I argue, is that describing a place also implicitly involves describing people. On a personal level, territorial stigmatisation is an emotionally painful experience involving feelings such as betrayal, shame, anger, worry, sadness and frustration. Or it can involve pride for those who manage to avoid displacement and are treated as part of the solution to the problem.

Besides having to deal with the stigmatising stories about the Gustaf Dalén area and (the impending risk of) displacement, the former inhabitants also had to make sense of being left out of the future vision – with the significant exception of Tahere. This is why it was important for us to research not just *physical* but also *discursive displacement*. As scholars like Chantal Mouffe (2005) and Eric Swyngedouw and colleagues (2002) have pointed out in their writings on post-politics, political visions can always be challenged, but when they are presented as the best – and perhaps only – solution, it is not so easy to do so. The dominant narrative of a journey from criminality to sustainability, necessary if Gothenburg does not want to be left behind in the global competition, denies every other possible future. Arto, Lamin, Tore, Roland and Tahere all had ideas about how the Gustaf Dalén area could have been released from the state of permanent provisionality that characterised it before the plans for New Kvillebäcken were introduced. Their different visions of the future were less dramatic than a complete redevelopment, and of course they included themselves, though not necessarily all their neighbours.

Notes

1 Between 2010 and 2012 I conducted walk-alongs with on the one hand representatives from the municipal developer and the private construction companies and on the other hand long-standing inhabitants of the area. The method of walk-alongs, first described by Margarethe Kusenbach (2003), combines interview and observation. See also my chapter in *Walking in the European City*, edited by Timothy Shortell and Ervick Brown (Holgersson forthcoming).
2 The names have been altered and when it comes to their associations and businesses I describe their character but do not include their full names.
3 This chapter has been written as part of the research project *Stadsomvandling som City branding, gentrifiering och upplevelsedesign. Fallet Centrala Älvstaden i Göteborg* [Urban redevelopment as city branding, gentrification and enchantment engineering: The case of central Älvstaden in Gothenburg], funded by The Swedish Research Council VR and led by Catharina Thörn.
4 However, in a column on the topic one of their journalists describes the expression as a play on words, referring to the motorcycle shops and clubs in the area – 'Gaza' is pronounced like 'gasa', which means 'to press the gas pedal' in Swedish (Fransson 2008).
5 Between 2004 and 2007 Gothenburg participated in the EU-project Waterfront Communities and made the Gustaf Dalén area its test case. For an analysis of this process, see Joakim Forsemalm's doctoral thesis *Bodies, Bricks & Black Boxes: Power Practicies in City Conversion* (2007).

References

Adlers, C. (2011) 'Från Slum till Hållbar Stadsdel', *Byggindustrin*, 24 June. Online. Available at www.byggindustrin.com/fran-slum-till-hallbar-stadsdel__8898 (accessed 1 October 2013).
Ahmed, S. (2004) *The Cultural Politics of Emotion*, Edinburgh: Edinburgh University Press.
Birgersson, L. and Wrigglesworth, T. (1984) 'Industrihistorisk Inventering av Göteborgsområdet', Report from the Country Administrative Boards of Göteborg and Bohus County.
Bradley, K. (2009) *Just Environments: Politicizing Sustainable Urban Development*, Stockholm: Royal Institute of Technology, School of Architecture and the Built Environment.
Bridge, G., Butler, T. and Lees, L. (eds) (2012) *Mixed Communities: Gentrification by Stealth?* Bristol: The Polity Press.
Checker, M. (2011) 'Wiped out by the "greenwave": Environmental gentrification and the paradoxical politics of urban sustainability', *City & Society* 23(2): 210–29.
Clark, E. (2005) 'The Order and Simplicity of Gentrification: A Political Challenge', in R. Atkinson and G. Bridge (eds) *Gentrification in a Global Context: The New Urban Colonialism*, Milton Park: Routledge.
Dahlström, C. (2004) *Nästan välkomna: Invandrarpolitikens retorik och praktik*, Gothenburg: University of Gothenburg, Department of Political Science.
Forsemalm, J. (2007) *Bodies, Bricks and Black Boxes: Power Practices in City Conversion*, Gothenburg: University of Gothenburg, Department of Ethnography.
Fransson, J. (2008) 'Gomorron Göteborg', PunktSE Göteborg, 26 February.
—— (2011), mail conversation 13 October.
Gilroy, P. (2006) 'Multiculture in times of war: An inaugural lecture given at the London School of Economics', *Critical Quarterly* 48(4): 27–45.
Gothenburg Municipal Government (2012) 'Göteborgsbladet – områdesfakta'.
Gothenburg Urban Planning Department (2001) 'Östra Kvillebäcken: Fastighetsinventering', Distrikt Norr.
Gothenburg Urban Planning Department (2009) 'Detaljplan för Östra Kvillebäcken, södra delen inom stadsdelarna Kvillebäcken och Brämaregården'. Diarienummer 0965/04.

Holgersson, H. (forthcoming) 'Challenging the Hegemonic Gaze by Foot: Walk-Alongs as a Useful Method in Gentrification Research', in T. Shortell and E. Brown (eds) *Walking in the European City*, Farnham: Ashgate.

Kern, L. (2012) 'Connecting embodiment, emotion and gentrification: An exploration through the practice of yoga in Toronto', *Emotion, Space and Society* 5(1): 27–35.

Kusenbach, M. (2003) 'Street phenomenology: The go-along as an ethnographic research tool', *Ethnography* 4(3): 455–85.

Kvillebäcken Consortium (2013), 'Pressinbjudan: Inflyttningsfest i Kvillebäcken – den 27 februari befolkas Göteborgs nya stadsdel', press release 20 February.

Lavadinho, S. and Winkin, Y. (2008) 'Enchantment Engineering and Pedestrian Empower-ment: The Geneva Case', in T. Ingold and J.L. Vergunst (eds) *Ways of Walking: Ethnog-raphy and Practice on Foot*, Aldershot: Ashgate Publishing.

Micu, P. (2006) 'I Folkmun Kallas Området "Gazaremsan"', *Göteborgs Tidning* 20 March.

Mouffe, C. (2005) *On the Political*, Milton Park: Routledge.

Mukhtar-Landgren, D. (2012) *Planering för Framsteg och Gemenskap: om den Kommunala Utvecklingsplaneringens Idémässiga Förutsättningar*, Lund: University of Lund, Department of Political Science.

Nora, P. (1989) 'Between memory and history: Les lieux de mémoire', *Representations* 26: 7–24.

Olshammar, G. (2002) *Det Permanentade Provisoriet: Ett Återanvänt Industriområde i Väntan på Rivning eller Erkännande*. Gothenburg: Chalmers Technical University.

P4 Göteborg (2012), 'Afternoon Session', *Sveriges Radio*, 27 December.

Peterson, M. (2010) 'Four centuries of multiculture', in H. Holgersson, C. Thörn, H. Thörn and M. Wahlström (eds) *(Re)searching Gothenburg: Essays on a Changing City*, Gothenburg: Glänta production.

Puwar, N. (2011) 'Noise of the past: Spatial interruptions of war, nation and memory', *Senses & Society* 6(3): 325–45.

Riverbank Development (2008) 'Vision Kvillebäcken'. Online. Available at www.youtube.com/watch?v=MPf-TaD5GFA (accessed 1 October 2013).

Schierup, C., Hansen, P. and Castles, S. (2006) *Migration, Citizenship and the European Wel-fare State: A European Dilemma*, Oxford: Oxford University Press.

Slater, T. (2006) 'The eviction of critical perspectives from gentrification research', *Interna-tional Journal of Urban and Regional Research* 30(4): 737–57.

Swyngedouw, E., Moulaert, F. and Rodriguez, A. (2002), 'Neoliberal urbanization in Europe: Large-scale urban development projects and the new urban policy', *Antipode* 34(3): 542–77.

Tunström, M. (2007) 'The Vital City: Constructions and meanings in the contemporary Swedish planning discourse', *Town Planning Review* 78(6): 681–98.

Vikingsson, K. (2007) 'Tredje mordet i år på Ångpannegatan', *Aftonbladet*, 7 December.

Wacquant, L. (2008) *Urban Outcasts: A Comparative Sociology of Advanced Marginality*, Cam-bridge: Polity Press.

Wilson, D. and Grammenos, D. (2005) 'Gentrification, discourse, and the body: Chicago's Humboldt Park', *Environment and Planning D* 23(2): 295–312.

Wright Mills, C. (2000 [1959]) *The Sociological Imagination*, Oxford: Oxford University Press.

8

'THIS BRIDGE IS JUST LIKE THE ONE IN VIŠEGRAD!'

Dwelling, embodying and doing home across space

Kristina Grünenberg

> ***Nedžad***: Just before the war started . . . just before it began, we had settled into our lives, we had worked hard both of us . . . and decided to open a private business. We refurbished our flat completely, we bought new furniture, new fridge, a new stove; everything was new, everything! . . . Even the washing machine . . . new! We bought a new car. We were getting older and had a bit more time to enjoy these things . . . We bought a machine for the private business, which we were setting up . . . an industrial machine . . .
>
> ***Edina***: We were really stupid! We just thought the war would stop. We saw what happened in Croatia and in Slovenia and yet . . .
>
> ***Nedžad***: We weren't stupid! We simply didn't think that something like this could happen.
>
> And then you think . . . you know, I was born in this town and I lived there for 45 years; it was 'my town'. But when I visited Bosnia several years later, I realised that I wouldn't be able to live there . . . not there!! Maybe not in Denmark, but especially not there . . . Because things have changed in this town of mine . . . people . . . the way of life . . . changed completely . . .
>
> *(Author's fieldnotes)*

In 1992 what was incomprehensible, unspeakable and unthinkable to most Bosnians happened. Fighting between different warring factions in shifting combinations, brutal paramilitary forces in-and-out of control, ethnic cleansing, massacres and mass rape, led to thousands of dead and wounded, and the flight of approximately 2 million out of 4.3 million inhabitants.[1] This chapter addresses the ways in which a group of Bosnian households transformed space into place in the context of exile in Denmark. It argues that processes of home-making took place through 'affective practice' implying relational and bodily processes, which enabled processes of 'learning to be affected' by new socio-spatial topographies.

The flight to Denmark and Temporary Protection Status

Approximately 17,000 of the refugees fleeing the former Yugoslavia, mainly Bosnian Muslims, arrived in Denmark at the beginning of the 1990s. The majority of these people were prisoners of war who had left Bosnia and Herzegovina (BiH) via the UNHCR and others, who had been 'ethnically cleansed' out of their homes. The Danish Parliament subsequently decided for the first time to implement a special policy of Temporary Protection Status for refugees from the former Yugoslavia (see Grünenberg 2006). The law provided the refugees with instant collective protection as a group and also suspended the normal asylum procedures for a period of up to two years. It furthermore implied a re-evaluation of the temporary status every six months. The normal asylum procedure at the time meant that, having obtained asylum, a refugee would have rights to equal participation in Danish society. In contrast, the special law of Temporary Protection Status focused explicitly on repatriation, and non-integration was perceived as a way of ensuring that this took place. In other words, an implicit perception of integration and repatriation as opposites permeated the political agenda at the time. Implicit in these notions were also assumptions about how the relationship between culture, identity and belonging relates to time and space. The political frame of Temporary Protection Status was constructed on the basis of a perception of identity, belonging, place and culture as being inextricably and naturally entwined making it impossible to conceptualise multiple belonging. Through the politics of Temporary Protection Status, and the placement in Red Cross managed refugee camps often placed well outside urban areas, the refugees' existence in time and space was controlled, thus conceptually hindering their potential 'rootedness in the wrong place' (see Grünenberg 2006: 68). In order to restore order, then, refugees from BiH were to return to 'their place' (see also Gupta and Ferguson 1992; Malkki 1994; Warner 1994, 2006). Through these practices Denmark was constituted as a 'non-place' while BiH was simultaneously constituted as the 'right place' for Bosnian refugees.[2]

Nonetheless, approximately five years later, most Bosnian refugees had been granted permanent leave to remain. The majority of the refugees decided to stay in Denmark, many of them visiting Bosnia on holidays. Yet another new beginning, this time as part of official Danish society was about to unfold.

In the field

The present chapter is based on ethnographic fieldwork directed at the everyday practices through which Bosnians gradually 'got a grip' on their new lives-in-the-making. In practice the empirical material comes out of two connected ethnographic fieldwork phases among Bosnian (mainly Muslim) refugees. The first phase took place between 1994 and 1997. During this period I followed and interviewed 20 Bosnian households from their initial stay in Danish refugee camps until they obtained permanent leave to remain, and thus permanent residence. The second phase took place from 2001 until 2006 during which I did the fieldwork for my PhD thesis. During this phase I followed the same households in their new lives in Denmark, and accompanied some of them to Bosnia and Herzegovina (BiH) and Croatia during the summer holidays. Through the multi-sitedness and expanded time horizon of the ethnographic fieldwork, this chapter is able to trace affective practices over time, as well as across space. As such the chapter provides insights into the processual constitution of places and spaces, senses of belonging and being in the world.

Focus

In this chapter I will argue that the search for home for these Bosnian households constituted affective practices made up of relational and bodily experiences, through which meaning and/or meaninglessness was attributed to the specific socio-spatial terrains, and localities of which the households formed part. I will furthermore show that these terrains transcended national boundaries in ways which shaped everyday lives.

I will do this by first taking a short tour into the ideas of movement, and stasis – some of the most important dichotomous positions within migration research on home and belonging. I will then move on to the empirical material, and show how Bosnian everyday lives, affective and sensory experiences transcended these seeming dichotomies as well as what is conventionally thought of as the two entities of home- and host-countries in particular ways. And finally I will argue that through a focus on 'affective practices' including bodies and senses and the process of 'learning to be affected' we might challenge conventional dichotomies and understand phenomena such as processes of home-making in – and belonging to – specific localities in new ways (see also Turan Hoffman, Chapter 9 this volume, for discussions on the constitution of home in diaspora).

Fixity, mobility, affect and the quest for home

> Spaces are claimed or 'owned' not so much by inhabiting what is already there, but by moving within, or passing through, different spaces which are only given value as places (with boundaries) through the movement or passing through itself.
>
> *(Ahmed 2000: 33)*

One of the core questions addressed in social research in the context of home is how people mediate between the experiences of a world in flux and perpetual change, and the simultaneous need for certain levels of predictability, continuity and coherence. The reason why the question has become interesting and relevant is inextricably related to the way in which globalisation has brought (at least certain types of) mobility and fluidity into focus. This focus has served to expose the arbitrariness of the conventional nation–state-centred political ways of ordering the world, such as for example in the Danish case, the juxtapositioning of integration and repatriation. At the same time it has meant an increasing critique of the notion of home as a place of stability (sometimes perceived as the nation state writ small). From a theoretical standpoint then, there has been a tendency to conceptualise and approach the notion of home either from the perspective of a 'sedentary paradigm' taking the nation state as a natural point of departure, or in terms of globalisation, mobility and 'mobile theorising' and its concomitant view of the postmodern as a world of things and people in flux, on the other hand (Appadurai 1991; Clifford 1992; Chambers 1994; Marcus 1998; Malkki 1992; Urry 2000).

In this context some researchers have argued that it is anachronistic to deal with the routinisation of space and place when dealing with the construction of belonging and being at home in a migration context (Rapport and Dawson 1998). Such arguments seem to operate with the assumptions that movement and mobility are somehow closer to the reality of daily life in the contemporary world, than tales of everyday routines and social practices, which are defined as 'signs of fixity'. I agree with, for example, Rapport and Dawson that we should keep our eyes open to fluidity and movement and to other ways of conceptualising homes, which the previous focus on the nation state may have overshadowed. Nonetheless in the following I will argue that one does not preclude the other. I have found that Margaret Wetherell's conceptualisation of 'affective practice' resonates with the reservations I have with the mobility focus. In her recent book on affect and emotion, Wetherell (2012) argues against a concept of affect focusing only at the fleeting and fugitive and on unfolding activity. She argues that too much is lost when 'semantics, social critique, repetition, stasis, sedimentation, regulation, pattern and coherence' is cut out (55). Hence in the following I will argue that both the realm of routine and of mobility might become part of specific contextual assemblages mobilising particular affective practices of belonging and home-making. Furthermore, Wetherell's definition of 'affective practice' as: '. . . a figuration where body possibilities and routines become recruited or entangled together with meaning making and with other social and material figurations . . . an organic complex in which all the parts relationally constitute each other' (Wetherell 2012: 19) seems useful to capture the relationality of the processes of home-making and senses of belonging which are at stake in my empirical material.

From space to place: 'This bridge is just like the one in Višegrad'

> People in a very competent manner make the places where they live into their homes, as they transform some of the conditions connected to the specific locality or specific place where they live.
>
> *(Les Back interviewed in Røgilds 2005: 16)*

Upon leaving the camps from 1996 onwards, and entering relatively new spaces, the Bosnian households I followed embarked upon a process of turning the unknown into the known – spaces into places. The region of Lolland/Falster, and the town of Nykøbing, situated near the refugee camps became the preferred place of settlement for these households.[3]

This process of transforming spaces into places was effected through, for example, bodily routine, that is, moving in and through the same spaces over time, creating personal routes out of roads, and the practice of naming and comparing. Through the gradual reconstruction of everyday life routines, space was increasingly appropriated. This happened as the habitual everyday routes and routines in the local area gave shape to the surrounding space and gradually transformed it into known places.

Going to work with Nedžad:

> It was six o'clock in the morning as we left the house, and ten minutes past six as we got into the car, just as Nedžad had predicted. Like every morning he had already got up at 5.15, had coffee, checked his horoscope, the news in Danish and the news in Bosnian on the tele-text.
>
> I was going to spend a day at work with Nedžad at the industrial laundry. His superiors had agreed to let me work with the women on the ironing rollers. As we were on our way, Nedžad put a tape in the tape recorder. It was a Bosnian song about Nedžad's town, sung in the classical and melancholic style of 'sevdah', traditional folk oriented music.[4] Nedžad said: 'Sometimes I am so much into my everyday life that I completely forget that I am not in Bosnia, even this [he makes a gesture with his arm towards the passing fields] is like the area around my town. Then I hear this song or something else, and I wake up . . . I have got very used to being here'.
>
> *(Field notes, June 2002)*

Nedžad's bodily movement through space during the day and the way he had incorporated material objects into it – the cup of coffee, watching breakfast TV – had become part of a routine which he took for granted. The large stretches of land, which he passed through on his way to work every day gradually merged with the surroundings of his old home town. This co-presence of the temporal as well as geographical 'here and there', imbued the surroundings with a sense of meaning and history, as Nedžad 'learnt to be affected' by his new surroundings. Drawing on the Belgian philosopher and psychologist Vinciane Despret's (2004) concept of 'learning to be affected' in an essay about the body, Latour describes how employees working in the French perfume industry were gradually trained to sense different, hitherto unrecognised, smells. The trainees in other words 'learnt to be affected by difference' and in this process were, according to Latour, not merely moved from inattention to attention, but instead Latour argues, that in this process a 'new nose' with a different sensual repertoire and with it a 'new world' came into being through particular assemblages (Latour 2004: 207). As

Nedžad moved through the temporal and spatial routines of his everyday life in exile, he gradually learnt to be affected by its particular material compositions and qualities, rhythms and sensations. In this context he also moved from simply being there physically to actually 'being in-the-world' (Richardson 2003: 76), a state which Ann Game describes as a 'doubled state of now and then, old and new at once' (Game 2001: 228). It implies she argues, the sensation of a self, not as a bounded, singular entity, but instead as a relational self – a self 'in connection' (ibid).

Nedžad's seemingly rather banal and undramatic everyday routines and practices, then, marked a way for him to bridge the gap between past and present, here and there.

The sense of connection in this case also implied what Ghassan Hage in an essay on home calls 'maximal bodily knowledge'. He illustrates this point in the following way:

> If I get up at night, my feet can take me to the toilet or to the fridge without me having to really wake up and think where to go.
>
> *(Hage 1997: 147, note 6)*

Nedžad's everyday routine, the bodily, material and spatial practices described, brought a sense of temporary unity and taken for grantedness into his world – not just a sense of physical presence, but also a sense of mere (unquestioned) being in the world. Just like when Hage's feet find the fridge on their own. As Ahmed eloquently puts it: 'The lived experience of being at home hence involves the enveloping of subjects in a space which is not simply outside them: Being at home suggests that the subject and space leak into each other, *inhabit each other*' (2000: 89; original emphasis). Subject and space are in this context no longer separate, but emerge as new 'wholes' like Latour's new French bodies (2004). The feeling of being at home produced in this context was as Ahmed argues for emotions generally: 'an effect of the repetition of some actions rather than others' (Ahmed 2004: 196). Nedžad's feelings of being one with the surroundings were in other words *the outcome of* everyday bodily and material routines and actions, rather than *the ground of action* (ibid). Seen from this perspective emotions are inherently relational, rather than a property of individuals and they are potentially based on routine repetitions of bodily and sensory activities. In Nedžad's case the feelings of 'being one with' were only made possible because he managed to establish recognised daily routines, in this case through employment. An important point here is, however, that these daily routines were not merely recognised and framed by him as valid, but also by the Danish political and public discourse with its focus on self-sustainability. In this sense Nedžad's emotions were inscribed and framed by powerful definitions of what constituted a normal and decent life.

Whereas Nedžad 'forgot himself' in his daily routines, Namira, a 35-year-old woman relocated from the camp to the same area, engaged actively with the surroundings by comparing the Danish town, Bridgetown, where she now lived to her former hometown. This comparison also marked a way of incorporating the Danish town into the category of 'the familiar' in a particularly intimate way. Hence Namira, as well as others, from the Bosnian town of Višegrad in eastern Bosnia, would often comment on the similarities between the two towns. The material setting mostly referred to in this context was a Višegrad bridge. Bridgetown was approximately the same size as Višegrad and also divided by a bridge. When Namira's father, who actually lived in Višegrad, visited her during the summer, Namira happily commented on his visit to me over the phone: 'Even my dad says that this reminds him of Višegrad because of the bridge.' By drawing together her former hometown with her present hometown, like Nedžad did through repetitious movement between the fields he passed by on his daily trip to work, Namira on the one hand imbued urban space with significance, attachment and meaning, and on the other 'bridged' two notions of home, which are according to Brah (1996) at play in exile. Hence feelings of home as: 'a mythic place of desire in the diasporic imagination', and as: 'the lived experience of a locality' (Brah 1996: 192) were brought together, through bodily and material practices, if only for short moments.

Sensory experiences, such as taste, were often part and parcel of these affective linkages, as we shall see in the following section.

Food and senses of continuity

The preparation of food – of known as well as hitherto unknown tastes – marked a socio-cultural as well as spatial nodal point in the daily or weekly routines, especially for the female members of the households. The preparation of food implied bodily, spatial as well as affective dimensions. The familiarisation with particular spatial routes through town made the weekly trip 'kod Turćina' (literally meaning at the Turks) possible. 'Kod Turćina' was the way the small Turkish-owned greengrocer shop in the centre of town was known by the Bosnian households, in spite of the name on the sign being 'Izmir Greengrocers'. In the shop they sold a host of products necessary for traditional Bosnian cuisine, among them *Bosna ajvar*, a type of paste made from peppers, aubergine and garlic. Ajvar is for many Bosnians unequivocally Bosnian or former Yugoslavian. The paste is put to multiple uses in Bosnian cuisine and experimental uses in the Danish context. Hence many Danish open sandwiches have been honoured with a taste of ajvar. The acquisition of particular consumer products and the routes thus established also constituted ways of appropriating space, just as the preparation of these foods was used as a way of tying little knots of continuity across times and spaces, that is, across and between the *here and there* and the *now and then*. These moments of continuity were mostly established at weekends, when there was, as Namira expressed it, 'finally time to cook a real Bosnian meal', given that everyday life was generally too busy for hours of cooking.

Ghassan Hage (1997) equally argues how the preparation of food contributes to processes of home-making among Lebanese immigrants in Australia:

> [the] production and consumption of ethnic food [constitutes] a locus of practices with which migrants try to make themselves feel at home in Australia.
>
> *(Hage 1997: 101)*

Along a similar vein Duruz (1999) argues how a Turkish family shopping for food in Australia draws a 'culinary map': '. . . on a regular basis a culinary map is drawn and redrawn – one that is textured with memories [in our case through consumption of indispensable ajvar] and possibilities [of e.g. consuming Danish open-ended sandwiches with ajvar]' (Duruz 1999: 308, my insertions). The weekend ritual of cooking a Bosnian meal then, implied specific routes through town, the practices of preparing, visualizing, smelling, tasting and consuming. Food in this context became a way of appropriating new spaces and remembering old ones, as Hage has also argued about the cooking of 'homeland foods': 'The aim is not to go back. It is to foster these homely intimations so as to provide a better base for confronting life in Australia . . .' (Hage 1997: 108).

Hage equates the preparation of 'homeland foods' with feelings of nostalgia. Whereas on the one hand, he understands nostalgic feelings as a way of creating a safe haven, on the other hand he argues that it is a way of establishing a platform '. . . from which to perceive and grasp [in this case] Australian opportunities' and thus part of the processes of home-making (see also Rhys-Taylor, this volume, for discussions of the mango as a figure accommodating the known and the new simultaneously). Hage's idea of nostalgia as a potential resource, pointing forward, is quite different from that of Game (2001) who defines nostalgia as something belonging to the world of conformity and closure, which hinders a life of connectedness and ardour (Game 2001: 230–1). These different ways of perceiving of nostalgia also seem related to the juxtaposition of the previously mentioned mobility and stasis perspective in migration research.

I would argue instead that 'homeland' food shopping, preparation and consumption could be seen as constituting affective practices which are used to establish important connections (Wetherell 2012). In this sense, the practices surrounding food consumption pointed to how the establishment of routines, the transformation of space into place and the maintenance and construction of new senses of belonging were entwined in processes of home-making. Rather than merely seeing the preparation of Bosnian food as an expression of nostalgia or of a result of sticking to 'Bosnian culture', thus unwittingly reifying and naturalising material practices as typical expressions of, for example, ethnic identity, we might instead suggest that cultural practices simultaneously perform and constitute (ethnic) identity, perform and constitute belonging and new ways of moving forward (Fortier 1999: 43). For example, when young women learnt how to make 'real' Bosnian 'pita' from their mothers, that is, a type of filo pastry, most commonly filled with either meat, cheese, spinach or zucchini, this did not mean that all Bosnian pitas were the same. Instead, as Fortier argues, rituals, reiterations and repetitions, in this case of pita making, never resulted in exact replicas; instead a difference always presented itself somewhere in the process (Fortier 1999: 43, 49).

These sometimes subtle differences, as Hage has suggested, make homeland cooking much more than a simple expression of nostalgia – if nostalgia is understood as a retrogressive and conformist affective state.

I have argued that subtle differences were installed into established everyday life activities and that appropriation of space took place through affective practices in the Danish context of exile and new beginnings. However in the context of visits to Bosnia much more overt and violent transformations and differentiations were encountered and had to be dealt with by the Bosnian households, as we will see in the following section.

Changing places, changing phrases: From place to space

I am on a train going from Sarajevo towards Prijedor to visit a friend of mine, Izmet, who is my neighbour in Denmark. From there I will move on to visit Sadeta and her mother, one of the households I have followed over the years, who are visiting the village they lived in and were forced to flee from into the forest when the war started.[5]

We are approaching the demarcation line between the Federation and the Serb Republic.[6] The train pulls to a halt at the station in a town called Doboj. We are now in the Serb Republic and, as I have experienced so many times when travelling between European countries, a person dressed in a different type of uniform gets on board, only this is not supposed to be a national border. I open the window to let in the warm summer air and look outside. The first thing that strikes me is the inscription on the station building in front of me, where the name of the station is normally written. It is still possible to make out the Latin letters, which have left a mark in the stone façade. 'Doboj' it says, or it used to say, before the letters were ripped off the façade and replaced with Cyrillic.[7] It still says 'Doboj' . . . now in Cyrillic, but what strikes me as a very tangible result of an appropriation and transformation of place gives me the impression that it is no longer a Doboj for everyone.

(Diary, August 2002)

In Sadeta's old home town, the tricolour of the Serb Republic has been planted on the hilltop above the village for all to see.[8] Today, after the war, the village is located in the Serb Republic. Sadeta's parents have, however, got their old plots of land back and are beginning to reconstruct their house where the old one, which was burned to the ground, once used to be. The same applies to her maternal grandparents, who lived a bit further down the road. The whole village was practically burnt to the ground during the war except for a few houses inhabited by Bosnian Serb households, whose doors were marked with a white cross and therefore, according to Senada, Sadeta's mother, left unharmed. However, while many of the former inhabitants live in exile scattered across Europe, since 1998 an increasing number of former inhabitants have returned and a housing project in the area had reconstructed many of the burnt down or bombed houses. This meant that today, after an intensive process of reconstruction, shiny new roof tops glitter in the sun when seen from the hills. This process also meant, however, that the village had changed considerably since the war, altering what for Sadeta and her family used to be known places into either 'empty spaces' or unknown, newly constructed places (see also Holgersson, Chapter 7 in this volume for similar issues in relation to gentrification). Thus a sense of being out of place formed part of the experiences of this and many other families on their summer trips to Bosnia.

> We were walking down the street of the village where Sadeta lived until the war. Sadeta was back for the first time since the war. Suddenly a young Bosnian man stopped us. He was obviously also living abroad by the way his hair was styled, his clothes and the number plates of the shiny white car he had just got out of. He asked us: 'Are you from here?' Sadeta replied: 'Yes, *I* am from here!' [Young man]: 'Well, could you tell us where we could find the nearest pizzeria?' [Sadeta]: 'I have absolutely no idea!' [Young man]: 'How can you not know if you are from here?' Sadeta [who had immediately recognised him as a diaspora,[9] was now a little upset about the probing questions and the insinuation that she could not really be from town, if she did not know its places] responded: 'For the same reason that you are asking me the silly question in the first place!'
>
> *(Field notes, August 2002)*

Small events like this joined her mother Senada's description of frustrating walks around town in search of the *ćevabdžinica*, a traditional local (fast-food) shop selling grilled, oblong-shaped meatballs in bread with raw onion and yogurt, because she no longer knew where it was, nor which one of them prepared the most savoury *ćevapi*. Her story took on a strong symbolic meaning due to the place occupied by *ćevabdžinice* in the life of most towns in Bosnia. *Ćevabdžinice* occupy a somewhat similar place in the Bosnian imagery as do local 'fish and chip' shops for many Londoners. *Ćevapčići* then not only constituted a marker of local knowledge, but also a sense of Bosnianness. Furthermore, eating *ćevapčići* is for many Bosnians (and certainly for the households I visited) one of the 'obligatory' sensory experiences of a visit to Bosnia. These stories and experiences all told the tales of the transformation of known places into spaces. It also hinted at the impossibility of: 'being inhabited in the same way by that which, in some ways, appeared as familiar' (Ahmed 2000: 91). Through violent and deliberate acts of transformation the familiar had in very tangible ways been made strange – the *heimlich* made *unheimlich* disjoining certain memories from physical places and materiality in the process (see also Jackson, Chapter 3 this volume). Not only materiality had transformed, however; a transformation of language had also taken place in the absence of the households, as the following example will illustrate. During another walk with Sadeta in her 'native' village, we passed an elderly man. She greeted him with 'Kako ste?' ('How are you?') and subsequently started telling me about her frustrations related to the changes in vocabulary which have taken place in the village:

We always used to greet our family members and older people we knew with 'Merhaba' (a greeting derived from Ottoman vocabulary and hence associated mostly with the Muslim population), but outside [in public] we would always say 'Dobar dan' [a common and general greeting in pre-war Yugoslavia]. Now you cannot use it any more. I went into a shop owned by Muslims the other day and said 'Dobar dan', and the shopkeeper looked rather sternly at me and said 'Merhaba'. A couple of days later I was in a different shop, which is apparently now owned by Serbs, and said 'Merhaba' and of course they didn't like it. You feel so stupid and out of place. It was really frustrating and irritating.

(Field notes, August 2002)

Having had these experiences, in which she was reprimanded for using the 'wrong phrases' at the wrong times, she subsequently decided to greet people with the less specific and more neutral 'Kako ste?' ('How are you?'). This phrase did not disclose anything about her cultural or religious affiliations, nor hint at anybody else's, would make nobody suspicious or hurt, and thus made it easier for her to navigate across a changed socio-cultural terrain, without constantly being reminded of her out-of-placeness.

Stefansson (2003) argues that the permanent returnees to BiH gradually came to terms with these and other changes and managed over time to re-inscribe themselves onto places. The possibility of this happening during short summer trips was much more limited, and senses of disjuncture and detachment generally pervaded the experiences of Sadeta and her family as well as many of the other households I visited. However, new ways of experiencing and feeling attachment were simultaneously made possible on these trips by the vast number of Bosnians living abroad. Hence social relations to other exiled Bosnians also visiting the former homeland during holidays were cultivated by the families I visited and kept alive between visits through the Internet or occasional social visits. Hence during the summer trips to BiH new transnational social relations permitted uncensored remembrance of the Yugoslavia shared in the past, discussions of conditions of exile and new homelands, as well as romantic relations between youngsters as well as parents. In this way new maps of belonging to – and familiarity with – localities around the world were drawn.

Christmas lunch, coming home and concluding

As illustrated by the story of Senada and also expressed in the opening quote by Nedžad, visits to Bosnia could turn out to become a complicated affair, leading to a rupture in the fabric of known affective practices and thus sensations of disjuncture and estrangement. The spatial and relational universe once ingrained in the skin had become unavailable. Conversely, as I have illustrated through the examples of both Nedžad and Namira, by learning to become affected by new spatial and relational topographies, which were made available through the possibilities of establishing daily routines, past and present – here and there were drawn together and sometimes new horizons of belonging were opened up. As I have shown, these horizons were opened up, for example, as exiled Bosnians met during annual holidays. However, Nedžad also provides a brilliant example of such new horizons engendered in the Danish context. In the following extract he describes his participation in a Danish Christmas lunch held for the staff of the industrial laundry, where he had managed to find employment:

> The Christmas lunch was to be held in a restaurant where I had never been before.
>
> It was cold, the snow was quite heavy . . . I lost my way . . . I arrived about 45 minutes late. When I finally arrived they were all concerned about me, waiting for me, outside in the cold . . . at that moment I felt I had been accepted. I was very moved . . .

(Author's fieldnotes)

Contrary to Sadeta, who was confronted with sensations of, as well as direct expressions of, misrecognition from what was, from a conventional point of view, her 'real homeland', Nedžad was included into a community of co-workers, at an event which is seen as one of the emblems of Danishness – 'the Christmas lunch'. Through Nedžad's experience of bodies, worriedly waiting for him in the snow, he was able to inscribe himself meaningfully into a context fraught with symbolic meaning, and new horizons of belonging were made available to him.

Throughout this chapter I have shown how places are connected and disconnected through affective practices. In this context I have argued for the usefulness of Wetherell's (2012) pragmatic focus on affective practices as assemblages, which potentially include the processual, the habitual, the relational, the brain, as well as the body within a single contextually sensitive framework.

These practices in my material involved transformations of space to place (and sometimes even place to space) through the (re-)establishment of routes and routines through, for example, bodily inscriptions and naming practices, meaningful social relations, recognition as well as power over place. I have shown how these processes generated varying intensities of attachment to and detachments from particular localities and how new horizons of belonging sometimes emerged in the process. I have furthermore argued how the affective practices in question brought together the *here and there, now and then* and thus transcended and challenged conventional dichotomies of stasis and mobility.

Notes

1 The number of deaths was a highly disputed and politicised issue throughout the 1990s with figures ranging from 25,000 to 280,000 (Pupavać 1998).
2 Marc Augé defines non-place as follows: 'If a place can be defined as relational, historical and concerned with identity, then a space which cannot be defined as relational, historical, or concerned with identity will be a non-place' (Augé 1995: 78).
3 Nykøbing Falster is a town with 16,400 inhabitants, located 128 km from Copenhagen in what is in political discourse known as 'outskirt Denmark'.

4 Sevdahlinka is a traditional genre of folk music from Bosnia and Herzegovina. Sev-dalinka is mostly associated with the Muslim population (Bosnjiak) but the style is popular across ex-Yugoslavia. For a short example listen to www.youtube.com/watch?v=FpC2FqnEVn0

5 Sadeta, who is 16 years old, lives with her 13-year-old brother, mother, Senada, and father, Mirzo, in Denmark. Her maternal grandparents who also fled to Denmark now spend most of their time in Bosnia.

6 Republika Srpska is one of two political entities in Bosnia and Herzegovina, the other being the federation of Bosnia and Herzegovina (mainly inhabited by Bosnjiaks and Croats) officially forged after the Dayton Peace agreement in 1994.

7 Cyrillic is the written form particularly used in Serbia, whereas Latin letters are predomi-nantly used in the rest of former Yugoslavia.

8 The flag is similar to that of the neighbouring country, Serbia, which today forms part of the State Union of Serbia and Montenegro.

9 'Diaspora' constitutes the colloquial phrase for Bosnians living in exile used by Bosnians who stayed behind (most often pejoratively). Notice how the term has changed into a noun, transforming 'diaspora' from a condition that people who fled the country *are in* to something *they are* (see Grünenberg 2005, 2006 for elaborations).

References

Ahmed, S. (2000) *Strange Encounters: Embodied Others in Post Coloniality*, London: Routledge.

—— (2004) *The Cultural Politics of Emotion*, Edinburgh: Edinburgh University Press.

Ahmed, S., Castañeda, C., Fortier, A.M. and Scheller, M. (eds) (2003) *Uprootings/Reground-ings: Questions of Home and Migration*, Oxford and New York: Berg.

Appadurai, A. (1991) 'Global Ethnoscapes: Notes and Queries for a Transnational Anthro-pology', in R.G. Fox (ed.) *Recapturing Anthropology: Working in the Present*, Santa Fe, NM: School of American Research Press, 191–210.

Brah, A. (1996) *Cartographies of Diaspora: Contesting Identities*, London and New York: Routledge.

Clifford, J. (1994) 'Diaspora', *Cultural Anthropology*, 9(3): 302–38.

Despret, V. (2004) 'The body we care for: Figures of anthropo-zoo-genesis', *Body and Soci-ety*, 10: 111–34.

Duruz, J. (1999) 'The streets of Clovelly: Food, difference and place-making', *Continuum: Journal of Media and Cultural Studies*, 13: 305–14.

Fortier, A.M. (1999) 'Re-membering places and the performance of belonging(s)', *Theory, Culture and Society*, 16(2): 41–64.

Game, A. (2001) 'Belonging: Experience in Sacred Time and Space' in J. May and N. Thrift (eds) *Timespace: Geographies of Temporality*, London: Routledge, 226–39.

Grünenberg, K. (2005) 'Constructing "sameness and difference": Bosnian diasporic experi-ences in a Danish context', *Journal of Balkan Studies*, 9(1–2): 173–93.

—— (2006) 'Is home where the heart is or where I hang my hat? Constructions of home and belonging among Bosnian refugees in Denmark', PhD thesis, Department of Sociology, University of Copenhagen.

Gupta, A. and Ferguson, J. (1992) 'Beyond culture: Space, identity and the politics of differ-ence', *Cultural Anthropology*, 7(1): 6–23.

Hage, G. (1997) 'At Home in the Entrails of the West: Multiculturalism, "Ethnic Food" and Migration Home-Building', in H. Grace, G. Hage, L. Johnson, J. Langsworth and M. Symonds (eds) *Home/World: Space, Community and Marginality in Sydney's West*, London: Pluto Press, 99–153.

Latour, B. (2004) 'How to talk about the body? The normative dimensions of science studies', *Body and Society*, 10(2–3): 205–29.

Marcus, G.E. (1998) *Ethnography through Thick and Thin*, Princeton: Princeton University Press.

Malkki, L. (1994) 'Citizens of humanity: Internationalism and the imagined community of nations', *Diaspora: A Journal of Transnational Studies*, 3(1): 41–68.

Rapport, N. and Dawson, A. (1998) 'Introduction', in N. Rapport and A. Dawson (eds) *Migrants of Identity: Perceptions of Home in a World in Movement*, London: Berg.

Richardson, M. (2003) 'Being-in-the-market vs. Being-in-the-plaza', in S. Low and D. Lawrence-Zuñiga (eds) *The Anthropology of Space and Place: Locating Culture*, Oxford: Blackwell, 51–74.

Røgilds, F. (2005) 'Charlie Nielsen's journey: Wandering through multicultural landscapes', Critical Urban Studies, Occasional papers, Goldsmiths, University of London.

Stefansson, A.H. (2003) 'Under my own sky? The cultural dynamics of refugee return and (re)integration in post-war Sarajevo', PhD thesis, Institute of Anthropology no. 25, Faculty of Social Sciences, University of Copenhagen.

Urry, J. (2000) *Sociology beyond Societies: Mobilities for the Twenty-First Century*, Routledge: London.

Warner, D. (1994) 'Voluntary repatriation and the meaning of return to home: A critique of liberal mathematics', *Journal of Refugee Studies*, 7(2/3): 160–74.

Wetherell, M. (2012) *Affect and Emotion: A New Social Science Understanding*, London: Sage.

9

DIASPORA TOURS AND PLACE ATTACHMENT

A unique configuration of emotion and location

Zeynep Turan Hoffman

Diasporas, people who have separated from their ancestral homelands, experience a physical loss that metastasises into a psychological craving for home. Diaspora tourism is an attempt to address the emotions arising from the change of locations – it triggers and fuels feelings that create new formations and connections with other people and places.

This dynamic can be used to challenge the stark dichotomy between 'tourist' and 'vagabond' posited by Zygmunt Bauman (1998), in that his framing presumes a rigid and ahistorical typology that forever distinguishes the powerful and the powerless. But diasporas may have been forcibly displaced in an earlier era and only in a recent period have they acquired the resources to undertake politically significant travel. Nevertheless, Bauman's interpretive frame does provide a language that helps to make sense of the strange interactions that result from cosmopolitan conditions. To that end, and in regard to the perspectives and contribution of this collection, this look at diaspora tourism necessarily investigates the emotions that cause and are caused by the tourism of 'vagabonds'. In this chapter, I present a theory and concepts for analysing the nature, meaning, and consequences of diaspora tourism by spotlighting the centrality of place attachment and fleshing this out through a parsing of contacts between tourists, place, and locals. To illustrate my analysis more concretely I critically examine the case study of Armenian diaspora tours to eastern Turkey, which explores the interactions of Armenian tourists and local Turks and Kurds in the context of contested place attachment, and considers the psychological, social, and political outcomes.

The word 'tourism' often evokes ideas of leisurely diversions and entertainment, however, certain forms of it are loaded with psychological and political meaning. This is especially the case with the phenomenon of heritage tourism. But, whereas for some such tourism in Europe may include warm embraces from distant relatives, in the case I will discuss, Armenian diaspora tourism in eastern Turkey (or 'western Armenia' as commonly used by Armenians), the experience is profoundly bittersweet – an emotional experience of anger, frustration, and sadness coupled with feelings of consolation or even closure. Armenians have a bond to this landscape not just through history or family ties but also through inheriting the trauma of a loss of land or the destruction of home. Understanding the power and process of place attachment is, therefore, an essential backdrop in appreciating how narratives of dispossession and the juxtaposition of diaspora tourism shape prospects for forging new ties with their ancestral homelands in modern day eastern Turkey.

Given that the chapter makes an argument about the utility of a new conceptual approach (place attachment) in applying an understudied phenomenon (diaspora tourism) via a case (diaspora Armenians visiting eastern Turkey), the chapter begins with theory, delves into empirical data, and then concludes with two lines of commentary, one on the specifics of the main example reviewed and one on analytical tools that blend emotion and location concerns in the study of cosmopolitan curiosities. First, I outline the salient concepts and theories. There is a dearth of theoretical tools to evaluate diaspora tourism through a discussion of place itself, but I have assembled a framework of concepts borrowed from the field of Environmental Psychology. Second, after a brief explanation of the methodology used to collect data, I depict the history and practice of Armenian diaspora tourism. In particular I detail two guided Armenian diaspora tours that took place in 2009 and 2011, discussing the significant activities and behaviours of tour participants. Third, I distil the affective and social–political consequences of Armenian diaspora tourism as well as those of all forcibly displaced peoples in order to draw two sorts of conclusions. On the one hand, the need for new types of analysis to explain the broader phenomenon of the innate quest for belonging and the role of heritage tourism in contested lands. On the other hand, a review of the practical steps that can be taken for identity-building and cultural survival for diaspora groups longing to make peace with memories of loss and the land where their ancestors lived and in some cases died.

Conceptual framework: Place attachment and diaspora identity

Identity is a key driver of behaviour – who we are indicates something about what we do and why we do it – and, thus, in attempting to conceive why certain actions are taken scholars consider the values and experiences that inform people. And, this premise holds true in trying to explain the behaviour of diasporas. Accordingly, the defining experience of being in diaspora – of having left voluntarily, been exiled from, and in some instances lost, a homeland – influences communities that have migrated. In terms of thinking about diaspora identity construction this leads to a key debate: is identity connected to the physical place they have left, or is it impacted more by a psychological place of having left the physical place? In the former camp, some scholars argue that diasporic identity is by nature based on the relationship with a geography other than the one in which the diaspora is located (Basu 2007:

iii). The latter perspective is upheld by others who contend that: 'Detachment from a particular home grants the nomadic subject the ability to see the world, an ability that becomes the basis for a new global identity and community. In such a narrative, identity becomes fetishised, it becomes detached from the particularity of places which allow for its formation as such' (Ahmed 2000: 88). However, I maintain that diaspora identity is not the exclusive result of either one, but is rather a hybrid product that derives from the land (location) and the social dimension that comes with being displaced from it (affect). Therefore, the term 'place attachment' is vital as it brings together 'place' as well as the feelings toward that place ('attachment').

Place attachment is a concept used in Environmental Psychology regarding the complex mechanics of a person's bonding to a place. Setha Low (1992) defines place attachment as culturally shared meanings and activities associated with places that derive their value from socio-political, historical, and cultural sources. In her analysis of cultural origins of place attachment, Low lists the following six processes: genealogical bonding through history or family; linkage through loss of land or destruction; economic ties through ownership, inheritance, and politics; cosmological bonding through spiritual or mythological relationships; linkage through religious and secular pilgrimage and participation in celebratory cultural events; narrative ties through storytelling and place naming. From Low's perspective place attachment encompasses other attachments, such as to family, community, social status, religion – all of which originate in a place. As such, place attachment should be understood as complex constructions of individual and social experiences, collective histories, and selective memory (Kahn 1996: 167). Meanings attached to the landscape unfold in language, names, stories, myths, and rituals. These meanings are embedded into shared symbols and ultimately link people to a sense of common history and individual identity (ibid: 168). Places capture the complex emotional behavioural and moral relationships between people and their territory. They represent groups, their actions, their hopes, and their relationship to other groups.

The influences of place attachments that propel identity construction for diaspora communities can be seen at three levels. First, it can be found in the cultural practices of those who experienced displacement or have become rooted and versed in a mindset of the displaced. This is apparent in how they understand the concept of 'home'. Second, the sway of place attachment can be viewed in the educating of the next generation, i.e. the descendants of the original diaspora that are born into diaspora. 'Mediation' enables second and third generation diaspora members to become familiar with and connect to the experience of diaspora. Third, the weight of place attachment can be observed in relations between the diaspora and those outside their community. Whether it is relations with those from the same ethnicity that did not leave the homeland, or those not ethnically related but in the areas of the former homeland, or those not connected whatsoever, how the diaspora community interacts with them reveals that state of the vitality of identity construction.

Diaspora tours and their role in identity construction force us to rethink what home means as a lived space and as a narrative place. Place attachment is based on sensoriality (how the senses of sight, smell, hearing, taste and touch are stimulated) but also sociality (person-to-person interactions and shared experiences, such as walking, talking, sharing a meal etc.). This is underscored by Avtar Brah who differentiates between home as where one lives and home as where one 'comes from' in terms of affect (1996: 192). Home is a mythic place of desire in the diasporic imagination. In this sense, it is a place of no return, even if it is possible to visit the geographical territory that is seen as the place of 'origin'. On the other hand, home is also the lived experience of locality, its sounds and smells. For diasporas, it is the locality where individuals immerse themselves in and also the locality that 'intrudes into the senses: it defines what one smells, hears, touches, feels, and remembers' (Ahmed 2000: 89). Ahmed argues that the lived experience of being-at-home resembles a second skin and 'the subject and space leak into each other'. This means that the boundary between self and home is permeable, but also the boundary between home and away is permeable. In other words, those in diaspora develop an identity that locates home in a social context replete with emotional and psychological meaning rather than in a geographic spot in which their culture and identity are repressed.

Mediation is the common way in which second or third generation diaspora tourists (who had previously not been on diaspora tours) form attachment to their ancestral homeland. Their bond to that particular land is based on stories they had heard and photographs they had seen as opposed to first-hand experiences of the actual landscape. Having an accurate sense of the landscape from the recounted tales they heard from their grandparents or parents is not possible and what is experienced during heritage tours might be quite different from what they had imagined these places to be.

For members of a diaspora community that experience displacement first-hand as well as for those were born into diaspora, religious and secular pilgrimages, and participation in community-wide celebrations, have been instrumental in the development of place attachment. Moreover, direct contact and communion with physical settings builds a deeper, more visceral form of place attachment than one founded purely on social networks. Such wholehearted bonds can be characterised as *topophilia*, the affective relationship between humans and their environment or love of place (Tuan 1990). As I will explain, diaspora tourism evidences the core importance of cultural, biological, and affective place attachment.

Encountering the other is an important aspect of the diaspora tours – especially for diaspora Armenians. Their contacts with Turks and Kurds alike are framed by the memory of the genocide and denial, as well as the consequent historical construct of Turks as 'the other' after the genocide. Therefore, a potential social encounter between a diaspora Armenian and a local can either deconstruct this rigid perception or, depending on the nature of the contact, will further embed the recognition of the local as the 'other'.

Place attachment gets to the heart of identity construction for diaspora groups, but operationalising an approach to study it requires some additional concepts that address how such attachments form, regenerate, and endure. Five methods are instrumental to the process of making contested spaces into singular places (and from the perspective of studying place attachment are behavioural markers):

- *Place enacting*: Carrying out cultural practices that are uniquely connected to a specific area.
- *Place naming*: Delineating an area with a particular label.
- *Place historicising*: Enumerating a history associated with an area.
- *Place possessing*: Occupying (or reoccupying) an area in a physical or metaphorical sense.
- *Place socialising*: Connecting with others in a way that links to and locates a specific area.

The concept of place attachment makes a crucial contribution to explaining diaspora tourism because it brings to the fore the interrelation of identity, place, and memory – these three elements motivate tours and, in turn, are nurtured by tours. Identity is reshaped at personal and group levels in a way that more greatly coheres the community. A sense of place is influenced through generating first-hand experiences in sites visited. Memory is preserved by acts that challenge rival histories. From this we can see that journeys operate and impact at many levels: for individuals, they undergo a personal psychological transformation in coming to terms with the loss of family and in developing kin-based ties; for communities, these trips sustain culture and in particular pass it on to the next generation. Furthermore, sowing a sense of place at personal and community levels continues the political struggle to reclaim an endangered history. In the next section I will evidence the idea of place attachment by showing how diaspora tourism realises these efforts through conscious and intended practices.

Empirical case: Armenian diaspora tourism and the power of place attachment

This section substantiates the power of place attachment as an engine of identity construction and as a goal of diaspora groups in the case of Armenian diaspora tourism to eastern Turkey. Here I demonstrate a methodology for witnessing place attachment processes and production, provide a short history of the emergence of Armenian diaspora tourism, and present a deep descriptive analysis of two recent tours. While the empirical evidence illuminates the particularities of the situation of Armenians in eastern Turkey – an ethnic group visiting an area that their kin were violently dispossessed of – it will also serve as the basis for drawing out conclusions about the value of place attachment analysis.

Methods

At the outset it should be noted that the study of diaspora tourism entails casting a wide analytic net in order to capture all the relevant aspects. The best way to study the affective dimension of diaspora tourism was to gather ethnographic data from the tour participants. The survey material used in this article builds on a collaboration with Dr Anny Bakalian, a sociologist, who is Associate Director of MEMEAC at CUNY and was born in Lebanon of Armenian parents who trace their origin to Gesaria (Kayseri) in Central Anatolia.[1] Dr Bakalian participated in two diaspora tours to eastern Turkey/western Armenian in May 2009 and June 2011. After Bakalian's trips emails were sent to her fellow diaspora tourists asking them to fill out a questionnaire with impressions and feelings about the trip. More specifically, the questionnaire solicited information about the surprises experienced during the trip, expectations before the trip and feelings for the Turkish state and Turkish people before and after the trip.

Participant observation was part of the research, however, it is not included in this chapter (for Dr Bakalian's field notes, see Turan and Bakalian forthcoming). I will, however, draw on testimonials and chronicles by travellers in Armenian American publications and reports in Armenian American newspapers and on the Web to gain a deeper sense of the Armenian community's views on relations with their ancestral lands.

Self-awareness of the participants is another factor contributing to the kind of responses received. Especially for the participants in New York who are exposed to the psychology and politics behind the issues I am studying, the interviews included acts of self-making, and 'form-finding' that Galen Strawson (2004) describes as the ability to detect developmental coherencies in the manifold of a person's life (14–15). Therefore, their answers involved the creation of coherent narratives that they knew would be a part of scientific data. Undoubtedly, Bakalian's position as a fellow Armenian and 'pilgrim' added to the way they responded to these questions. I believe these answers reflected both their conscious and unconscious as well as the political and moral responsibility they felt for their collective group.

Historical background

For centuries Armenian and Turkish populations lived side by side in a relative state of peace – each community maintained their own cultural values and engaged in trade with the other. However, in the nineteenth century, as the Ottoman Empire was slowly pushed from Europe and felt the encroachment of newly formed Christian states in eastern and southeastern Europe, it sought to quell any internal threats from minorities. In sporadic instances in the 1890s and culminating in extreme violence and displacement in 1915, Armenian populations were victimised by the Ottoman Empire. The 1915 episode, what Armenians term 'the Aghet' (which translates as 'catastrophe'), has become a touchstone for Armenian identity, particularly for those whose families were victimised. Although the official narrative of the Turkish state attributes the Armenian deaths and exodus from Anatolia during the First World War to mutual civil unrest between the two ethno-religious groups, several Turkish historians including Taner Akçam (2006) and Müge Göçek (2011) contend that the 1915 events were, in fact, a genocide carried out as official policy of the Ottoman Empire. By contrast, those who deny that it was a genocide – though considerably fewer in number – including Guenter Lewy (2005), Justin McCarthy (2006), and Stanford J. Shaw (1992), argue that the violence was merely the product of the chaos of reciprocal ethnic hostilities and attacks.

This historical and political backdrop is relevant in understanding what is at stake in regard to Armenian diaspora tourism in eastern Turkey or what Armenians refer to as 'western Armenia'. Both diaspora Armenians and Turks claim the same historical lands. Moreover, disputed historiographies remain thus rendering any relation of Armenians to the land controversial. In short, the territory of historic Armenia (now eastern Turkey and the Republic of Armenia) is among the most significant pillars of Armenian identity (Panossian 2006: 228). For diaspora Armenians, who have been displaced from these lands, the so-called Aghet, has become a second cornerstone of their identity. Hrag Varjabedian (2009: 511) argues that Armenian Americans travel to Anatolia not 'to claim their ancestral homes, but to reconnect with their history and genealogy, creating a sense of wholeness within their familial history and identity'. Furthermore, the denial of the genocide by the Turkish state has played a large role in sustaining the narrative of loss because this keeps grievance current – the displacement experienced by the diaspora is not only the physical distance from the land but also a historical displacement that obscures their attachment to their ancestral land. Thus, the objective for the travellers is not framed as creating new bonds to a foreign place but rather is seen as revitalising historic ties through conducting rituals and other forms of performance.

The first known diaspora tour from the United States dates back to 1967 and was organised by the National Association for Armenian Studies and Research (NAASR).[2] From the 1970s until the 1990s, due to internal and external political factors, there were very few diaspora tours to eastern Turkey. First, armed conflict between the Turkish government and the Kurdistan Workers Party (PKK) in the 1980s, and continuing into the 1990s, deterred travel of all kinds to the region. However, after the capture of Kurdish leader Abdullah Öcalan, the violence had greatly abated by 2000. Second, the Armenian Secret Army for the Liberation of Armenia's (ASALA) assassinations of Turkish diplomats from 1975 to 1983 in cities like Paris, Geneva, Los Angeles, and Belgrade to demand public acknowledgement of the genocide and to take back the territory unleashed public rage against Armenians and made travel to Armenian sites untenable. The initiation of a rapprochement between the governments of Turkey and Armenia during the late 1990s led to a decline in tensions.

Consequently, in the last decade, eastern Turkey has become far more stable and safe for tourists, enabling Armenian Americans to visit and explore their ancestral lands.

Recent tours

Although safety issues are no longer paramount, there remains a serious knowledge-based challenge in organising Armenian diaspora tours: there are no maps or guidebooks, and very little substantial documentation of the Armenian presence beyond a handful of landmarks. There are not many tour operators that are well educated in Armenian history, culture, ruins, and relics in contemporary Turkey. This is partly because the names of villages, streets, and other place-markers of the early twentieth century have been changed in transition from the Empire to state with deliberate efforts to reinforce a new collective memory.

Currently the leading tour operator for Armenian diaspora tourism is Armen Aroyan. Through his travels in the 1990s, Aroyan has built an encyclopedic knowledge of remnants of Armenian culture in eastern Turkey. He gathered information from both Ottoman Armenians who participated in his earlier tours and also Armenians who were able to remain in that region of Turkey and converted to Islam or were left as children and raised by Turkish or Kurdish families. He knows both the Armenian and Turkish names of all the villages and towns in the region; moreover he maintains up-to-date information about the Armenian communities and cultural monuments that existed in the area prior to 1915.

Aroyan has arranged well over 80 such tours in the past 20 years. He tailors his tours – he takes people to their actual ancestral village/town, not simply historic Armenian sites such as Mount Ararat (symbol of Armenia for patriots and nationalists) and Ani (a medieval Armenian city on the Silk Road). Before each excursion, Aroyan contacts each participant to formulate an itinerary that encompasses where their families are originally from as well as other culturally significant places. Another important aspect of the three tours I look at is that each one included a scholar of Armenian history accompanying the group. In short, the tours are designed to not only familiarise participants with history, but to connect them at a personal and community level to the places they visit.

Heritage tours to eastern Turkey implicitly have the goal of facilitating place attachment. These temporally short trips cover psychologically great distances – a busy and intense couple of weeks may be life-changing for individuals and pivotal for the long-term sustenance of the community. A deeper look at the tour activities, and especially the conduct and reactions of participants from two Armenian diaspora tours in 2009 and 2011, supplemented with additional narratives, demonstrates the range of place attachment making practices.

Place enacting

One significant element of these tours is performing praying or chanting in Armenian churches, some of which are now converted into mosques. It is common for tour participants individually or as a group to offer a prayer at Armenian sites. An online testimony from a 1999 trip is a good example of this dynamic:[3]

> In 1839, Surp Kevork was renovated. While excavating, the workers found a container of Holy Muron (Chrism) bearing the seal of St. Nersess Shnorhali (the Graceful). Also found was a parchment on which was inscribed the seal of King Hetum II (1289–1297). Within these sacred walls, I offered

Hokehankisd [requiem service] for the souls of my parents, grandparents, other members of the Kherdian family, and for all the inhabitants who lived and died on this land. It was a very emotional moment to be at the very place of my roots where my father and generations of Kherdians had lived.

These invocations are religious in nature but the effect is psychological and geographical as the liturgy is given greater meaning by the enactments being held on land that has been dubbed as sacred to Armenians. The act of cultural identification at these sites roots participants to the land.

Place naming

Maps and other geographical identifiers are powerful representations of how place is controlled, and in eastern Turkey the names of towns, topographical features, and regions are no exception. Armenian diaspora tours present an opportunity to engage in the symbolic struggle by referencing places according to their Armenian names.

An instance from Bakalian's 2009 trip exemplifies this renaming. Two tour participants switched the Turkish name of *Anı Örenyeri* (Anı means ruins in Turkish) of the medieval capital of Armenian Kingdom back to its original Armenian name Ani on a signpost. This simple yet significant political act of dotting the "ı" was achieved using a couple of Band-Aids and a pen.

Place historicising

Telling the history of a place while visiting it is another means to cultivate bonds. The literal grounding of a narrative by affixing it to a place and having that place embody it powerfully links people to the land. Several participants stated that they did not have a real sense of the landscape from the tales they heard from their grandparents or parents and what they saw was quite different from what they had imagined these villages to be. Their experience was a physical confirmation and it felt like a homecoming. A male participant in the 2011 diaspora tour wrote:

It was very emotional knowing that they have lived within these walls, walked the same streets, past the same buildings and prayed in the same church . . . For the first time, I could see through their eyes and I imagined what they had witnessed and only reluctantly spoke about. I think what I gained was being able to put all of what I had ever heard or read, or seen in photographs together into a current image.

A second illustration of place historicising (and also indicative of topophilia) is apparent in an online testimonial of a diaspora tourist in Ani:

That afternoon I was sitting in the window of one of the ruins overlooking the vast area below. Never have I seen a sight more beautiful. In front and above us were the mountains of Armenia. Below flowed the peaceful Akhurian River which separates Ani from the rest of Armenia. It was a place I did not want to leave. The words of a song my father used to sing came back to me, 'Ani kaghak nusder goolam . . . I am the city of Ani sitting and weeping.'[4]

The adage that it is the 'victors' of history that write it signals the magnitude of the power of defining it. For Armenian diaspora tourists, their very presence in these places enables writing a history of their own, and thus, proclaims the survival and resilience of their culture.

Place possessing

Land has an enduring quality that cultures value – it is a persistent surrogate of people, a reminder that their society had a place. To possess it has great importance to communities that have been displaced from it. In a physically small but metaphorically meaningful way Armenian diaspora tourism allows reclaiming of land, repossessing of place. This is exemplified by a photo taken by tour participants in 2011 in which they pose wearing the three colours of the Armenian flag (red, blue, and orange) with Mount Ararat in the background. This seemingly harmless gesture is in fact a not so subtle attempt to reclaim Armenian heritage in the region, as significant as if they had planted a flag in the ground or constructed a formal memorial.

Another display of this place possessing is planting flower seeds in memory of people who were killed, leaving burning candles at Ani to claim that 1915 is not forgotten, and leaving shoes or socks in front of the door of the participant's family home in their ancestral village – which was meant to suggest that the family still lived there.

A third manifestation of place possessing is collecting dirt. A participant remarked on the comfort provided by bringing back Ziploc bags filled with dirt to spread on his father's burial plot in California. Taking the soil from the ancestral homeland and putting it on graves of those who were born there completes a metaphorical circle that had been broken.

An online travel blog from a half-Armenian diaspora tourist incorporates photographs into her chronicles of her trip to Kharpert (now Harput) where her paternal grandmother was born. She talks about how she is looking at the same view her grandmother looked at 100 years ago as if she is connecting with her grandmother through the place. She adds, 'I thought it was the most beautiful sight I've ever seen.' On a different photograph, we see her footprints in the snow, which she titles as 'My own footprints in this town'.[5]

Through these acts, participants create genealogical and historical continuity based on the land (Varjabedian 2009: 528–9). In short, the tour affords the dispossessed to repossess, and this repossession cements and makes tangible what has been a seemingly obscure connection to the land.

Place socialising

Place is a social construct and asset; its significance in a psychological and social sense is based on its role in generating meaning for people. Thus, though land itself may have inherently valuable characteristics, such as being fertile or rich in minerals, it is through the prism of identity, culture, and politics that land also has worth. However, the experience of place – the attachments to people felt through the attachments to land – can also be felt in social interactions. In other words, place may substitute for people (a way to connect to forbearers), but people can also be a proxy for place (a social contact recalls the place where the sense of community is felt). Armenian diaspora tourism engages in place socialising on two levels.

First, the journeys to Armenian places engender bonding between tour participants. The conditions of the tour are ripe for building a sense of community; participants share not just a bloodline but also a similar worldview – as descendants of genocide survivors they all have a perspective grounded in loss. Moreover, these tours have been more popular for Armenian Americans than other forms of travel for practical logistical reasons. Given these factors, the site visits, communal meals, and long bus rides give the trip a ritualistic quality. Everyone makes an effort to share and mix, friendships are developed, and as one of the participants remarked, 'much laughter and tears are exchanged among the pilgrims'.

A second form of place socialising occurs in interactions between Armenian diaspora tourists and local Turkish and Kurdish populations; in visiting formerly Armenian areas, visitors come into contact with those that presently live there. Although Armenian Americans have contact with local populations throughout their tour, the quality of contact seems to be more superficial than genuine. First, diaspora tourists travel in a group and have a very busy itinerary. Second, there is a language barrier between locals (villagers) and tourists. The most genuine contacts they have are with the bus drivers (Kurdish), service personnel, and with locals who can speak English. However, when genuine contact does occur between a tourist and a local (e.g. a Turkish person apologising after learning the tourist was Armenian), it leaves a significant impact on the tourist. Mostly contact engenders heartening flashback or comfortable reminiscence as the Armenian tourists see much of themselves, their families, and their community in the foods, lifestyles, and customs of Turkish society.

This is epitomised in *A Family Erased*, a documentary by George Kachadorian.[6] The documentary follows the director's family as they journey from the United States to find their grandparents' home in the village of Huseynik (now Ulukent) based on the maps their grandparents drew from memory. When his father and his two aunts arrive in Ulukent, they see that the village has 'not changed much in one hundred years, [and it] looks just like in the pictures in the old books'. The father summarises his experience: 'When Armenians go to Turkey, everything looks familiar. They know what the food is, they like the food, they know what the music is, they like the music. People look like relatives of ours. It is not an unfamiliar place.' His aunt then chimes in and says:

> The most moving thing were the children. Again, very familiar. They look like our kids, they really do. Beautiful brown faces, beautiful eyes. Kids were bringing us flowers, holding our hands. You do feel very connected to not only the place but to the people even. And that is also a little confusing.

The aunt's puzzlement is not uncommon when we look at the post-trip impressions of diaspora tour participants. Their connection with the landscape and with Turkish people seems strange to them because it challenges their diaspora identity as Armenians. The newfound bond with people formerly seen as enemies is not something they could foresee before their trip. Confirming this sentiment, a tour participant from 2012 wrote:

> It is easier to humanise Turks when you're surrounded by them. I grew up hearing stories about the Genocide, seeing images, developing strong feelings about Turks and Turkey. From the airport in New York, where I started the journey, surrounded by Turks on the same flight and a Turkish man being friendly with me, to whom I had a terrible reaction, to the time when I found myself in Turkey surrounded by millions of Turks, the intensity of my reaction changed. I was at times appalled by individual Turks, a soldier, for example, or a certain villager, who reminded of the Turks I had learned of from my grandparents and others, but more often I saw that they're people living their lives, just as do we . . . families, children, parents, workers, couples, etc.

And another participant from 2012 tour wrote, 'I have mixed feelings on my trips. It is so familiar; the food, the culture, the music, the way people act, it is [all] so familiar.'

This is a perfect illustration of the experience of diasporic homeland as juxtaposition first as a memory of lived experience through senses and also as a narrative through re-creation of the 'other' (bad Turk) and finally, embodying the stranger. Armenian diaspora tourism, therefore, withers the narrative of mutual animosity and threat, and yields unanticipated feelings of understanding. The contested lands that had so violently divided Armenians and Turks bring them together as the visitors come to see what they lost and in the process sometimes discover a new, albeit strange, appreciation for those who now inhabit those lands. This is not to suggest that in witnessing and having dealings with Turkish culture the genocide is suddenly forgotten or forgiven, but that the pursuit of place attachment creates opportunities for Armenian diaspora tourists to encounter Turkish populations, and that potentially furthers more friendly relations and abets prospects for reconciliation.

Conclusions: Place attachment through the emotion and location prism

This section reflects on the framework of the first section and the evidence of the second section so as to make two types of contribution. First, to the understanding of Armenian diaspora tours to eastern Turkey; what it means in terms of identity for this sector of Armenians as well as how it influences ongoing disputes between the Armenian diaspora and the Turkish government and local populations that control key parts of historic Armenia. Second, to making sense of the power and process of place attachment; how it impacts identity and what is the research agenda for this line of inquiry.

Why Armenian diaspora tourism matters

One of the most important outcomes of a diaspora tour for participants is the multi-faceted nature of place attachment to eastern Turkey. Their first-hand experience of the landscape, the people, the food, and the music opens up new possibilities for these individuals to form healthier attachments to the place that are not just based on the narrative of loss and destruction. This has developmental significance in re-defining an individual's narrative in a more positive light.

Based on surveys, the overwhelming majority of the respondents state that the tour in which they participated had a meaningful impact on them. Some even reported that the experience was 'life-changing'. The heritage tours normalise the new experiences in a psychological sense; the new experience replaces the burdens of the past. The individual is able to move forward although this does not mean for-getting. While the memories of the trauma of the Aghet remain, they are no longer debilitating. Cuisine, music, dance – shared by Armenians, Kurds, and Turks alike – are part of the favourable experience.

Diaspora Armenians grow up hearing family and friends recount Turkish atroci-ties, 'their psyche and identity are organized around these stories' (Topalian 2004: 227). Consequently, trips to Turkey are loaded with implications at the level of immediate personal reactions of tour participants and, more importantly, wider rami-fications for the Armenian diaspora and the preservation of Armenian identity.

These journeys help individuals liberate themselves from the constraints of the genocide paradigm and create their own life narrative or counter-narratives in order to reinvent themselves the way they understand themselves to be (Varjabedian 2009: 203). Many Armenians, discover on their heritage tour that they had an understanding of locals (Kurds, Turks), and others had a similar reac-tion in encountering common physical and cultural elements. Media and technol-ogy provide a space in which these narratives can be devised and disseminated as texts and video clips on personal blogs or YouTube. Furthermore, digital storytell-ing contributes to the interpretation of cultural heritage by allowing actors to bring to light new meanings within their own cultural, material, and virtual environment (Cunningham 2010: 198).

Diaspora Armenians who take these tours, however, do not stop demanding recognition of the genocide. On the contrary, almost all of the participants who completed our survey stated that they continue to insist on acknowledgement, if not apology, from Turkey for the injustices carried out by the Ottoman Empire. To that end, we asked the participants to describe their feelings toward the state of Turkey and the Turkish people before and after their trip. Before the trip, the words they used to describe their feelings toward the state are 'anger', 'negative', 'hostility', 'fear', 'frustration', 'terrible', and 'bitterness'. Their post-trip responses mostly include the word 'same' and one person said, 'more aggravated seeing the level of destruction'. When it comes to the second part of the question that refers to the Turkish people, most participants struck a discernibly more positive note in stating that they have no problems with the average Turk, but they maintain their grievance against the government of Turkey. They felt less negative toward the 'average man' on the street. They were able to distinguish the Turkish people from the government. Thus, although diaspora tourism builds cultural bridges between the descendants of Armenians and the landscape and local populations of Turkey, it has not unlocked the door to political reconciliation between Armenia and Turkey.

Why place attachment matters

The findings that stem from an analysis of diaspora tourism point to far more complexity in gauging the significance of identity and its two-way relationship with place. Moreover, it showcases the intricacy of how identity is constructed, maintained and changed. However, as my analysis shows, a way forward in interpreting diaspora tourism is place attachment.

Identity can be derived from many sources: gender, ethnicity, culture, class, etc. And, indeed, not just many sources, but multiple sources simultaneously. But place has a special and distinctive role – everyone is from somewhere though not everyone is necessarily sensitised to their position in society or the economy. Other sources of identity aside from place should not be discounted, but place, particularly for groups that have experienced a shared trauma that led to their displacement, plays a fundamental part in defining and cohering the group. That is to say, while the identity of individuals tends to layer different components (ethnicity, gender, etc.), group diaspora identity is usually based on their one enduring commonality – their homeland.

Place attachment provides a window into diaspora identity. In the first part of this chapter I enumerated five behaviours associated with place attachment – place enacting, place naming, place historicising, place possessing, place socialising – so that they could be traced in evaluating the present condition of the identity of diaspora communities, and specifically those of Armenians from eastern Turkey in the case I have examined in detail. But this is not the only case where these dynamics are at work, and the research agenda for those who study forcibly displaced diasporas should include applying place attachment concepts to measure group behaviour, group coherence, and socio-psychological and political outcomes.

The grievances of these forced diaspora groups can lead to them transforming the lands from which they fled into battlegrounds. For there to be any hope of resolving these sorts of conflicts, there must be a greater understanding of what motivates belligerence on both sides, and in these instances it is often place attachment. Through a greater appreciation of place attachment and new analytical tools to make sense of its value, its means, and its ends, there is a better chance at addressing the problem of lost homelands. Maps of current political geography in many ways do a disservice to our understanding of the world because without knowing the emotions behind locations, place attachment is neglected, identity is obscured, and the ability to see the world as it really is, is lost. The lens of place attachment does not promise to right all wrongs for the forcibly displaced, but by offering a potential path to comfort, space for peace and reconciliation becomes possible.

Note

For a more extensive treatment of the ethnographic data and also field notes of Anny Bakalian please see Z. Turan and A. Bakalian (forthcoming) 'Diaspora Tourism and Identity: Subversion and Consolation in Armenian Pilgrimages to Eastern Turkey', in A. Gorman and S. Kasbarian (eds) *Contextualising Community: Diasporas of the Modern Middle East*, Edinburgh: Edinburgh University Press.

Notes

1   Dr. Bakalian and I began our collaboration on this research project in 2009. Some of the data gathered in that undertaking informs the findings of this chapter.
2   Founded in 1955, NAASR is the only national non-profit organization dedicated to the advancement of Armenian Studies through education, research, and cultural programmes. It is also interesting to note that for the first NAASR heritage tour in 1967 'Turkey' is used as a destination. In a 2012 announcement, for example, the trip is to 'Historic Armenian Communities of Asia Minor and Cilicia'. This shows how the discourse of the specific geography has changed over the years. The 50th anniversary commemoration of the genocide has a symbolic meaning in that sense. Up until then in the USSR, the genocide commemorations were banned as they were deemed 'nationalistic' and the Soviet regime was deemed by Armenian nationalists as the central power against the nation. However, as local liberties were extended to individual states within the USSR in the 1970s, the forming of ASALA in Lebanon focused on Turkey as the greatest enemy (see R. Peroomian (1993) *Literary Responses to Catastrophe: A Comparison of the Armenian and the Jewish Experience*, Atlanta, GA: Scholars Press).
3   'Bittersweet Journey' by Archdeacon Charles Hardy. Available at www.bvahan.com/armenianpilgrimages/hardy2.htm (accessed 1 October 2013).
4   Available at www.bvahan.com/armenianpilgrimages/hardy2.htm (accessed 1 October 2013).
5   Available at http://brittanygoesglobal.com/pictures-from-the-town-my-great-grandmother-was-born-harput-turkey (accessed 1 October 2013).
6   Available at www.pbs.org/frontlineworld/watch/player.html?pkg=rc74turkey&seg=1&mod=0 (accessed 1 October 2013).

References

Ahmed, S. (2000) *Strange Encounters: Embodied Others in Post-Coloniality*, London: Routledge.

Akçam, T. (2006) *A Shameful Act: The Armenian Genocide and the Question of Turkish Responsibility*, New York: Metropolitan Books.

Basu, P. (2007) *Highland Homecomings: Genealogy and Heritage Tourism in the Scottish Diaspora*, London: Routledge.

Bauman, Z. (1998) *Globalization: The Human Consequences*, New York: Columbia University Press.

Brah, A. (1996) *Cartographies of Diaspora: Contesting Identities*, London: Routledge.

Cunningham, P.A. (2010) 'The impact of media on cultural heritage: Disruptive or synergistic?', *Journal of Heritage Tourism*, 5 (3): 189–201.

Göçek, F.M. (2011) 'Reading Genocide: Turkish Historiography on 1915', in R.G. Suny, F.M. Göçek and N.M. Naimark (eds) *A Question of Genocide: Armenians and Turks at the End of the Ottoman Empire*, Oxford/New York: Oxford University Press.

Kahn, M. (1996) 'Your Place and Mine: Sharing Emotional Landscapes in Wamira, Papua New Guinea', in S. Feld and K. Basso (eds) *Senses of Place*, Santa Fe, NM: School of American Research Press.

Lewy, G. (2005) *The Armenian Massacres in Ottoman Turkey: A Disputed Genocide*, Salt Lake City, UT: University of Utah Press.

Low, S. (1992) 'Place Attachment in the Plaza', in I. Altman and S. Low (eds) *Place Attachment*, New York: Plenum Press.

McCarthy, J. (2006) *The Armenian Rebellion at Van*, Salt Lake City, UT: The University of Utah Press.

Panossian, R. (2006) *The Armenians: From Kings and Priests to Merchants and Commissars*, New York: Columbia University Press.

Shaw, S.J. and Shaw, E.K. (1992) *History of the Ottoman Empire and Modern Turkey*, Cambridge: Cambridge University Press.

Strawson, G. (2004) 'A Fallacy of Our Age: Not Every Life is a Narrative', *Times Literary Supplement*, 15 October, 13–15.

Topalian, S. (2004) 'Daughters and Granddaughters of Survivors: From Horror to Finding Our Own Voices', in M.A. Mamigonian (ed.) *The Armenians of New England: Celebrating a Culture and Preserving a Heritage*, Belmont, MA: Armenian Heritage Press.

Tuan, Y. (1990) *Topophilia: A Study of Environmental Perception, Attitudes, and Values*, New York: Columbia University Press.

Turan, Z. and Bakalian, A. (forthcoming) 'Diaspora Tourism and Identity: Subversion and Consolation in Armenian Pilgrimages to Eastern Turkey', in A. Gorman and S. Kasbarian (eds) *Contextualising Community: Diasporas of the Modern Middle East*, Edinburgh: Edinburgh University Press.

Varjabedian, H. (2009) 'The poetics of history and memory: The mutual instrumental of Armenian genocide narratives', PhD dissertation, University of Wisconsin, Madison.

PART IV

Cosmopolitanism in the home
North American belongings

10

CRIME WATCH

Mediating belonging and the politics of place in inner-city Jamaica

Rivke Jaffe

Introduction

From the 1980s onwards, Jamaican gangs became notorious for their success in building transnational crime networks. The gangs' geographical reach largely corresponded with the cities and countries where Jamaican immigrants settled. Their networks built on and extended earlier patterns of narcotics trafficking, but became more geographically diverse and more violent as the focus shifted from marijuana to cocaine. Drugs, guns and people began to travel along cross-border circuits that stretched from Downtown Kingston to inner-city neighbourhoods in New York, Toronto and London. The notoriety of the so-called 'yardies', as Jamaican gang members came to be called, grew as they received increasing attention from North American and European media. Various mass-mediated representations, from televised specials to mainstream movies and investigative journalism, have framed Jamaican gangs for non-Jamaican audiences. On the whole, these accounts depict Jamaican criminals as extraordinarily violent and ruthless, much to the distress of many Jamaicans at home and in the diaspora. Such stereotypical representations of ghettos and gangsters reflect and reinforce dominant imaginative geographies that depict Jamaica as a lawless, criminogenic space, and, many feel, they both diminish the appeal of the island as a tourist destination and cause difficulties for Jamaicans who live or travel abroad.

The residents of Jamaica's most stigmatised inner-city neighbourhoods are rarely the intended audience of these circulating representations of Jamaican crime. Nonetheless, they too engage actively with these representations. Based on ethnographic research with residents of a West Kingston neighbourhood that gave birth to one of the island's major 'posses', this chapter discusses such engagements. I explore how mass-mediated depictions of crime intersect with what can be understood as a transnational affective geography. Residents with whom I socialised were eager to watch crime documentaries, expressing empathy, intimacy and disappointment as they discussed their relationships with, and knowledge of, the featured criminals. I understand residents' responses to these images of transnational Jamaican crime as part of a process of relational place-making, in which belonging to Downtown Kingston is construed through connections to a broader network of urban places and through licit and illicit translocal flows. From this perspective, these representations do more than just reproduce stigmatising images. They also connect marginalised urban populations across borders, framing place attachment to Jamaican 'ghetto' space and inscribing circuits of transnational belonging.

Various authors (Massey 2004; Amin 2004) have emphasised the relational character of urban places. Ash Amin (2004: 34) writes of cities 'as nodes that gather flow and juxtapose diversity, as places of overlapping – but not necessarily locally connected – relational networks, as perforated entities . . . [They] come with no automatic promise of territorial or systemic integrity.' Places such as Downtown Kingston and its 'ghetto' neighbourhoods are constituted in part through the transnational networks and mobilities of people, goods, ideas and money. These networks include the transnational communities of Jamaicans who reside primarily in urban areas of the UK, US and Canada. In UK cities, neighbourhoods with a strong Jamaican presence have included Peckham and Handsworth, described elsewhere in this volume by Emma Jackson and Kieran Connell. They are also shaped by transnational criminal networks and economies through which guns, drugs and cash come to travel, and by the transnational media that produce and circulate images and imaginaries about these people, places and criminal activities.

Through a discussion of residents' engagements with these representations, I seek to extend work in geography that has focused on the mediation and communication of space and place, by emphasising not just media texts but their consumption, and by showing how precisely this consumption, interpretation and appropriation of media is central to a relational politics of place. Ethnographic research is especially useful in understanding the emotions that structure this mediated place-making. However, such research – especially in and on high-crime areas – also inevitably has an affective impact on the ethnographer herself. Following a discussion of crime, media and place, I turn to the Caribbean and its dominant representations. I focus on the ways that residents of 'Brick Town', where I did most of my fieldwork, construct local and transnational forms of belonging. In exploring these place-based processes of identification, I emphasise the effects of emotions such as excitement and happiness, as well as fear, on both residents and the ethnographer.

Crime, media and the politics of place

I seek to understand how emotion and location intersect by focusing on transnationally circulating media representations and their more local appropriations. The relationship between media and place is a main concern of the emerging field of media and communication geography. Various scholars have begun to concentrate on 'how communication produces place and how space produces communication' (Jansson and Falkheimer 2006: 9). Different types of media are also always emplaced and characterised by specific spatialities. They are produced, distributed and consumed in specific places, and through spatially specific networks (Adams 2009). These geographies of production and consumption are often power-laden. The capacity to create and distribute representations, and access and exposure to them, are unevenly distributed and often reproduce inequalities along lines of gender, class and ethnicity (see e.g. Mahtani 2009). Despite the democratisation of media production that the Internet has enabled, much of the media that we are able to watch, read or hear is produced in a relatively limited number of newsrooms, publishing houses and music and film studios. These spaces are often socially exclusive and tend to be peopled by relatively homogeneous groups of producers. Similarly, our access and exposure to mass media – newspapers, television channels, radio stations – still tends to be largely structured through the urban or national spaces, as well as the transnational circuits, in which we dwell.

While media, then, are always spatially embedded, our experiences of space and place are always mediated. Television, movies, songs, books, paintings and the Internet all shape the ways in which we understand regions, places and mobilities by imbuing them with emotion and meaning (Zimmermann 2007). These 'imaginative geographies' (Gregory 1995), from stigmatising narratives about neighbourhoods on 'the wrong side of the tracks' to imperial discourse that posits a hierarchy of 'West' over 'East', have real material influences. They influence how we interact with specific places and people seen as 'other'. However, these imaginative geographies also help people recognise who is *not* other: processes of place-making, drawing on shared place-associations and territorially based identities, are central to framing and mobilising community (Martin 2003). In addition, the use of media and communication technologies, from print media to the Internet, enables the development of new social or virtual spaces and associated communities, from the nation to Second Life (Anderson 1983; Boellstorff 2008).

These various connections between space, place and media are often political (Rosati 2007), not least because of the ways in which affect, politics and space are connected (Thrift 2004). Where and by whom are the most popular media produced and circulated, and how is access regulated? Which place narratives and imaginative geographies become dominant, and how does this bolster existing power structures? Conversely, how do counter-narratives destabilise power structures? A critical geography of media and communication addresses such questions. However, the focus in this field, like in much of broader media studies, has tended to be on cultural analyses of the content of media texts themselves, followed by analyses of the political economy of media production. Less attention has gone to studying how these media texts are consumed, appropriated and interpreted in a range of contexts.[1]

In analysing representations of Jamaican crime, I want to understand their discursive power, and in what broader political contexts these representations are produced. In so doing I want to think through what type of imaginative geography comes to stand in for Jamaica, and how this ties into longer colonial histories. However, I want to focus most closely on how people who live in those places and who are indirectly the topic of those representations engage with them actively, and how we can understand the effects of those engagements. I am interested in how crime documentaries, as aesthetic objects, 'do not just provide evocations of times past or moral reckonings but affective senses of space, literally territories of feeling' (Thrift 2008: 11). Such a focus on the consumption and appropriation of these representations can help us understand the entanglement of affect and mediation in processes of place-making.

In addition, in thinking through the connections between media and the politics of place, I want to draw on the work of authors such as Ash Amin (2004) and Doreen Massey (2004) who argue for relational, processual, multi-scalar understandings of place. This approach sees places – cities, neighbourhoods, countries – not as stable or fixed, but as processes, with multiple meanings and fluid boundaries constituted through translocal relations. A place is only constituted relationally, through multiple connections and flows; cities in this view are continuously changing spatial formations, nodes where different relational networks overlap. Places are the dynamic outcome of ongoing negotiation and, accordingly, place-making is always a contested process. If we understand place relationally, and as a process of contestation, this also has consequences for how we approach mediated place narratives, emplaced media consumption, and the political implications of both.

Representing the Caribbean

The representation of Caribbean islands has remained remarkably constant. They have long been imagined as tropical Edens: lush, tropical, green spaces that stand in contrast to the urban, civilised, temperate spaces of Europe and North America. This exotic imaginary of the Caribbean – which is echoed and reworked in the tropical abundance of contemporary London markets described by Alex Rhys-Taylor in this volume – attracted colonial adventurers from botanists to planters, and it continues to draw millions of tourists to the region annually. However, the trope of paradise has also long been accompanied by a complementary form of representation that emphasises danger and lawlessness (Sheller 2004; Thompson 2006). Jamaica, in particular, has often been depicted as a wild, unruly space where both climate and inhabitants may pose a threat to visitors. Such representations also have their roots at least partly in the racialised imagery of colonialism, when slave uprisings and Maroon attacks on plantations threatened the colonial fantasy of a productive tropical paradise. They continue, however, in postcolonial depictions of the urban poor, of gang wars and drugs traffickers, of a violent dystopian Jamaica that serves as a counterbalance to the Edenic tourist trope.

These more dystopian representations of urban squalor and violence are evident in popular culture, both locally and internationally. As Deborah Thomas (2011: 147) notes, 'violence is central to many popular representations of Jamaica within contemporary film and fiction, not only in those stereotypical representations produced by so-called outsiders'. The emphasis on violence is prominent in a range of local and international movies focusing on Jamaican gangsters, from the 1970s classic *The Harder They Come* to more recent productions such as *Shottas* and *Rude Boy* (Harewood 2008; Mennel 2008: 170–4). The sometime glorification of violence within the musical genre of dancehall (a more fast-paced, electronic version of reggae) has also reinforced perceptions of Jamaica as an aggressive, ghettoised space. The reputation of Jamaicans (and Jamaican men, in particular) as deviant and violent has also been bolstered through decades of journalistic reports of urban poverty and crime. These reports, which have often been sensationalist and racialised, have served to stigmatise and criminalise African-Jamaicans, both in Jamaica and in relation to Jamaicans in the diaspora (Murji 1999; D'Arcy 2007). It is on these journalistic representations that I want to focus here, drawing on fieldwork I conducted in the context of a larger project on crime and citizenship in urban Jamaica.

Crime watch

Most of my fieldwork was focused on a neighbourhood I will call Brick Town, a West Kingston 'ghetto' (the names of the neighbourhood, the local gang and the people quoted in this article are all pseudonyms). Until a few years ago, this neighbourhood had been governed by a man I will refer to as 'the General', a prominent 'don', as local leaders associated with criminal organisations are known. The General was associated with a gang I call the West Side Posse, which dated back to the 1940s and had strong connections with one of Jamaica's two main political parties. I spent a lot of my time in the neighbourhood hanging out at cookshops, informal restaurants where many residents would stop by to eat or chat. One of these cookshops had a TV and a DVD player, and there were always people watching the illegally copied DVDs that could be bought in Kingston's markets or from street vendors for less than a pound. In 2010, I worked with a number of research assistants from different inner-city neighbourhoods throughout Kingston, and one of them had given me a copy of a DVD titled 'Lords of the Mafia Jamaica'. I had never got around to watching it, but then I got the idea of watching it together with residents in the shop.

On the day I showed up with the DVD, the player was broken but I was able to persuade one of the people living in the yard surrounding the shop to lend us his DVD player. Various regulars grouped around the TV to watch it with me, including the cookshop owner. The crowd included market vendors who had stopped by to take a break, as well as employees coming off their shift at a nearby hospital. Most ate our cooked lunch from Styrofoam boxes, while the regulars had their rice served into their own bowls made from calabashes. Together, we crowded onto wooden benches and improvised seats made from crates and buckets to watch the show. The DVD turned out to contain a series of documentaries, starting with a BBC show from the 1980s on the 'yardie' gangs, interviewing many different people in Downtown Kingston. This was followed by a series of American cable TV shows focusing on yardie crime in the US, especially New York. The final set of programmes appeared to be a Canadian series, linking Jamaican gangs in Toronto to Kingston.

Some parts of the DVD, especially the American shows, were quite sensational, with dramatic voiceovers, spectacular shots of guns, drugs and squalor, and scenes in which armed law enforcement figures hunted down alleged criminals in suspense-filled chases. I was wondering if the men I was watching it with would be offended at the ways in which Downtown Kingston, and Jamaicans more generally, were being represented internationally. However, they did not really seem to be watching it this way at all – they were more interested in recognising and commenting on the various individuals and places featured in the DVD.

For instance, the 1980s shows featured Chubby Dread, a prominent don from the central Kingston neighbourhood of Southside, who had died in the 2000s. Watching these scenes, the viewers all started pointing to the people they recognised: 'Chubby that!' 'Chubby right hand that!' A little later a female politician appeared in the show and one of the men exclaimed: 'She did mawga dem time deh!' – she was skinny in those days. Spotting many people they recognised from decades ago, they commented on what had happened to them in the meantime. Recognising someone called 'Uzi' from the Renkers Crew, for instance, one of the men informed the others that Uzi was now in prison in the US. A man called Broomie came up on the screen, and someone explained to me that 'Oh, he's from Tel Aviv [a central Kingston neighbourhood[2]], he got shot in his belly.' It was almost like watching old family videos and reminiscing on how relatives' or friends' appearances had changed, and what had become of them in the meantime.

The comments were also quite critical, as people started talking back at the screen, similar to how many viewers at home might also habitually talk back to their television. One of the DVD's shows featured a don explaining how he and his men would take up weapons in election time, to get out the vote for the politicians to whom they were affiliated (see Sives 2002, 2010; Harriott 2008 on the 'garrison politics' that connect politicians, criminal leaders and the urban poor). 'And what you get in return?', someone shouted back, implying that it had all been for nothing.

While the men were critical of the way dons and so-called *shottas* [gunmen] let themselves be used by *politricks*, they also reproduced some of the attitudes intrinsic to the rule of the don. Within the so-called garrisons over which these dons preside, the golden rule is that you may never talk to the police about the illegal activities that go on in the neighbourhood. To do that is to be an informer, and the rule is *Informer fi dead*, informers must die. When Tony Brown, a don from Rockfort, a neighbourhood in East Kingston, appeared on the screen and started explaining how some aspects of the illegal economy worked, various people started shouting at the screen: 'A informer ting that!' [That is an informer thing!] 'Informer!'

More broadly, the group of men viewing the DVD with me were not so much concerned with denying any of the illegal acts being portrayed in the documentaries. One scene included an exposé of passport forging, after a whole set of passports disappeared from the US embassy in Kingston: 'Dem times deh did nice! Yu cyaan do that again . . .' [Those times back then were nice! You can't do that anymore . . .].

However, the crime and conflict were still not their main focus. As we watched a DEA raid in Brooklyn, with heavily armed security forces knocking down a door and running through a brownstone building in order to arrest Jamaican drug dealers, Nicholas, one of my friends in Brick Town who was also watching, started smiling. 'A my likkle corner that!' he exclaimed. 'Your corner?' I asked. I knew he had lived abroad but I did not know that it had been in Brooklyn. 'Yes man, that is where all the West Side Posse men ended up', Nicholas answered, referring to the Brick Town gang, which had indeed had a prominent presence in New York in the 1980s. So again, he was watching the shows not so much to learn about raids, drugs and guns; nor did he express any obvious distress about the rather lurid ways in which Jamaicans were being depicted. Rather, he was engaging intimately with the people and places portrayed in these quite sensational documentaries, and it made him happy to see faces and streets that he hadn't seen in a long time. One of the younger viewers was also quite enthused and was emphatic that 'mi must get a copy a dis' and made arrangements with a friend of mine to have it copied.

Born fi' Dead

Not all responses to foreign depictions of Jamaican crime are equally positive. On another day, earlier in the same year, I drove into Brick Town and parked my car in front of a business owned by the neighbourhood's former don, who has been in prison for several years now. The business was now run by one of the General's relatives, Lorraine. I had been introduced to Lorraine the year before – she was never very talkative but I always tried to greet her politely and we had what I felt was a cordial relationship. As I parked I saw Kevin, a young man I had interviewed the year before. I bought him a fried chicken lunch and we sat at Lorraine's business talking about his attempts to get a visa to go to the US. Though more formal than the cookshop, Lorraine's place was another main neighbourhood hangout where many residents would pass through to greet each other, eat lunch and catch up on the news. While we were waiting for Kevin's meal I saw Benjamin, a young man who used to work at Lorraine's business, but whom I had not seen for a while. He told me he had started to work at a sandwich shop in Southside, the neighbourhood in central Kingston where he was from. He was just in Brick Town to say hi to his old boss. Lorraine's daughter, who also worked in her mother's business, started teasing Benjamin about how dangerous Southside was. Benjamin laughed and said it wasn't true and made me promise to come look him up. Just then Lorraine passed by and told him 'No, don't take her to Southside, we don't want no *Born fi' Dead*, it mash up di ting' [it messed everything up].

Born fi' Dead (Gunst 1996) – literally, 'born to die' – is a book that came out in the mid-1990s. It was written by Laurie Gunst, a white American woman who was teaching history at the University of the West Indies in the 1980s, but embarked on researching the relationship between drugs, gangs, politics and violence as sort of a side project. The book is written in a largely empathetic, ethnographic style, and it became a bestseller.

I did not quite understand what Lorraine was saying. I thought I heard her also mention something about writing a book, but I did not think it had much to do with me going to Southside to visit Benjamin. Was she issuing an indirect warning to me that I should not be too nosy? But surely, I thought, after having seen me all the time last year she must have had some idea that I was doing research and not just hanging out for fun. In fact, I had interviewed one of her sons, and he had seemed fine with everything. Maybe she had been talking to Danny, a recent deportee from the US whom I had met, who was also an associate of the General, and he had mentioned that book?

I felt a little bit shaken after Lorraine's comment, especially since she usually never said much to me at all, even indirectly as was the case that day. Perhaps, I worried, I should get in touch with the General's brother who had been my introduction to the neighbourhood but who had moved to the US in the meantime. In the end, I ended up more or less avoiding that side of neighbourhood until I left for the Netherlands three weeks later. On my next return visit, almost a year later, she greeted me warmly and never made mention of Gunst's book or my writing project. So the issue remained unresolved – to what extent was Lorraine using a previous, harmful representation of Jamaican crime to communicate some kind of message to me?

Emotion and ethnography

My experiences in Brick Town with different media 'texts' demonstrate how place attachment and transnational connections are mediated. The cookshop viewing of documentaries showed me that people can engage with stereotypical representations in a positive way. The crowd I was watching with mostly disregarded the documentaries' hackneyed clichés and stigmatising depictions to co-narrate the history of Downtown Kingston. Their happiness and excitement at seeing famous figures with whom they had grown up, or at least heard many stories about, was part of a process of place-making and inscribing belonging. This is an emotional process that involves connecting oneself to the space of the neighbourhood and its history, *and* into the transnational network of places that Brick Town became connected to over the last few decades. The fact that these famous figures, histories and networks involve criminals is not necessarily salient in the mediation of place-based belonging. In Lorraine's reference to *Born fi' Dead*, however, the focus on illegality is important, but it also serves to demarcate the borders of belonging to Downtown Kingston. Her remark suggested a delineation of insiders and outsiders, an allusion to the difference between those who write about a place and those who might suffer the consequences.

Such entanglements of emotion, media and place always also involve the researcher. As an anthropologist, based in the Netherlands, but returning to Brick Town frequently and staying in touch with its residents, I have a complicated role of 'familiar outsider'. I am part of the place-constituting relational networks that authors such as Amin and Massey talk about, both through my personal connections and through the representational politics of my research. Neither these connections nor my research are dispassionate; ethnography is often an emotional experience and this affects both the researcher and the research. The two fieldwork situations described here point to some of the emotions this involves. Christopher Moreno (2007) speaks of watching television together as an 'affective media field', a space that shapes social connections. Crowding around a television together with cookshop regulars – not just to watch crime shows, but also to watch kung fu movies, the Jamaican news, or the lottery results – provided me with a space of conviviality, in which I could take part in exclaiming on a particularly unbeliev- able scene or muttering snide comments at the presenters. Such shared spaces and the positive relations they facilitate were crucial in allowing me to feel comfort- able in an area generally depicted as 'volatile' and 'lawless', and they were equally important in allowing others to feel comfortable around me. In contrast, Lorraine's seemingly casual but loaded remark scared me and underlined my sense of precarity in 'belonging' in the neighbourhood, however temporary my stay. The power of emotions to shape an ethnographic relation to place came together in my deci- sion to avoid that part of the neighbourhood before returning to the Netherlands. Feelings of safety and a certain level of 'homeness' are not always discussed in great detail by ethnographers, but the relation between ethnography and 'place-feelings' are critical factors in research. In researching the affective senses of space, the terri- tories of feeling that Thrift (2008) speaks of, we should be attentive, then, not only to the senses and territories of our research participants but also to our own.

Conclusion: Mediating belonging

In the two brief fieldwork descriptions I have included in this chapter, we see two different kinds of circulating media and responses to them. Both cases involve representations of Jamaica and Jamaicans that are produced in the global North – by American and European publishers, by major British, American and Canadian broadcasting corporations. These representations feed into stereotypes of Jamaican crime and transmit negative place narratives about the island and its people. In the first case, the documentaries were originally produced and broadcast on television for national audiences, and the producers probably did not expect many inner-city Jamaicans to view them.[3] However, as illegally copied DVDs (or YouTube clips) these programmes are able to circulate internationally and are eagerly viewed by some of the people most affected by the negative place narratives they contain. In the case of *Born fi' Dead*, this is a semi-academic book that was produced by an author who perhaps did not give enough thought to the repercussions of the book on the lives of those it depicts. While I have never seen a copy on sale in Jamaica, the rumours of its contents circulate just the same. It has been alleged that persons were murdered because the author, Laurie Gunst, disclosed incriminating informa- tion about her protagonists, whom she did not anonymise sufficiently. Well aware of previous depictions of Kingston's gangs and ghettos and the possible reper- cussions of such representations, inner-city residents seek to contest, control or appropriate these representations. Some residents refer to previous studies, presumably to warn the anthropologist obliquely that she should not ask too much. Others are eager to watch crime documentaries together, expressing empathy, intimacy, excitement and disappointment as they discuss their relationships with, and knowledge of, the featured criminals.

The production, in the global North, of these globally circulating representations of Jamaican crime, connects to a context of Jamaican transnationalism. In this case, marginalised urban populations in Kingston are connected to Caribbean migrants in similar 'ghetto' neighbourhoods in New York, in London, in Toronto, through transnational networks that go back decades. Various strands of these networks are engaged in criminal activities, but of course they are much broader; global criminal networks are always intertwined with larger social, economic and political networks (Nordstrom 2007). While produced in a context of transnationalism, I would argue that, through their consumption, these mass-mediated depictions of crime also write and reinforce durable circuits of transnational belonging.

These circuits involve many more people than criminals alone – even as sensational reports such as the television shows I described here stigmatise entire nations (Jamaica) or swaths of urban landscape (Downtown Kingston) they also serve to connect inner-city residents across and through the transnational shadows. In so doing, they show how media are central to a relational sense of place, in producing a 'Jamaica' and a 'Kingston' through transnational connections and circulating representations. Doing ethnographic research within this longer time frame of mobile representations of Jamaican crime has its complexities – it can potentially endanger the researcher, who may be associated with earlier, possibly harmful depictions. Yet active ethnographic engagement with these representational practices can also open up new methodological and theoretical avenues, expanding geographies of communication and media to help us understand the politics produced by the intersection of the mediation of place and the emplacement of representations.

Notes

1 Media anthropology has of course a much longer tradition in emphasising media consumption.
2 Many inner-city neighbourhoods in Kingston are named after violent places throughout the world, e.g. Angola, Vietnam, Mexico. In Chapter 7 in this volume, Helena Holgersson notes a somewhat similar process of global referencing in Gothenburg, where the Gustaf Dalén area came to be labeled as the 'Gaza Strip'.
3 However, the Canadian documentary does seem to have Jamaican Canadian viewers in mind at times.

References

Adams, P. (2009) *Geographies of Media and Communication: A Critical Introduction*, Chichester: Wiley-Blackwell.
Amin, A. (2004) 'Regions unbound: Towards a new politics of place', *Geografiska Annaler: Series B, Human Geography*, 86: 33–44.

Anderson, B. (1983) *Imagined Communities: Reflections on the Origin and Spread of Nationalism*, London: Verso.

Boellstorff, T. (2008) *Coming of Age in Second Life: An Anthropologist Explores the Virtually Human*, Princeton: Princeton University Press.

D'Arcy, S. (2007) 'The "Jamaican criminal" in Toronto, 1994: A critical ontology', *Canadian Journal of Communication*, 32 (2): 241–59.

Falkheimer, J. and Jansson, A. (eds) (2006) *Geographies of Communication: The Spatial Turn in Media Studies*, Göteborg: Nordicom.

Gregory, D. (1995) 'Imaginative geographies', *Progress in Human Geography*, 19 (4): 447–85.

Gunst, L. (1996) *Born fi' Dead: A Journey through the Yardie Posse Underworld*, New York: Owl Books.

Harewood, G. (2008) 'Constructions of violent Jamaican masculinity in film and literature', unpublished thesis, University of Maryland, College Park.

Harriott, A. (2008) *Organized Crime and Politics in Jamaica: Breaking the Nexus*, Kingston: Canoe Press.

Jansson, A. and Falkheimer, J. (2006) 'Towards a Geography of Communication', in A. Jansson and J. Falkheimer (eds), *Geographies of Communication: The Spatial Turn in Media Studies*, Göteborg: Nordicom, 9–25.

Mahtani, M. (2009) 'The racialized geographies of news consumption and production: Contaminated memories and racialized silences', *GeoJournal*, 74 (3): 257–64.

Martin, D. (2003) '"Place-framing" as place-making: Constituting a neighbourhood for organizing and activism', *Annals of the Association of American Geographers*, 93: 730–50.

Massey, D. (2004) 'Geographies of responsibility', *Geografiska Annaler: Series B, Human Geography*, 86 (1): 5–18.

Mennel, B. (2008) *Cities and Cinema*, London: Routledge.

Moreno, C. (2007) 'Affecting and affective social/media fields', *Aether: The Journal of Media Geography*, 1: 39–44.

Murji, K. (1999) 'Wild Life: Representations and Constructions of Yardies', in J. Ferrell and N. Websdale (eds), *Making Trouble: Cultural Representations of Crime, Deviance and Control*, New York: Aldine de Gruyter, 179–201.

Nordstrom, C. (2007) *Global Outlaws: Crime, Money, and Power in the Contemporary World*, Berkeley and Los Angeles, CA: University of California Press.

Rosati, C. (2007) 'Media geographies: Uncovering the spatial politics of images', *Geography Compass*, 1 (5): 995–1014.

Sheller, M. (2004) 'Demobilizing and Remobilizing Caribbean Paradise', in M. Sheller and J. Urry (eds), *Tourism Mobilities: Places to Play and Places in Play*, London: Routledge, 13–21.

Sives, A. (2002) 'Changing patrons, from politician to drug don: Clientelism in downtown Kingston, Jamaica', *Latin American Perspectives*, 29 (5): 66–89.

—— (2010) *Elections, Violence and the Democratic Process in Jamaica: 1944–2007*, Kingston: Ian Randle Publishers.

Thompson, K. (2006) *An Eye for the Tropics: Tourism, Photography and Framing the Caribbean Picturesque*, Durham, NC: Duke University Press.

Thrift, N. (2004) 'Intensities of feeling: Towards a spatial politics of affect', *Geografiska Annaler: Series B, Human Geography*, 86 (1): 57–78.

—— (2008) 'The material practices of glamour', *Journal of Cultural Economy*, 1 (1): 9–23.

Zimmermann, Stefan (2007) 'Media geographies: Always part of the game', *Aether: The Journal of Media Geography*, 1: 59–62.

11

AGENCY, AMBIVALENCE AND EMOTIONS IN A PUBLIC HOUSING ANTI-DEMOLITION STRUGGLE[1]

Melissa Fernández Arrigoitia

An ending

On 25 July 2011, after a decade of legal and community battles, Las Gladiolas – the last four public housing high-rise towers located in San Juan, Puerto Rico's financial district – were demolished. The impressive implosion, carried out with 3,500 pounds of explosives, was broadcast 'live' on television into people's homes and fed into tents and relocation areas. Traffic was stopped and viewing points designated along the neighbouring Martin Peña Bridge for curious spectators to stop and watch. For days, newspapers and television reports anticipated the demolition event with detailed coverage of the security measures it would entail, including the temporary relocation of the Las Monjas neighbours and their pets; the aviation permits obtained due to the building's location within a flying corridor; the cordoning off of nearby streets to limit the effects of building projectiles and 'fugitive dust' resulting from the explosion; and the firefighting and police mechanisms set in place to support the operation. Besides some concern voiced by neighbours about the potential failure of the event or the damage the shaking ground and debris could cause their homes, local authority personnel, demolition experts and contractors were all quoted confidently attesting to the technical safety of the intervention. Their design-driven language side-lined years of contestation over the dismantling of those towers, emphasising instead the mainstream belief that early public housing developed in the island was a 'mistaken vision' that required material demolition.

Once the booming explosions were over, a cacophony of car alarms, applause, hooting and expressions of awe followed. The few ex-residents watching the event from a nearby tent, who were also long-time members of the anti-demolition *Gladiolas Vive* (Gladiolas Lives) activist organisation, were immediately focused on by the cameras. Their tears and wails filled the screens and, later, printed media.

The group's leader, Myrta, underscored the temporal meaning of this 'unbuilding'[2] event with the following words: 'These walls hold the memories of this community. It is an end and a beginning. We are sad, but we also know that what is coming is better.' Under the new banner of *Gladiolas Renace* (Gladiolas Reborn) and in line with the US federal HOPE VI housing policy, a new lower development (which would house less than a third of the original residents) would be built where the towers had once stood.

At first sight it would seem odd that the most vociferous opponent of this demolition would pronounce any aspect of its afterlife as 'better'. After all, it was she who had engaged in a long-term media battle of words with the local housing authority director of the time, repeatedly denouncing his authority's actions against the permanence of Las Gladiolas. But if we take a closer look at the tumultuous trajectory that led to this event, a raw emotional battleground over urban space and belonging is revealed. This chapter dwells on some of the elements of that process to highlight dimensions of affect and emotion that were part and parcel of the fight over these stigmatised urban homes. Drawing on ethnographic material from research undertaken between 2006 and 2008, it focuses particularly on the emotional aspects of residents' ambivalent positions, and on the role played by affective memory in co-producing conflict and resistance. To do so, I look at three sets of emotions – fear and defiance, pride and attachment, insecurity and care – centred on experiences that made sense of and mobilised the conflict in individual and collective ways. The feelings brought to bear in these moments gave the struggle over urban space a meaning that cannot be captured by simply focusing on the causes, manifest forms or results of an activist movement.

Historical interlude

To understand the nuances fuelling this emotional journey it is first necessary to provide a brief historical context to the emergence of public housing in Puerto Rico and its relationship to cosmopolitan place making in urban space. The colonial relations linking the island and the United States since 1898[3] – at once political, economic and cultural – were influential in framing that modernist housing programme within a specific moral discourse of propriety that rejects signs of gendered and racialised 'backwardness' and encourages aspirations and desires towards US-styled middle-class home-ownership as a form of civic urban belonging.

The latter was especially true from the 1950s onwards, when the idealised visions of ordered urban landscapes and suburban homes contrasted sharply with the reality of sprawling slums spotted across the growing urban region of San Juan. The rural and poor coastal populations lured into the city by the promise of employment were quickly depicted as gendered and racialised outsiders (black, poor, dependent, feminised and uneducated) prone to immorality (Santiago Valle 1994). It was amidst this environment of fear and loathing that the US-sponsored construction of new public housing as a way to regulate, control and restrain their living spaces was instituted. Since then, the resistances made by the poor to official forms of relocation were classified as inappropriate, illegitimate or illegal.

Beyond design, locating public housing next to higher-income communities and incorporating social programmes like training workshops for women was meant to provide the correct managed environment of 'orientation' that would lead to the idealised state of home-ownership. But the principles guiding these new practical, economic and sober structures as a way of extirpating social difficulties, erasing the so-called 'culture of poverty' (Lewis 1966) and 'fixing' certain problems fed into the 'underlying cultural unease' (Vale 2000: 333) that racialised and gendered 'others' in a way that actually perpetuated its stigma.

In Puerto Rico, the relentless reality of unemployment and structural inequality that remained meant that the policy of public housing as a temporary stepping-stone towards home-ownership was impossible for most. Soon, the real inability to move up the normalised owner-occupation ladder meant that anything outside that model got construed as flawed dependency (Hastings and Dean 2003) or, more commonly, as stubbornly resisting modernisation and progress. This growing anxiety over public housing's apparent 'failure' was communicated through images and discourses that depicted them as increasingly suffused by criminality and deviance.

Las Gladiolas was not the exception to this story. It went from being heralded as a place of advanced technology and socio-physical design (a 'promise') to being condemned as a space of socioeconomic marginality and physical deterioration (a 'failure'). Like the modernist thrust that drove the construction of Mexico City's CUPA housing project (see Kaasa, this volume), these four 17-storey towers, built in the new 'model city centre' of Hato Rey during the late 1960s, emerged during a moment of renewed optimism in public housing's architectural design where, 'to housing officials, the high-rise tower was a visible expression of economic efficiency and social order; to the architects, it was a breakthrough in modern design . . . the new prototype of the central cities' (Wright 1981: 236). As one of the island's first public housing high-rises, this multi-family, multi-storey building was envisioned as the 'solution' to the identified 'problem' of public housing. But these new tall, prefabricated building technologies were also considered to be fundamentally incompatible with the 'rural' or 'slum' populations it was meant to house. Indeed, the question of public housing high-rise as 'culturally inauthentic' entered public discussions and debates from their inception. Thus, despite the original hopefulness they materialised, the towers quickly became framed according to the same discourses of failure already in circulation about public housing more generally. And, within a neo-liberal logic of progress and urban 'modernity', classifying public housing 'failure' as a social problem is not just an abstract exercise, but a necessary step in creating an environment that justifies any subsequent policy interventions like demolition, displacement and the construction of new mixed-income walk-ups (Flint 2006; Jacobs et al. 2003).

Creating fear and moral panic justified the physical and security interventions that followed. This was made particularly tenable in Las Gladiolas by emphasising the humanity and decency of *some* good public housing residents that deserved to be 'saved' by an altruistic government from the decay set forth by their more unsuitable and delinquent 'bad' neighbours, seen as responsible for the towers' socio-physical deficiencies. These good/bad contrasts conformed to and reproduced the moralistic paradigm that defined slum dwellers through an essential (raced, classed and gendered) difference. Such moral dualisms appealed to common emotional registers of empathy and antipathy and have had lasting consequences in the contemporary practices of urban exclusion.

This desire to make a clear divisive line between being good and legitimate versus bad and unworthy was very important to many of my respondents when expressing their strong anti-demolition sentiments and desire to stay in Las Gladiolas. On various occasions, it was pointed out to me that the blame-worthy neighbours expected 'to get things on a silver plate without doing anything to earn it' and that this lazy 'uncooperative' attitude had to do with them being *mantenidos* (dependent on welfare). In Puerto Rico, itself called a 'welfare island' (*The Economist* 2006), this popular accusation of assistentialism is full of scorn and contempt for those who are seen to be working against the mainstream capitalist tenets of personal and national progress and advancement (Santiago-Valles 1994; Alegría Ortega 2003: 178). This 'good/bad' framework facilitates the rejection and acceptance of 'others', fixes meaning and obscures the blurry ambivalence that actually informs lived senses of loss and community, such as that influencing the contours of residential struggle and resistance. It is this productive sense of ambivalence I now turn to.

Fear and defiance

The struggle to remain in place had begun in 2005, when without any order for demolition being formally consulted or announced, a *realojo* (relocation) office occupied an area in the communal entryway of Gladiolas tower A. From there, displacement was planned, coordinated and carried out. Its workers' main tactic was the use of printed letters distributed personally to neighbours or under their doors (often with police officers in tow) offering information or threatening resettlement, depending on the individual case:

> They tell me I have to go. They send me letters almost every day. Sometimes two of them come, sometimes one, telling me I have to move. They ask me where I want to go but when I tell them they say 'no no no, not there'. I feel bad when they come around . . . How am I going to go to a place I don't know?

Ana 'felt bad' and resisted moving out because Gladiolas was 'where all my people are'. She feared the severing of social ties. Residents already knew the force and power of occupations all too well. Since the 1990s 'rescue and restore' policy *Mano Dura Contra el Crimen* (Hard Hand Against Crime), they had been forcefully and repeatedly exposed to occupations in which SWAT teams raided their towers, controlled access points and perimeter walls with razor wire were erected, and police were stationed indefinitely inside the buildings. Occasional 'invasions' were still taking place in 2005. In one resident's words:

> The last 'operation' brought 300 police officers. They brought dogs; they brought fire trucks, ambulances, and the civil defence. They surrounded Las Gladiolas with patrol units . . . it looked like the Vietnam or Kuwait war . . . After breaking everything and pointing their huge guns at children, in hallways, they occupied all of the halls in all four towers . . . the purpose was to create a negative image of us . . .

Fear and intimidation were a powerful and familiar combination. With relocation and police literally knocking on their doors, most gave in to the sustained pressure, which also came in the form of deterioration. As another resident put it, 'One doesn't want to live in stench, in dirtiness. If you're filling me up with that everywhere, then you're forcing me to go. So I go . . . because I cannot take the tension.' This same tension, another young woman told me, led to her blood pressure rising so much she '*que por poco estiro la pierna*' (almost died). So I ended up with yet another problem cos my pressure went up so high now I have to go to a psychiatrist.' Both of these comments linked negative psychological and physical effects to the environment of pressure and filth they were being subjected to. In fact, every neighbour I spoke with told me about at least one condition they felt had initiated or deteriorated since relocation began, including diabetes, blood pressure, rheumatic conditions, heart problems, brain strokes, depression, psychosis and even the death of others. Pharmacy bills and prescriptions were often pulled out of pockets and purses to show me proof of what authorities tended to deny – real suffering and economic need.

There was a gendered angle to these experiences, as only women admitted depression and were readily able to raise diseases as something that was interlinked with the anti-displacement struggle. In private, they spoke of their afflictions in terms of the solitude associated either with their age or with the lack of partners or caregivers to support them. In public forums, many raised the issue of medical costs and the need for psychiatric support without a decent public health system: 'Medicaid doesn't cover anything at all, except the visit to the doctor – not even a five dollar pill . . .'. As caregivers responsible for their children, their parents or other individuals like their neighbours and friends, financial instability and a deteriorated sense of health increased their sense of physical and emotional strain.

For many of those that remained, the encroachment of the relocation office was a reminder of 'the enemy within' – an abusive form of coercion for which they took the Puerto Rican Housing Authorities to court:

> because according to them they said they were not offices of relocation because they're there to help people that *voluntarily* want to go . . . and we were like, 'No way! – that's a lie!' You can't imagine the confidence with which they'd just say that in court. And everyone wanted to just scream out: 'You liars!'

The anger and repressed frustration expressed by Lara above was the result of having to look official forms of injustice in the eye. She described the personal and communal experiences thereafter as a gradual and definitive process of political awakening – the beginning of a long period of activist and legal resistance to relocation. Visits by relocation officials that had once been met by feelings of fear and intimidation were now described by her with pride, as an opportunity to demonstrate her knowledge of her rights:

> They've told me, 'when are we gonna move you?' And I say, 'Whenever I feel like leaving.' The other day they said, 'Oh, now [after seven months without electricity] we can look for a place wherever you want.' And I said, 'No, not yet. I still have to take care of something.' They said, 'You can resolve whatever once you're gone.' And I said, 'No, the problem started here. The problem ends here.'

She had not only learned to effectively challenge authority, but also to use her recently acquired legal know-how (facilitated by a pro-bono lawyer) to play with the agents and 'make them work overtime' for her. She would come to the door armed with letters that declared her right to be in her apartment, even if she knew certain conditions for her stay were running out. Other residents similarly faked an interest in moving out not to spite the authorities, but to remind them that they could – 'a matter of dignity', one said. These small moments of joy in the exercise and recognition of power were immensely important in providing confidence for the larger collective efforts to stay put. For Lara and others, then, the original experience of deception within court had affectively catalysed the course and form of the events that followed. Specifically, the offensive misuse of the word 'relocation' had created a sense of aggravation, which set the tone for years of acrimonious relations between dwellers and *realojo*.

But defiance against a common enemy was not a straightforward affair. Those who literally stayed at home were still subjected to displacement pressures and unknown futures. At all times, 'staying' was in fact a prolonged period of 'waiting', with ups and downs variously characterised by wishful expectations, hopes and anxieties which, in turn, led to shifting allegiances; to feeling 'kind of both for and against it', as I was sometimes told. Despite believing in *Gladiolas Vive*, they were inhibited and 'afraid of attending demonstrations', lest they be blacklisted and not offered a suitable housing alternative if leaving became inevitable. The choice of moving through one of the many housing options being offered was so confusing and polarising, that it was not uncommon to hear of a neighbour surreptitiously taking off during the evening to avoid potential confrontation or questioning. During that time, losing neighbours overnight transformed home into a precarious day-by-day experience coloured by the mixed emotions that these shifting events presented them with.

The fear that inhibited residents' participation and fostered tenuous connections also precipitated changes in the tactics used. The leaders of *Gladiolas Vive* began to actively mediate the ambivalence of individuals who preferred to look out of their balconies than descend stairs into the community centre by hosting meetings in the open courtyards overlooked by all towers, using loudspeakers to facilitate audibility and spread the word about the latest developments. At the same time, they realised that with real numbers dwindling, it was important to expand and strengthen their struggle to include new networks of solidarity with a variety of other groups, communities and movements. In the 'Puerto Rican Day for the Eradication of Poverty' (October 2007), for example, one of the leaders insisted that 'as long as we continue to be stepped on, we will unite even more because we have the same needs . . . Now we have support networks between marginalised sectors that we did not have before.' While originally born out of need, their growing presence in activities hosted by other areas threatened by displacement also led to the belief that the law was at their disposal and could be used to achieve real political gains. The backing of the University of Puerto Rico's pro-bono Legal Assistance Clinic and Amnesty International armed many in the group with a sense of confidence that allowed for certain claims of belonging to be made.

Pride and attachment

In 2006, one year after *realojo* was installed in their towers, Gladiolas residents waged the island's first class-action law-suit against both the local and American housing agencies, based on the claims that they had not been properly consulted before the demolition decision was made and that the Housing Authority had been deploying a de facto demolition over the years through maintenance negligence. This legal protestation accused both the federal and local agencies of performing intentional disrepair, and was presented by residents as a counter-discourse to the historical and localised accusations made against them as irresponsible or immoral.

At the more informal level, many residents resented the fact that, despite a desire to keep their common areas tidy, private companies officially in charge of maintenance had stopped lending the tools needed to do so, and argued that this was directly responsible for negative impacts on communal life. To Arcadio, one of the two Gladiolas community leaders who had been living in the towers since their inauguration, the paint on walls (or lack thereof) *stood in* for the buildings' overall state of care or neglect. The discoloured walls, he told me, were a material manifestation of authority's abandonment while the fresh yellow and blue on the entrance section was a product of their own communal efforts; a sign of their ability to 'take some responsibilities and enable this ourselves'. He had also taken matters into his own hands by fixing-up some spaces where windows were being stolen; installing make-shift fences in their place; painting those red so they would be undesirable to thieves; and covering rail posts in the back part of the buildings that people were using to jump into apartments with frying oil so as to make them slippery and unusable. These crude DIY solutions were born both out of an attempt to maintain order and demonstrate control (albeit fledgling) over the community. He talked about those actions with a strong sense of satisfaction and pride.

Another resident, Carla, similarly attested to residents' everyday hands-on understanding of how to live – to dwell – in high-rises by pointing out to me the multiple celebratory and creative uses of the buildings that had once taken place:

> Here, we were a family – everybody. We would even do Christmas parties with competitions for the best decorations in the towers. We'd decorate the hallways, raffle off plant pots, adornments; we'd put arches and light – lots of things we'd make here ourselves . . . A friend would cook *arroz con gandules*, the other *pernil'*, the other would make Halloween costumes. The kids wouldn't have to go anywhere else but could just get their candy here. We'd do Valentine's parties. When they'd say, 'let's all paint that', it meant we painted, or cleaning . . . I'd make the floor shine. Had my plants as well. Arcadio used to get kids to plant trees and *recao'*, *ají'* plantain . . . and that was all cut down . . . All that's left is a skinny cherry tree.

The description she offered countered the cultural 'incompatibility' debate originally leveled against Las Gladiolas where, like in the United States, despite all amounts of public scrutiny and opinion opposing apartment blocks, 'among its inhabitants: most did not feel uncomfortable living in serial high-rises . . .' (Urban 2012: 30). To her, it was a familiar setting that provided joy. Her fond recollections of a better time were also inseparable from the opportunities and freedoms that proper physical maintenance had granted mothers like her. This gendered and affective aspect of place making highlighted the political issues of public housing maintenance as both material *and* personal; as object and subject; as physical and emotional.

For both Carla and Arcadio, the material deterioration of the buildings contained a vast range of emotional memories and affective registers of the past and present that allowed them to actively challenge the dominant 'irresponsible tenant' discourse. Their activities and memories existed within a larger discourse of care, enacting responsible conduct (while challenging irresponsible conduct) around two principal rationales: that of self-agency or self-responsibility, and of tenants as 'good' duty-laden members of communities. This 'politics of behaviour' (Flint 2004: 895) responds to the 'good/bad' moral logic defined before, and has been noted as an important strategy 'against the onslaught of revanchism and an economy and governing regime that seems anything but caring' (Staeheli 2008: 13). In other words, they were both aware and critical of the everyday mechanism of 'ethopower' (the power of ethical behaviour) that had forced them to take matters into their own hands to protect themselves from circumstances they felt were caused by government's neglect. While resentful, their experiences and memories expressed prideful senses of attachment to the shared spaces of home.

In Carla's account of sociality and cleanliness, the role memory plays is also very relevant. As King (2008: 138) has proposed, *dwelling* is an active relational activity of the now enhanced through memory, where 'we retain past dwelling whilst living in the present'. Her emphasis on the interrelation between the building's upkeep and happy experiences of community and belonging illustrate the linked roles that memory and materiality play in actively negotiating a process of home loss. The current state of isolation and disrepair that depressed her and brought her to tears in our meetings was powerfully given meaning through what was there before. The sadness and loss that formed part of the resistance was made more bearable when it was actively put in dialogue with memories that reminded her of her attachment to that space. The emotional narratives contained in and expressed through those rec-ollections can be considered subversive in that claims to place-attachment through a sense of past unity and responsible, organised collectiveness challenge the grounds upon which public housing has been historically stigmatised as dysfunctional. For her and many others I spoke with, holding on to these versions of the past granted the grim material contours of the present a stronger sense of common loss and shared grievances. It also helped to mediate the unsettling impact of the ambivalent emotions described in the previous section.

This shifting but ever-present sense of place and belonging attached to their buildings came out more forcefully when, in late 2006, during an anticipated evening launch of the *Las Gladiolas* documentary held in the towers' courtyard, a maintenance squadron quietly entered the housing complex in order to paint over a mural painted by the children, which featured a hamster and the initials of the youth social project, COPADIM. This otherwise unimpressive painting was sym-bolically significant because, after they had been evicted from their offices in the towers, this was the last palpable trace of COPADIM's much respected and loved social work(ers). The children who had painted the wall saw what was happening, alerted the adults gathered around the documentary screen and ran to defend it with their bodies. In an act of militant defiance, many hooded their faces, chanted 'Gladiolas Vive!' and waved their arms in a 'throwing out' gesture directed at the workers. The scene was electric and loud; residents were not scared. Instead, interpreting the act as cowardly and strategically provocative, they vociferously demanded explanations and cried out 'Abuse!' (see Plate 4).

In this case, the space of the wall had provided the canvas upon which to express competing senses of property and attachment. For the maintenance agents (who said they'd been ordered there by the 'higher' Housing Authorities), this was an assertive act of power through humiliation and disruption (of one of the few moments of excited unity amongst neighbours who were seeing themselves on a big screen, in public protest). It imposed moral rules, boundaries and urban aes-thetic imaginaries for maintaining 'others' in their place. For residents, it allowed for a concrete confrontation in a form not usually allowed – a mass unleashing of anger against the repressive forces they felt were trying to dispossess them. In the weeks that followed, new unexpected forms of solidarity emerged from this event and the legal issue of removing public housing murals became heavily debated in social movement meetings, in the media and in court. Although their wall was eventually painted over under the bright sun of a normal week-day, this event highlighted the contested and fluctuating meaning of walls, and how the emotions they elicit in different contexts and through distinct power relations can make them take different forms.

Insecurity and care

Feelings about how things were at any point in time during the conflict – the pulse of residents' (shifting) attitudes towards resistance and how that affected the rest of the movement – could be gleaned in how they negotiated their ambivalent emotions and memories *as mothers*. This dominant gendered self-identification amongst women, the most populous group in the towers, was the most commonly used to express senses of approval or repudiation of the present or past. In Puerto Rico, there is strong external but also internal resentment against *madres solteras* (single mothers) – *the* local cultural proxy for 'welfare recipient' – or *hombres vagos* (lazy men), both seen to perpetuate and reproduce undesirable behaviour. Like the slum subjects before her, the 'welfare mother' in particular is vilified as a low-class over-breeder who reproduces or enables public housing's degeneration. She is seen as a failed over-consumptive homemaker who embodies the collapse of a programme that tried to educate and domesticate its subjects along white, middle-class rules of social propriety and upward mobility. Contained within four public housing walls, she is condemned through capitalist tenets that criticise the jobless, and an underlying moral (Catholic) and cultural unease with being a single woman. One male interviewee from the housing agency told me that these women try to dupe the system by being single by day and married by night 'purely in terms of the benefits that they get as participants of different assistance programmes'. Deception and dubious sexual morality makes her fall outside the desired moral order. These discourses recall those historically raced, gendered and classed signifiers of appropriate urban place and progress – what it should look like and which bodies belong to it. They remind us of Hall's account earlier in this book where discourses of depravity and stigma attached to London's estates feed into exclusionary urban redevelopment initiatives.

Women in Las Gladiolas were not unaware of this popular belief and, as mothers, went to great lengths to distance themselves from those associations. They did not see themselves as part of *that* class, or *those* problem people with the *real* welfare mentality. For those who had lived in the towers for a long time, this was compounded with the assertion that when housing policies had been worker- rather than welfare-oriented (i.e. when they were first instituted), times were better because the quality of residents (their education levels, civility) was higher. They condemned each other privately sometimes for behaving in accordance with those stereotypes, but, as single women, they were also proud and unapologetic about their identity. In the context of the anti-displacement conflict, it provided a filter through which to resist the power, control and domination of the government and men. The links between physical deterioration, isolation and criminality were the most common nexus through which these commentaries took place.

No one denied that drug lords and drug wars once dominated the towers, and all the mothers I spoke with mentioned the damaging impact this had on children. One resident said she felt more comfortable with the growing isolation of the towers because, with less drug hustling taking place, she no longer had to fear for her children when they played in the courtyard downstairs or at night without her supervision (see Plates 5 and 6). Another showed me the crack on the wardrobe of her daughter's room where a bullet had once entered and become wedged while the girl slept – unusually so – in her mother's room. She had immediately barged into the courtyard below where the drug hustlers stood guard to scream at them and demand that whoever was responsible be 'given a lesson'. While that moment had produced fear and rage, she spoke proudly of how she was able to go out into the communal space, demand explanations, and that someone would have to answer for it. At the same time, she feared that the deteriorated and isolating condition of the towers which, with serious leg and back problems meant she needed to stay in her eighth floor apartment most of the time, could somehow put her youngest son at risk – and that she would not be able to protect him. For her, the first anecdote had provided a sense of empowerment as a mother who could talk back with a real sense of power to those who threatened her children; whereas the second felt like a loss of control, where living without the alternative of 'resolving daily injustices in the local arena' (Goldstein 2003: 190) felt like a threat. A third interviewee similarly said:

> I had three children here, brought them up all on my own. But before, I didn't mind staying alone, even when you had to come running because shootings would break out when you least expected it. But now, I tell you, I've never felt so scared as now . . . There's no respect anymore. And right next door to me used to live a *chulo* (pimp); people were injecting themselves right there, and yet they'd always say 'Good Morning, good afternoon'. All drugged up they'd just go back into their houses and never tried to jump a fence or a door . . . You look at me with a double lock, with those windows, I barely sleep thinking someone might be robbing me . . . Because the people that are getting in are no longer from here and they're stealing *hasta los cables* (even cables, from elevators). Now you don't know who is who.

She felt that the system of control instituted by criminals, while faulty and reproachable, was more conducive to an internal sense of cohesion, control and respect than the one that was at play during the current moment of advanced deterioration. In this sense, there was a simultaneous and ambiguous attraction *and* aversion to those past elements that had provided security but, also, had produced severe problems, especially when children were concerned. What some experienced as a loss of security and safety, others felt as liberation. In all three cases, mothers' relationships to the memory and experience of violence, insecurity or crime did not allow them to categorise each other in a simple black and white fashion because, to them, 'criminality' was not simply 'good or bad' but recalled in contradictory, relativised ways.

They expressed different senses of control, power and security depending on their particular interaction with 'criminal' space and people in the past and present.

Conclusions

This chapter started with an ending – the sudden 'unbuilding' demolition of Gladiolas. What followed highlighted the importance of capturing, recognising and recuperating the complex narratives and emotional states of being that actually shaped that public housing space, its politics and its demise. What becomes evident is that the emotional upheaval produced by a decade-long legal and community battle must be understood not as a byproduct of urban displacement, but as central to and constitutive of it. In all of the sets of emotions presented here – fear and defiance, pride and attachment, insecurity and care – both sides affected and became involved in the politics of relocation.

For residents, remaining actively ambivalent amidst an imminent relocation was not a cynical or disinterested emotional standpoint. It was a mechanism that responded directly to the tug and pull of removal pressures; a practical, flexible and productive tool that proved crucial when their homes were under threat. At the same time, affective and highly gendered memory disrupted any linear or straightforward account of the way space was lived, felt or struggled over. It was at once an unsettling and stabilising arena that filtered thoughts and emotions, an active agent in the co-production of community resistances, conflicts and affective responses.

Beyond the cosmopolitanism inherent in the unequal and unstable power relations embedded in Puerto Rican public housing, where what happens in the United States affects the social, economic and spatial relations of the island, and vice versa, Gladiolas residents can also be considered 'cosmopolitan vagabonds' in one of the senses described in this book's introduction – an involuntarily mobile and forcibly relocated population that 'travel across space and time, create new formations and new working global connectors, simply in everyday being'. Their quotidian 'travelling' took place not only in the connections they forged and felt with movements far away struggling to stay at home, but also in the affective registers of individual memories, where the latter existed as an emotional boundary state and space that allowed for the strong fluctuating feelings of the past and present to coexist while uncertainty continued to reign.

Notes

1   The interviews in this chapter took place in San Juan, Puerto Rico between 2006 and 2008.
2   For more on the socio-technical 'unbuilding' of modernist high-rises, transnationally, see Jacobs and Cairns 2011 and Jacobs et al. 2007.
3   As part of the Spanish-American war, the colony of Puerto Rico was handed over to the US as a territory. The first 50 years of this relationship led to the Estado Libre Asociado (ELA [Free Associated State]), a new political status 'halfway' between statehood and independence that grants American citizenship to all islanders without the right to vote for the American president, as well as allowing partial political autonomy through

self-administration with an ultimate adherence to the US federal machinery (judicial, monetary, political and tariff systems).

References

Alegría Ortega, I. (2003) 'Ideología y Política: La representación de las mujeres', in L. Martínez Ramos and M. Tamargo López (eds) *Género, Sociedad y Cultura*, Rio Piedras: Publicaciones Gaviota.

Flint, J. (2004) 'The responsible tenant: Housing governance and the politics of behaviour', *Housing Studies*, 19 (6): 893–909.

—— (2006) 'Maintaining an arm's length? Housing, community governance and the management of "problematic" populations', *Housing Studies*, 21 (2): 171–86.

Goldstein, D.M. (2003) *Laughter Out of Place: Race, Class, Violence, and Sexuality in a Rio Shantytown*, Berkeley, CA: University of California Press.

Hastings, A. and Dean, J. (2003) 'Challenging images: Tackling stigma through estate regeneration', *Policy and Politics*, 31 (2): 171–84.

Jacobs, J.M. and Cairns, S. (2011) 'Ecologies of dwelling: Maintaining high-rise housing in Singapore', in S. Watson and G. Bridge (eds) *The New Companion to the City*, Oxford: Blackwell.

Jacobs, J.M., Cairns, S. and Strebel, I. (2007) 'A tall storey . . . but, a fact just the same: The Red Road high rise as a black box', *Urban Studies*, 43: 609–29.

Jacobs, K., Kemeny, J. and Manzi, T. (2003) Power, discursive space and institutional practices in the construction of housing problems, *Housing Studies*, 18 (4): 429–46.

King, P. (2008) *In Dwelling: Implacability, Exclusion and Acceptance*, Aldershot: Ashgate.

Lewis, O. (1966) *La Vida: A Puerto Rican Family in the Culture of Poverty – San Juan and New York*, New York: Random House.

Santiago-Valles, K.A. (1994) *'Subject People' and Colonial Discourses: Economic Transformation and Social Disorder in Puerto Rico, 1898–1947*, Albany, NY: State University of New York Press.

Staeheli, L. (2008) 'Citizenship and the problem of community', *Political Geography*, 27: 5–21.

The Economist (2006) *Trouble on Welfare Island: The Condition of Puerto Rico*. Online. Available at www.economist.com/node/6980051 (accessed 9 May 2013).

Urban, F. (2012) *Tower and Slab: Histories of Global Mass Housing*, London: Routledge.

Vale, L.J. (2000) *From the Puritans to the Projects: Public Housing and Public Neighbors*, Cambridge, MA: Harvard University Press.

Wright, G. (1981) *Building the Dream: A Social History of Housing in America*, New York: Pantheon Books.

12

REVOLUTIONARY AFFECT

Feeling modern in Mexico City

Adam Kaasa

> To impute a mirroring relation between affective activity and emotional states under-describes the incoherence of subjects – their capacity to hold irreconcilable attachments and investments, the complexity of motives for disavowal and defense – and the work of the normative in apprehending, sensing, tracking and being with, the event
>
> *(Berlant 2008b: 4)*

Our beloved

For a few days every September since 1949, residents, government officials, musicians, and neighbours gather at the Centro Urbano Presidente Alemán (CUPA), a set of modernist housing blocks in the south-centre of a sprawling Mexico City. They gather to mark the anniversary of the inauguration of these towers built by a young architect, Mario Pani, and an even younger and unknown engineering firm, Ingenieros Civiles Asociados (ICA) between 1947 and 1949.[1] On 2 September 1949, then President of Mexico Miguel Alemán (1946–1952) presided over government and union representatives, and a crowd flowing through the landscaped gardens, up the stairwells and along the 'streets in the sky'.

For nine days in August and September 2010, the CUPA marked its 61st anniversary with a range of activities including a football tournament, a photography exhibition, and film screenings. The week culminated on a Saturday full of official presentations, lingering into the night with music, dancing, food, and drinks. Listening to conversations, one overhears the oft repeated phrase '*mi multi es mi multi*' ('my estate is my estate'), the tag line for the 60th anniversary celebration in 2009, and a kind of invocation of pride.[2] The poster outside advertising this weeklong celebration ended with the following invitation:

> Neighbours, let's participate with joy and peace in the Events for the 61st Anniversary of Our Beloved '*Multifamiliar Miguel Alemán*'![3]

Listening to the stories shared that night, I wondered first how a community might sustain this annual celebration of a building over some 60 years and multiple generations? And second, how this celebration came to manifest itself through the language of love (*nuestro querido*)? There are similar housing estates in Mexico City, including others by Mario Pani, that do not evoke comparable reactions.[4] There is, equally, an overwhelming perception of the failure of the modernist housing block in other geographic contexts (Prudon 2009). But here was a group of residents and neighbours who referred to their mass housing estate as 'Our Beloved'. As I reflected on the week's celebrations, it became increasingly unclear to me to what, or to whom, they were directing this love? On the surface, the answer seemed obvious: the CUPA. Still, I began to question whether or not I knew what the CUPA was, or indeed if it was any 'thing' at all.

I began to reconsider the location of this emotion given the name of 'love'. Where was it, and to what was it directed, if indeed it was directed at someone or some 'thing'? In her oral history of the CUPA, Graciela de Garay (2002, 2004b) presents several narratives of residents that evoke the excitement, joy, and pride sustained through their lived experience. However, equal notes of anger, loss, and frustration pepper their accounts. I had visited the estate several times prior to the celebration, and met informally with residents who had complained that the pool was often closed due to insufficient maintenance, half-mentioned that some of the elevators no longer work, or despaired that the garbage incinerators had been malfunctioning for years, leading to accumulations of trash. I could not simply argue, then, that this 'love' was a quotidian response to a material object, that residents and neighbours of this estate simply 'love' the CUPA. Where 'love' erupts is at the anniversary, as if the coming together of bodies, the memorialization of the CUPA's narrative produces, or brings forth this 'love'. Turning to Sara Ahmed, love, in this case, does 'not positively inhabit any-body as well as any-thing' (Ahmed 2004a: 121), but is an effect of its circulation, and that is, perhaps, before we begin to question the 'thing-ness' of the CUPA itself (Berlant 2004: 448; Jacobs 2006). We are left then with two questions, which I will not properly address, but which act as guides to the comments below: how does 'love' erupt year upon year, and where does it go when the celebration ends?

The CUPA is, again and again, invoked as a 'thing'. The image of the estate, like most architecture, privileges its façade, and aerial photography highlights the shape of the towers from the sky, creating a visual metonym for the CUPA itself. This visual form appears on the poster for the 61st anniversary, a black and white aerial image taken upon its completion in 1949 (see Plate 7).

Equally, the exhibition about the CUPA comprised photography and newspaper clippings from its inauguration. Rather than attempt to argue location in terms of space, I began to consider it in terms of time, positioning the anniversary week, the collection of bodies, bricks, photography, and memories, as a kind of affective economy tied to the moment that an anniversary purports to celebrate: the beginning, the birth, the origin. If an affective economy emerged over the course of several days in August and September 2010, and if the circulations of these affects themselves resurfaced year after year, then perhaps a kind of circulatory system that beats once a year imbricates a multiplicity of subjects and objects into the response whose only response is '*mi multi es mi multi*'. In thinking through the 'where' of this 'what', then, I decided to follow the gaze of those participating in these annual anniversaries, to look to the very first celebration, the inauguration of CUPA in 1949, a moment relived some 61 years later through old photographs, exhibitions, and narratives. It might be argued that 'thinking about feeling historical', or presenting affect within an architectural history can be limited. Affect cannot reside outside the gift of the present, structured in the circulations between signs, bodies, and objects (Ahmed 2004b), and in the autonomy of the nervous system itself (Massumi 2002). To this end, I take a cue from Berlant's claim 'that affect, the body's active presence to the intensities of the present, embeds the subject in an historical field, and that its scholarly pursuit can communicate the conditions of an historical moment's production as a visceral moment' (Berlant 2008a: 846). The inauguration returns, then, as the original 'building event', in Jacobs' (2006) terms, repeated year after year after year; and therefore, I want to try to understand what processes created the CUPA then as an object, so that now it becomes an object of love.

Affect, modernity, circulation

There seems to be a consensual mimetic trope among scholars of affect and affect theory, that affect is imbricated in movement, motion, circulation (Ahmed 2004a: 120; 2004b; Anderson 2006; Thien 2005: 451; Thrift 2004: 64). Equally, historical and contemporary notions of modernity have aligned themselves with the trope of motion (see chapter by Jones, Jackson, and Rhys-Taylor, this volume). As figured by Otto Wagner in mid-nineteenth century Germany, modernity is a '*process of abstraction, circulation and movement* and *monumentality*' (Frisby 2001: 20; original emphasis), or, in Baudelaire's words, the 'ephemeral, the fugitive, the contingent' (Baudelaire 1995: 13). Contemporary theorisation of affect as constituted in and through movement is, perhaps, a very 'modern' one. In this sense, the 'love' of the 'beloved' CUPA is necessarily the making sense of a spectral affect. The sign 'love' lingers, the trace of a movement. And so perhaps emotion can be located precisely in times and spaces where people are left to configure their sense of the world through language, by encrypting affective economies into dialogic and reciprocal deployments of, in this case, love. Affect, then, cannot be pinned down; talking about it brings it into language, and into space. Instead, affect is the beside-ness of making sense, the swirls circulating through watery relationships, whose motion only we can meaningfully trace.

In many ways, the CUPA, too, can be interpreted as constitutive of and constituted by circulation. At its urban scale, it was designed, in part, as a systematic decantation of central city 'slums', considered the first of many attempts to move people within the city, opening up land for development and 'rational' urban planning. Equally, as a 'city' within the city, the idea was to reduce the number of long trips for daily services like education, health care, leisure and groceries, all amenities that were built into the complex as part of the original design. Here, in reducing unnecessary movement of people in and out of the city centre for basic services, the idea was to decongest the burdened roadways and improve circulation for others. Architecturally, CUPA demonstrates innovative attention to the way people would move through, in, and around their apartments and the estate. The tall buildings were designed so that circulatory hallways were only necessary every three floors, meaning that the elevators on a 13-storey building would only make five stops. This innovation increased the efficiency of moving up and down buildings, and also meant that every apartment was a duplex, entering on one storey, usually into a small kitchen space, and then climbing up or down a flight of stairs to the private living and sleeping rooms, spanning the full width of the building. This organisation had the added effect of windows on either side of the apartment increasing the circulation of light and air, central tenets of International Style modernism, and particularly that of the architect Le Corbusier. The ground floor was raised up on pilotis, column-like concrete structural pillars, allowing air, light, and people to flow and circulate on and through the landscaped gardens, the buildings not creating linear barriers to movement. Finally, the hallways themselves were placed on the outsides of the buildings, not in an interior core, such that the flow of people was likened to 'streets in the sky', extending not just along one's own building, but connected along the full length of the zigzagging set of tower blocks. As an early example of large-scale modernist housing in Mexico, the CUPA was built around the circulating body, and the efficient rationale of circulation itself.

In what follows, I work to see architecture not for its 'thingness', as a thing to be uncovered or decoded either as political referent or as bearer of affect (Lees 2001), but, rather as a '*claim* to the idea of being architecture or a building' (emphasis mine; Jacobs 2006: 22; Kraftl 2010). That is, to think the architectural object as an incoherent assemblage with work being done to create its 'thingness' and to 'sustain that claim materially' (Jacobs 2006: 22). At its heart is the image of the non-coinciding reflection of Berlant's mirror that refuses to figure an affect-emotion reflection, an epistemic mirroring that she argues 'under-describes the incoherence of subjects' (Berlant 2008b: 4; see also Chapter 1 by Hall, this volume). Extending this image to the CUPA anniversary event, thinking about love's 'location' allows us to make visible the incoherence of location itself.

Inauguratory details

On Friday 2 September 1949, President Miguel Alemán and Esteban García de Alba, the Director of the *Dirección de Pensiones Civiles*,[5] unveiled a plaque to open the 1,080 new apartments. After a series of speeches, the festivities were marked by a presentation of the national ballet, and the Mexican Olympic swimming team. The CUPA was, according to the architect Mauricio Gómez Mayorga writing in the Mexico City daily newspaper *Excélsior* two days later, 'a building built from a better Mexico, of the only Mexico that should be of interest to living men: the Mexico of tomorrow' (Mayorga 1949).

Anyone present that day could not possibly miss the building. Its mass alone commanded attention, particularly in that space at that time, surrounded as it was with farmland, and a sprinkling of low-rise development. In his official capacity as the representative of the state, García de Alba noted that in the first two years and nine months of the Alemán administration, they 'invested more than 90 million pesos into solving the problem of housing public servants' (Lomelí 1949). He began by outlining the detailed statistics of the building, impressing its mass and scale on the already awed audience:

> The estate is formed by nine buildings of thirteen storeys with 936 apartments serviced by twenty elevators and 3,400m^2 of ground floor space for commercial use. Six buildings of three storeys with 144 apartments. Total of 1,080 apartments, with 98,987m^2 of construction . . . The total cost of the construction – not counting the cost of the land – is \$18,800,000.00, equal to a cost per square metre of \$189.92.[6]
>
> *(Lomelí 1949)*

Addressing the crowd outside the buildings, the power of these numbers fused with the material image of the modern housing block. In the difference between seeing and knowing, the audience saw its mass, the image of modernity, but now they knew its details. Elements like square footage and cost are the unseen details as important as the mass of brick and mortar to funnelling the attention of those present at its inauguration. Modernity here is as much about what is made to appear, the image of the modern city, and those equally modern unseen details: the efficiency, for example, of the building technique and materials through mass standardisation.

Considerable time is spent explaining the modern amenities of the CUPA at the inauguration, a systematic representation of the CUPA as a building 'from tomorrow'. García de Alba mentions 'hot and cold water, a deep well, telephones, electric light, garbage incinerators, central gas and a swimming pool' (Lomelí 1949):

> On top of all this, there are additional buildings for annexes and special services: two schools . . . A furnished nursery. A fully equipped playground . . . administration, the police, a fully equipped medical unit, and spaces for the post and telegraph offices. A theatre space and gymnasium. A laundrette equipped with individual automatic machines and drying rooms . . . As well, the swimming pool has changing rooms, water purification, a heater . . . The building has modern automatic boilers to provide hot water . . . The adjacent streets are illuminated, and two of them are now paved . . . Each apartment is equipped with radio and sound systems. The ground floor is prepared for commercial services.
>
> *(Lomelí 1949)*

I quote this passage at length to demonstrate the number and variety of details that were described about the building.[7] The narrative was not just about the revolutionary wonder of the building itself – a building that was worked on every day for two years by over 1800 workers (Pani 1952: 8) – but of the intricate and hidden systems of modern life materially embedded in the structures of the building.

During the inaugural weekend of CUPA in 1949, the newspapers were awash with images of the housing estate. The images rely on monumentality, mass, and the appearance of the 'whole'. Rarely, however, is there a photograph of detail, of intimate space, or the image of a 'part'. One of these appears on Sunday 4 September 1949, on the tenth page of the third section of *Excélsior*. The image is of one of the protruding stairwells on a 13-storey block, the staircases climbing in vertical diagonals, zigzagging up beside concrete rows of the 13 floors, and alongside singularly straight concrete columns, lifting the building off the ground (see Plate 8).

The caption of the stairwell reads, 'Note the clarity of expression in the concrete structure' (*Excélsior* 1949). A small caption, on a small image in the back section of a daily newspaper on a Sunday in 1949 in Mexico City, the idea of 'clarity' falls short. Indeed, the invocation of 'clarity', meaning at once coherent and intelligible, certain and definite, transparent and pure, belies the layers of inchoate and incoherent meaning embedded in the depth of this flat newsprint image.

A consideration of the image of the stairwell in some detail might lead to any number of interpretations. Walter Benjamin's assertion that 'what is crucial in the observation of architecture is not seeing but rather the coming through of traces and structures' (in Frisby 2001: 7), brings us some way back to Berlant's quote on the uncritical 'mirroring relation' invoked between 'affect activity and emotional states' (2008b: 4). Both are arguing that there is nothing 'clear' in that relationship, both using the metaphors of visuality: Berlant in the trickery of the mirror, and Benjamin on the gap between what we 'see' and what 'comes through', between seeing and knowing. In some way, Benjamin allows us to reconsider the effect of the built structures of modernity that were listed in detail at the inauguration. The boilers, the pool, the medical facility, the schools, the garbage incinerators, the radios and telephones: this is, perhaps, one superficial instance of the 'coming through of traces and structures'. The image of the stairwell paired with the caption of clarity leaves us to consider the inauguration less as a presentation of a building, of a finished and whole 'thing', and more as work towards its production.

The double revolutionary

While the presentation of detail marks the building's modernity, there was another, equally modern, trace made manifest in that inaugural weekend in 1949: the trace of revolution. In describing the inaugural event, the editor of the *Excélsior* wrote that the inaugurated building 'represents a revolutionary idea in resolving the problem of a scarcity of rental units' (Lomelí 1949). Alfonso Martínez Domínguez, the head of the union of the workers for the Departamento del Distrito Federal, speaking on behalf of the 80,000 bureaucrats in that department, congratulated the President on delivering this building: 'In effect, in no other country do the public servants benefit as much as we do from the judicial and social guarantees that the Mexican Revolution granted us' (Lomelí 1949). In his article 'The Biggest Material Realisation of Collective Housing, in Latin America,' the architect Mauricio Gómez Mayorga wanted to:

> underline in the most vigorous way possible the importance that realizing a project like this holds for our city and our country, destined to revolutionize in our medium[8] the concept of housing even, to convert itself into the most important collective experiment carried out.
>
> *(Mayorga 1949)*

In the same Saturday 3 September 1949 edition of the *Excélsior*, the engineer Robles Martínez declared a 'magisterial joy' for the inaugurated building, defending its originality against housing projects in Vienna, Le Corbusier's then unfinished Unité d'Habitation in Marseilles, mass housing in the USSR, or tower blocks on the Hudson in New York (Martínez 1949). Martínez concluded with a reminder that bureaucrats are 'also a sector in the revolutionary movement that . . . has the duty to support the governments emerging from this movement, to fulfil the principles of the Mexican Revolution' (Martínez 1949).

We have, in these invocations of revolution, the 'revolution' in multiple forms. First, the notion of a revolution in terms of a transformation in thought or practice, in terms of newness. That the CUPA is deemed 'revolutionary' as a housing project is an attempt to mark it as distinct to what has come before. While the CUPA is indeed a prototype of massification (Frisby 2001: 161–2) – Pani delivered 1080 apartments more cheaply and on 20 per cent of the land that was proposed in the original brief for 200 single family homes (Pani 1952: 27)[9] – mass alone does not make a thing revolutionary: change does. The inaugural commentary suggests this was not simply a change in scale, but a change in kind. Martínez's defence of CUPA's revolutionary originality posits its 'advanced place in the resolution of the problem of popular housing, not only in Mexico City, but globally' (Martínez 1949). In 1952, Pani himself defended the originality of CUPA arguing that:

> From an urbanistic point of view, the solution of the *Centro*, with a population density of more than 1,000 people per hectare, signals the true path that all major modern cities should follow.
>
> *(Pani 1952: 32–3)*

The thrust in the inaugural invocation of the CUPA as a revolutionary architectural and urban object is evident in the descriptions of it as such, and in the efforts to demonstrate its originality in a field of modernist housing developments internationally.

The second sense of the word 'revolution' reveals why it is so important that the CUPA is seen as 'revolutionary' in the first sense. That is, revolution in Mexico always already hosts the official reference to the Mexican Revolution (1910–1920), both as an event, but also as an ongoing process of everyday governance (Joseph and Nugent 1994). Every speaker at the inauguration of the CUPA praised the government with direct or indirect gratitude for fulfilling 'the principles of the Mexican Revolution' (Martínez 1949). Martínez ends his long article about the CUPA in the *Excélsior* as follows:

> [A]s the revolutionaries we are, we should recognise Miguel Alemán as the actual leader of the Mexican Revolution in the flesh and we are obligated to conduct our political actions conforming to the line that the revolutionary movement follows in his government, in his leadership.
>
> *(Martínez 1949)*

As a rhetorical trope, then, the 'revolutionary' acts as both an adjective – the CUPA is a revolutionary architectural object – and a noun 'as the revolutionaries we are'. The framing of the CUPA in these terms admits the character of the *double revolutionary*. First, the architect, the engineer, the resident are depicted, and indeed depict themselves, as forward thinking innovators, as urban revolutionaries. Second, in figuring CUPA in relation to the legacy of the capital 'R' Revolution, the character becomes embedded within a national imaginary linking the social progress of the Mexican Constitution of 1917 to the architectonic structure structuring a response to a then contemporary national housing crisis.

If part of the 'work' that is needed to sustain a claim to 'architecture' is precisely the work of the everyday, then I argue that this everydayness of the CUPA is inflected with the rhetorical circulations of revolution by double revolutionaries. It is signalled in the non-hierarchical list of modern amenities that posits the laundrette as being as revolutionary a device as the paved road, the garbage incinerator, or the tons and tons of concrete soaring like magic in the air (see Plate 9). The work of sustenance delivers the claim to revolution through the everyday movements of the body in this defiantly 'modernist' space. Washing clothes in a communal but automatic laundrette for example, and the rhetorical discernment of that movement as 'revolutionary' (in both senses), uncovers 'the precarious conditions of alliance that allow [the CUPA] to cohere (or not) into a built form, housing, architecture' (Jacobs 2006: 22).

Through its adherence to modernist notions of functionality and circulation, the design of the CUPA preordains some of the 'terms' of living for low-level bureaucrats in Mexico City. If the washing was going to be done some way, it is precisely because it will be done this way that matters. If the radio would be switched on, or the post fetched, or the garbage taken out, or an afternoon spent in the playground anyway, then it is the 'terms on which things *must* be done at the most everyday of levels' (Sayer 1994: 375; original emphasis) that signals the location of power. These terms are not just the material limits of what is possible, but the political limits as well. The continual quotidian construction of the CUPA as architecture is, in this sense, entangled in the everyday construction of the state, and the architecture of nationalism (see also chapter by Fernández Arrigoitia). Architectural revolutionaries whose domestic bodies are being conditioned by the very limits and possibilities of material modernity stand in for the revolutionaries doing the *work* of producing the state as they hang their linens to dry. The inauguration of CUPA worked in some way by defining the 'boundaries of the possible' (Sayer 1994: 375) squarely within the rhetorical power of the Revolution and the state, such that a 'revolutionary' affect circulated freely under the pilotis of these towers.

CUPA's role as Berlant's, perhaps imperfect, rhetorical mirror is made all the more manifest as a nationalist reflection through the assertions and celebrations in several newspaper articles that the architect, the engineers, and the construction workers for the CUPA were all Mexican: no foreign technical or material support was used (Lomelí 1949; Mayorga 1949). In these brief but important descriptions we are presented with an architecture of nationalism constructed through the national 'provenance' of the CUPA. The building's nationality is figured as Mexican based on the embodied 'national' at work in each of the bodies that worked on the CUPA, rationalising the attempts to disentangle the intellectual provenance of CUPA from any traces of a foreign accent.

This architectural nationalism sits beside contemporaries like Hannes Meyer, a German planner living and working in Mexico between 1939 and 1949, arguing that '[c]onstructive form is not peculiar to any country; it is cosmopolitan and the expression of an international philosophy of building' (in Overy 2005: 55). The architect Bruno Taut, having lived and worked in Germany, then exiled to Japan and Turkey in the early twentieth century demonstrates this particular paradox of modern architecture as both a cosmopolitan universal, and a deeply national force, writing that '[t]he more architectural forms correspond to the nature where the building is located, to the light and air, the more they are universal' (Akcan 2012: 269).

The CUPA, a self-referentially international modernist style housing block, *appears* national (read original) because we are told it is built by Mexican hands, with Mexican technical and architectural expertise. During the inauguration, work was being done to cement the nationalism of the CUPA as Mexican and, therefore, as part of the ongoing Revolution. Work was also being done to situate CUPA not just within a world of architectonic brethren, but at the forefront of innovation. This is a symbiotic modernity that makes use of the international and universal as precisely that which stands in so stalwart as national. We might understand the Revolution too not just as a national event, but as a cosmopolitan construction itself, an assemblage manifesting the scaffold of the nation state. On 2 September 1949, President Miguel Alemán was not just inaugurating an international style modernist housing block for 5,000 public servants in the south-centre of Mexico City, he was inaugurating the Revolution, already, and again.

Revolution. Love

In *On Revolution*, Hannah Arendt produces a genealogy of the concept trying to understand how it was 'that the idea of freedom and the experience of a new beginning should coincide' (1965: 21–2). Transplanting her project to one that considers the Mexican Revolution and its implications, modern architecture and urban planning become particularly adept at fulfilling the promise of that coincidence. The CUPA being one such promising object, newness radiating from its form and materials, and freedom promised (if not delivered) to its residents and, in equal measure, the nation. Early on in the genealogy, Arendt returns to etymology, reminding us that 'revolution' was a term whose original usage was in astronomy:

> In this scientific usage it retained its precise Latin meaning, designating the regular, lawfully revolving motion of the stars, which, since it was known to be beyond the influence of man and hence irresistible, was certainly characterized neither by newness nor by violence. On the contrary, the word clearly indicates a recurring, cyclical movement . . .
>
> *(Arendt 1965: 35)*

Adding to the deployment of 'revolution' as adjective and noun above, Arendt introduces the verb. Arendt marks the difference between two kinds of revolutionary 'movement' – the cyclical moment of (planetary) bodies, beyond the influence of the human, and the notion of revolution as movement of another kind – movement forward, rupture and progress – the precondition of the coincidence of newness and freedom. Returning to the consideration of the 'location' of the affective 'beloved' deployed and reconstituted throughout the present day anniversaries for the CUPA in Mexico City, I want to argue that it is precisely through movement that this affectivity persists. Here I do not necessarily want to rely on an image of 'movement' through space as the metaphor, but, perhaps, the movement, motion, and 'irresistible' circulation of other intransient objects. It is not that there is somewhere, some in-betweenness of a body and a building, the location through which affect 'moves' and we, committing to that trace, call its spectre 'love'. But, I want to suggest, something more chaotic, nonlinear, the image of the patient planets, but a trace of explosive chaos that pre- and post-dates their present solar rotations. As an image metaphor, this location is perhaps not between, but beside. Affect is that which allows objects, bodies, and signs – the speeches and exhibition, the glass and brick and concrete, the bodies, and memories, the daily movements, the lingering state officialdom – to appear as 'beside' one another, to cohere like objects in a swirl of water, seemingly moving on their own, but for the circulation of the liquid revolving between them.

Berlant reminds that '[i]t seems hard to talk about the sociality of emotion without presuming the clarity and coherence both of it and the world in which it is intelligible. It is hard for thought to abandon its desire to intensify the thingness of its thing and thus its value' (Berlant 2004: 448). In the narrative of CUPA, there persists a desire for 'thingness' – both of the architectural object itself, and of the emotions narrated in and around it. This desire is perhaps emblemised by the caption discussed earlier: 'Notice the clarity of expression in the concrete structure' (*Excélsior* 1949), it reads. The declarative voice allowing us to see what cannot be seen, telling us to 'notice the clarity', our brows furrowed, our eyes peeled, and finally our heads nodding slightly as if to convince ourselves of this collective fiction, the 'thingness' of the assemblage coming into view. Similarly, the inauguration acts as a kind of 'caption' to the building event declaring in more overt ways the coherence of meaning that ought to be interpreted, felt even, in the building.

This desire for 'thingness', however, does not necessarily lead to the 'thing' – and yet we find ourselves appreciating the clarity of the lines, the structure, the landscape design, and the concrete, grateful to 'the State' (that other 'thing') for its revolutionary clarity, and somehow able to articulate an emotion called 'love'. Affects like happiness and joy, pride and gratitude circulating at the time of the inauguration do the work of creating the appearance of unity, allowing us to link things that appear beside one another: the 'thingness' of the CUPA, the revolution, the 'cement of the Nation', and its cosmopolitical provenance. The repetitive circularity of the anniversary, the annual 'revolution' of the familial bonds of residents towards 'Our Beloved' *multifamilar* produces the conditions for an intergenerational affective economy. In looking at the details of one historical 'building event' – the inauguration of the CUPA in Mexico City in 1949 – and its re-inauguration each and every September, we start to see the way in which the perceived coherence between an emotion and a location comes into view, a coherence as fragile as the building event itself. It is, then, moving through the curvilinear gardens, or under the buildings, along the streets in the sky, or gazing out towards the mountains in the distance, that we start to notice the objects in the swirl, traces of incoherence of a revolutionary affect, in the double sense of the word, as the caption for a revolutionary architecture and a revolutionary state.

And yet I return to Berlant's rhetorical mirror, the gesture of the incommensurability between affect and emotion. I return to it in order to undo my argument at the very moment that it makes its claim. As Lees (2001) made clear in her study of the Vancouver public library, official claims on buildings about their meaning, and their use, are as immaterial as, perhaps, the building itself. The performance of architecture through its use, through its inhabitation, through dwelling transforms its meaning. I do not wish to add any more claims than there are already onto the CUPA. As, perhaps, a modest intervention in the thinking about one built object in Mexico City in 1949, my intentions were not to uncover a new historical 'truth' about it, but rather to think through the opening made by the affirmation of 'love' in the present, to consider the multiple ways we lay claim to, and are claimed by, the materialities beside us.

Notes

1   The architect-planner Mario Pani (1911–1993) is widely historicised as having more impact on the urban form and architecture of Mexico City than any other in the twentieth century. For more on Mario Pani, see Garay (2004a), Larrosa (1985), and Noelle (2008). Pani's architectural journal *Arquitectura/México* was the longest-running architectural serial in Mexico with 119 issues between 1938 and 1978.

2 *Mi multi es mi multi* is also the title of a film by historian Graciela de Garay, a compilation of her oral history work with residents of the CUPA. Her oral history is presented in two written volumes (Garay 2002; Garay 2004b).
3 All translations are the author's unless otherwise noted.
4 See for example the discussion by Rubén Gallo (2010) on the 'dystopia' of Nonoalco Tlatelolco, a 100,000-person housing estate in the north of Mexico City designed by Mario Pani and opened in 1964. On 2 October 1968, a public square in the estate played host to a devastating show of state violence when student protesters were gunned down, beaten, and arrested, just days before the city opened the Olympic Games.
5 The *Dirección de Pensiones Civiles* was the department responsible for the CUPA's construction.
6 The currency here is Mexican pesos.
7 For more details, see Pani (1952: 17–38).
8 Here, Mayorga speaks on behalf of the architectural community, our 'medium' being 'architecture'.
9 Pani argues in his 1952 book on the *multifamiliar* that if his dense typology of housing was rolled out across Mexico City, the city could be five times smaller with 80 per cent of the land given to green space (Pani 1952: 32–3).

References

Ahmed, S. (2004a) 'Affective economies', *Social Text*, 22 (2): 117–39.
—— (2004b) *Cultural Politics of Emotion*, Edinburgh: Edinburgh University Press.
Akcan, E. (2012) *Architecture in Translation: Germany, Turkey, and the Modern House*, Durham, NC: Duke University Press.
Anderson, B. (2006) 'Becoming and being hopeful: Towards a theory of affect', *Environment and Planning D: Society and Space*, 24 (5): 733–52.
Arendt, H. (1965) *On Revolution*, New York: Viking Press.
Baudelaire, C. (1995) *The Painter of Modern Life and Other Essays*, London: Phaidon Press.
Berlant, L. (2004) 'Critical inquiry, affirmative culture', *Critical Inquiry*, 30 (2): 445–51.
—— (2008a) 'Intuitionists: History and the affective event', *American Literary History*, 20 (4): 845–60.
—— (2008b) 'Thinking about feeling historical', *Emotion, Space and Society*, 1 (1): 4–9.
Excélsior (1949) 'Perspectiva de Conjuntos', Editorial, 10.
Frisby, D. (2001) *Cityscapes of Modernity*, Cambridge: Polity.
Gallo, R. (2010) 'Tlatelolco: Mexico City's Urban Dystopia', in G. Prakash (ed.) *Noir Urbanisms: Dystopic Images of the Modern City*, Princeton: Princeton University Press, 53–72.
Garay, G. de (2002) *Rumores y retratos de un lugar de la modernidad: Historia oral del Multifamiliar Miguel Alemán, 1949–1999*, Mexico City: Instituto Mora.
—— (2004a) *Mario Pani: Vida y Obra*, Mexico City: Universidad Nacional Autónoma de México.
—— (2004b) *Modernidad habitada: Multifamiliar Miguel Alemán ciudad de México, 1949–1999*, Mexico City: Instituto Mora.
Jacobs, J.M. (2006) 'A geography of big things', *Cultural Geographies*, 13 (1): 1–27.
Joseph, G.M. and Nugent, D. (1994) *Everyday Forms of State Formation: Revolution and the Negotiation of Rule in Modern Mexico*, Durham, NC: Duke University Press.
Kraftl, P. (2010) 'Geographies of architecture: The multiple lives of buildings', *Geography Compass*, 4 (5): 402–15.
Larrosa, M. (1985) *Mario Pani, arquitecto de su época*, Mexico City: Universidad Nacional Autónoma de México.

Lees, L. (2001) 'Towards a critical geography of architecture: The case of an ersatz Colosseum', *Cultural Geographies*, 8 (1): 51–86.

Lomelí, R.B. (1949) 'Inauguróse el Gran Edificio Multifamiliar: El Presidente Abrió el de 1080 Casas, en la Colonia del Valle', *Excélsior*, 1, 15.

Martínez, R. (1949) 'Expresó el Ing. R. Martínez el Júbilo Magisterial por el Edificio Inaugurado Ayer', *Excélsior*, 1, 5.

Massumi, B. (2002) *Parables for the Virtual: Movement, Affect and Sensation*, Durham, NC: Duke University Press.

Mayorga, M.G. (1949) 'La más Grande Realización en Materia de Casas Colectivas, en América Latina', *Excélsior*, 10.

Noelle, L. (ed.) (2008) *Mario Pani*, Mexico City: Universidad Nacional Autónoma de México.

Overy, P. (2005) 'White Walls, White Skins: Cosmopolitanism and Colonialism in Interwar Modernist Architecture', in K. Mercer (ed.) *Cosmopolitan Modernisms*, Cambridge, MA: MIT Press, 50–67.

Pani, M. (1952) *Los Multifamiliares de Pensiones*, Mexico City: Editorial Arquitectura.

Prudon, T. 2009 'Modern housing redux: The (un)loved and the (un)learned', paper presented at (Un)Loved Modern Conference in Sydney, Australia.

Sayer, D. (1994) 'Everyday Forms of State Formation: Some Dissident Remarks on "Hegemony"', in G.M. Joseph and D. Nugent (eds) *Everyday Forms of State Formation: Revolution and the Negotiation of Rule in Modern Mexico*, Durham, NC: Duke University Press, 356–66.

Thien, D. (2005) 'After or beyond feeling? A consideration of affect and emotion in geography', *Area*, 37 (4): 450–4.

Thrift, N. (2004) 'Intensities of feeling: Towards a spatial politics of affect', *Geografiska Annaler: Series B, Human Geography*, 86 (1): 57–78.

CONCLUSION

Creeping familiarity and cosmopolitan futures

Emma Jackson and Hannah Jones

In some ways our book has come full circle. We started in a Southwark housing estate and ended in a Mexican housing project, with two chapters chronicling the labelling of places that are 'home' to some, and hideous to others (and for some, both at the same time). In both of those chapters, and other chapters throughout the book, the authors unpick the emotions bound up in the discursive and physical production of both 'home' and 'other', and within this, the emotional resonance of local and transnational visions of past and future. The journey we have taken criss-crosses migratory routes, belongings and dislocations, all the while attempting to marry the perspectives of 'above' and 'below', 'near' and 'far' outlined by Back and Keith in their opening reflections. Following this journey reveals some recurring motifs: first, the emotional resonance of how places become stigmatised – and the emotional labour that can go into dealing with that stigmatisation or reclaiming positive associations. Second, the ways that movement between places and change within places are intertwined so that nostalgia, loss and longing are about lost moments in time, as much as places on a map. Third, occasions when the very multiplicity and difference within urban spaces become a mode of belonging in which to be 'different' is to have something in common. And finally, the 'creeping familiarity' in which movement, change and transruptions (Hesse 2000) begin to be recognised as part of everyday life, perhaps offering the possibilities for a more open, unfinished and growing cosmopolitan imagination.

Stigma and spoiled identity

In the opening chapter, Hall offered an analysis of how 'registers of relegation', the means by which certain places and their inhabitants become stigmatised, are challenged by the 'registers of the everyday'. These registers, imbued with emotion, echoed through the rest of the book. The register of relegation is bound up with the processes of a disinvestment by the state, followed by the labelling of place – often calling on resonances of other negatively felt places (e.g. 'the Gaza Strip' (Holgersson), 'The Kremlin' (Hall)) that then slips and sticks onto people and is experienced as shame and hurt. The emotion is not just expressed by those who are tarnished by a place's spoiled identity but rather circulates, with political and social consequences. Official discourses of relegation and of regeneration occupy a key role in these circuits of 'emotionality' (Ahmed 2004), deploying highly emotionally loaded imagery. For example, in Holgersson's chapter a construction representative vividly sets out a story of the neighbourhood as moving from 'hypodermic needles bobbing in the creek to being a modern energy-efficient residential area'.

Drawing out how emotion is harnessed and circulated by those who seek to intervene in place is important. As argued in our introduction, emotion is too often associated with the personal as removed from power relations. The 'enchantment engineering' (Lavadinho and Winkin 2008) taking place in Kvillebäcken is not directed at producing unnameable affect but specific emotions which justify the remaking of place and the erasure of other (cosmopolitan) histories. Nor, as Jones' chapter shows, is the production of emotion by agents of government or industry as disembodied as we might sometimes imagine. The social production of emotion to engage residents in a relationship with place also uses emotional resources of 'place-shapers', and by considering the emotional negotiations made by those in positions of (relative) power, another angle on the complex social relations of place and place management can be opened up.

Stigmatisation and the hurt it engenders can be challenged, or at least made liveable, in the register of the everyday. Such everyday registers and responses can be conscious acts of resistance, such as the 'return' to a reimagined Africa in the face of racism and the relegation of Handsworth (Connell), or the fierce love expressed by the Las Gladiolas residents in Puerto Rico and CUPA residents in Mexico City for their homes. However, there can also be more banal, alternative ways of living in a neighbourhood, the development of new socialities and tastes, as in Hall's Walworth Road or in Rhys-Taylor's street market, or the refusal of hegemonic media images by simply seeing another set of connections and experiences (Jaffe).

Explicit re-claiming of pride in otherwise stigmatised places is a political and deeply emotional act, as one of the musicians quoted in Connell's chapter makes clear:

> We called the album 'Handsworth Revolution' because [if] I wasn't in the band and came from Handsworth, and a group called their album that, it would make me feel good and give me something to aim for.

But the registers of relegation and the everyday do not always sit in stark opposition. Certain populations can be excluded from personal narratives of place in order to preserve a sense of pride and a sense of fit between self and local place. For example, in Jackson's Peckham, Marjory complains that while some might celebrate the Nigerian-ness of aspects of her neighbourhood, 'I don't want to live, and a lot of people round here don't want to live, in the grime of Lagos'. She and others in the study experienced the sights, smells and debris around her as 'filth', specifically associated with migration, polluting 'her' streets.

Furthermore, emotional responses of those struggling with place stigmatisation can be ambivalent, as in Kaasa's chapter where, beneath the strong attachments expressed to 'the Beloved' housing development, were other stories and emotions, of frustrations with closed swimming pools and broken lifts. Throughout the book are examples of people using different techniques to try to navigate, infiltrate or influence the process of the remaking of place, as in Holgersson's chapter when Tahere the butcher succeeds in inserting her business into the redevelopment – but at a price.

The chapters by Holgersson, Hall and Fernández Arrigoitia serve as cautions of how these alternative accounts, feelings and lived complexities of place, can remain unrecognised, not valued or simply erased by more powerful interests. But the stories of those affected do not end with the demolition of a building. People have to find ways to make this liveable and to adapt to change. In the opening scene of Fernández Arrigoitia's chapter, a campaigner for saving Las Gladiolas expresses mixed feelings: 'We are sad, but we also know that what is coming is better.' As Fernández Arrigoitia argues:

> [R]emaining actively ambivalent amidst an imminent relocation was not a cynical or disinterested emotional standpoint. It was a mechanism that responded directly to the tug and pull of removal pressures; a practical, flexible and productive tool that proved crucial when their homes were under threat.

Thus, this volume foregrounds the role of emotion in processes of stigmatisation, the use of emotion by powerful interests and the emotional labour that can go into dealing with stigmatisation that slips from place onto people, or into reclaiming positive associations. It also highlights the importance of working with, and seeking to unpick, ambivalence in accounts of place in order to better understand social processes of change.

Nostalgia and places in time

The power of nostalgia and longing cut through this book. They are bound up in experiences ranging from migration, sometimes forced, and nostalgia for a place that has been lost to those remaining in places where the neighbourhood has evolved into something new. In the chapters by Grünenberg and Turan Hoffman, two groups of displaced people, first generation Bosnians returning to visit their old homeland and a new generation of Armenian Americans returning to the land from which their ancestors were evicted, negotiate the erasure of their histories from place. Both groups seek to reconnect across time to homelands that have been reconfigured. Conflicts over signs – literally modified with a sticking plaster (in Turan Hoffman's chapter) – demonstrate how naming place is tied to claiming place. For the Bosnian refugees this is a dual process of negotiating a changing landscape of home while making new connections in Denmark. Indeed Denmark provides a means to reconnect with the homeland as similarities (such as a bridge) are seized upon, or old rituals are resumed in the new context.

Jaffe's chapter foregrounds belonging across places brought about by migration in a rather different way. Here, one version of the Jamaican diaspora presented in the media – including images that have the potential to cause offence – are reinterpreted and reclaimed, as recognised familiar faces and places in TV images from other continents resonate with those watching ('A my likkle corner that!').

Notably, two of the locations where the narrative of nostalgia for a lost neighbourhood is present are geographically close to one another (Redbridge and Barking). However, while in Jones' chapter Michael mourns the loss of a working-class white community in Barking of which he felt part, Saha and Watson's Redbridge respondents evoke another version of the past, a more multicultural place that they feel is being lost as more Asian people move into the neighbourhood. Both of these chapters also serve as reminders of the importance of not fixating on cities but also looking to the suburbs for emerging forms of cosmopolitanism.

Across all of these chapters we are reminded that the past is not just lying there waiting to be found (to paraphrase Walter Benjamin) but is 'up for grabs', being constantly worked over and retold. However, some accounts carry more weight than others. Who is written out of official histories of place? Which aspects of the past are erased? To what ends? And what are the effects on people who are deleted from the past? As Holgersson reflects in Chapter 7:

> Stories of displacement were hardly considered likely to sell any flats. Nor, it appears, were the stories of the everyday multicultural life of the 1990s and early 2000s. As we stopped outside a building remaining from before, which at that time still housed a garage and a mosque, a man from a construction company told me that they might skip over the last 30 years in the marketing of New Kvillebäcken.

Migrants here are seen as out of time, belonging to the past, as well as out of place, and not part of the bright, white future imagined by developers. Thus the past as well as the future gets remodelled through processes of regeneration/gentrification.

Processes of erasing cosmopolitan pasts and influences can be tied to particular projects of nationalism. In Kaasa's chapter the modernist building of CUPA is part of promoting a Mexican identity (and part of the ongoing revolution) without 'any traces of a foreign accent'. Upholding the building as 'The Beloved' and as Mexican takes work, its status is reinscribed on the building through the anniversary celebrations. This chapter shows the emotional labour that goes into making emotion and location appear to cohere.

Anonymity in multiculture, and cosmopolitan belongings

Multiculture (and multiculturalism) are regularly criticised by politicians and others as separatist, creating fractured and isolated populations. By contrast, the stories in this collection suggest not just that multiculture and the traces of migratory histories are everyday; but that 'super-diversity' itself can be a way of creating belonging, making oneself feel at home. For instance, in Jackson's chapter, Dr Huang 'likes living in an ethnically mixed neighbourhood, she says as a refugee you have to live in the big city where you don't stick out'. She adds 'Unless you live in a big town, being a foreigner sometimes is kind of . . . [sticking out] like a sore thumb? If you go outside everybody is Caucasian and things, what am I going to do there?'

In Holgersson's Gothenburg study, in the period that Kvillebäcken had been overlooked by developers, its corners had been curated by those with little in common except their lack of economic and political capital, but each had been, to some extent, unremarkable to one another in their places of worship, businesses and cultural activities. The advent of development in New Kvillebäcken meant these activities were once again noticed and 'othered', the cosmopolitan traces of migration and reinvention shuttered away, as the 'scent of fresh coffee' emanating from the Finnish association was erased in favour of the property developers' projected future coffee scents and balcony views of wealthier owner-occupiers.

This is similar to how, in Hall's street in Walworth, the cosmopolitan connections and activities of entrepreneurs and their customers are seemingly invisible to the local state's imagination of 'economic development'. Hall's and Holgersson's examples demonstrate the sometime invisibility of cosmopolitanism, when in forms not valorised by the state or by large-scale private capital. Whereas for Dr Huang, complex multiculture meant that she was able to feel comfortable because she did not 'stick out' – since everyone 'stuck out' in various ways – for the shopkeepers, residents and community centres in Holgersson and Hall's encounters, being unseen means their claims to space become overlooked too.

Rhys-Taylor's mangoes embody perfectly the phenomenon of how being 'from somewhere else' can be felt as exactly what people have in common in 'being here'. The consumers of mangoes in his market each savour a taste with pungent associations, yet those associations are intersemiotic and resonate in both the local-ness of the shared mango and the distant places and times it recalls. The mangoes, bought in a street market in London, hold different associations for those who buy them and represent different migration histories. But the coalescing of particular tastes and of histories in a particular place remakes a specifically local cosmopolitanism. This challenges definitions of multiculture that figure it as about population flows that remove a sense of place, or claim that transnational connections have led to 'omnivorous cosmopolites with little emotional investment in anything specific' (Rhys-Taylor, this volume). Rather, the local is remade through the remaking of transnational tastes while places become linked through these new emerging connections, in which to be 'different' is to have something in common.

Creeping familiarity and cosmopolitan futures

What cosmopolitan futures are hinted at in this volume? Stuart Hall's concept of 'multicultural drift' can be used to describe the creeping ordinariness of Peckham that slowly reworks Linda's feelings towards her new place of residence (Jackson) or Sharmila's recollection of an Asian girl playing Lord Nelson in a school play (Saha and Watson). But these processes of the formation of new tastes and the remaking of place over time are not always smooth, and particular places can become symbolic of uncomfortable change. Places can evolve into a version of local cosmopolitanism that can be difficult for those who are left feeling as if they do not belong. We hear this in Marjory's distaste for what she experiences as 'the grime of Lagos' in her locale (Jackson), or in Jean's disdain for gold-tipped fences and paved-over gardens (Saha and Watson), or in Michael's fraught account of feeling alienated and planning to leave Barking (Jones). Michael's sense of being left behind was reflected through anxieties about the way his son was starting to talk about the world:

> I think that it come home to me really really hard to me, really really hard, when one day my little boy came home from school at Christmas and said, oh, I've been doing about Christmas at school, Oh alright, so I went, that's nice, so what's Christmas all about then? And what he said was, he said CHRISTIANS believe. That's what he said. And for me that's like – that's a real check-up. That's a real, oh, hang on a minute.

Michael expresses feelings of being disconnected from where he lives, not just because of the changing place 'out there', but as change enters and remakes his own family, as his son becomes part of the new unfamiliar neighbourhood/cosmopolitan future that he finds so difficult to contemplate.

These examples reveal tussles over what is imagined as legitimate and positive cosmopolitanism, or about how much cosmopolitanism is too much. So Saha and Watson's respondents worry about the area becoming too monocultural (Asian), Holgersson's cosmopolitan Kvillebäcken is devalued in favour of an imagined exclusive future, and Jackson's Peckham interviewees praise diversity as represented by neighbours, but consider Rye Lane to be excessively African.

While some of these examples point to the closing down of versions of cosmopolitanism, within other chapters changing configurations of place open up new opportunities for belonging. A cosmopolitan Christmas, that contrasts with Michael's story of loss, is that of Nedžad's Christmas lunch (Grünenberg). He recalls the worry of his colleagues:

> It was cold, the snow was quite heavy . . . I lost my way . . . I arrived about 45 minutes late. When I finally arrived they were all concerned about me, waiting for me, outside in the cold . . . at that moment I felt I had been accepted. I was very moved . . .

This memorable and emotionally charged moment represents for him the possibility of belonging, of carving out a place for himself in a new place; the visible invention of new traditions.

For Amrit (in Jones), living within a changing and cosmopolitan environment and with a complex identity is part of everyday life. Rather than only harking back to a fixed point in the past where place and self cohere, he relates to his past, present and future. He reflects on being Ugandan Asian, the brother of single mothers and the Muslim husband of a Christian ('I don't actually only live a double life, I sort of live a multifaceted life, and all that then is modified and influenced by where I come from, and where I'm going'). Amrit shows the potentials of the emergence of new solidarities from emerging cosmopolitan lives and places. In Connell's chapter we saw an instance of this forging of a place being done on a collective level through forms of cultural expression, where music expressed the possibility of new syncretic belongings transcending the here and now.

These examples lead us to reconsider what the figures of cosmopolitanism might be. While for Bauman the tourist and the vagabond are the figures of our times, this volume provokes the reader to go beyond these categories in thinking about figures of cosmopolitanism. Perhaps more than any other chapter, Turan Hoffman's problematises this distinction. The heritage tourists are tourist/vagabonds, the descendants of families that were displaced, now returning. But these contradictions are also lived by other people across the volume: Dr Huang in Jackson's chapter was a refugee from Vietnam and this continues to affect her life and sense of place, however she lives this in conjunction with having the status of a retired doctor, and being able to regularly visit her family in different parts of the world. Scattered through these chapters are people such as Amrit and Nedžad, who both came to their countries of residence as refugees and are living complex cosmopolitan lives. Doreen Massey's concept of 'power geometry' can unfold differently throughout such cosmopolitan lives. It is possible to be vagabond *and* tourist . . . and ordinary.

References

Ahmed, S. (2004) The *Cultural Politics of Emotion*, New York: Routledge.

Hesse, B. (2000) 'Introduction', in B. Hesse (ed.) *Un/Settled Multiculturalisms: Diasporas, Entanglements, Transruptions*, London: Zed Books.

Lavadinho, S. and Winkin, Y. (2008) 'Enchantment Engineering and Pedestrian Empowerment: The Geneva Case', in T. Ingold and J.L. Vergunst (eds) *Ways of Walking: Ethnography and Practice on Foot*, Aldershot: Ashgate Publishing, 155–168.

INDEX